Playful Parenting

. . .

Playful Parenting

*Turning the
Dilemma of Discipline
into Fun and Games*

Denise Chapman Weston, MSW
and Mark S. Weston, MSW

Jeremy P. Tarcher/Putnam
a member of
Penguin Putnam Inc.
New York

To Arielle and Emily—our best recipes yet!

Most Tarcher/Putnam books are available at special quantity
discounts for bulk purchases for sales promotions, premiums,
fund-raising, and educational needs. Special books or book excerpts
also can be created to fit specific needs.
For details, write or telephone Putnam
Special Markets, 200 Madison Avenue,
New York, NY 10016; (212) 951-8891.

These activities are not intended to take the place of
professional interventions (counseling or psychotherapy).
Parents will need to use their best judgment to determine
when to seek professional help.

Jeremy P. Tarcher/Putnam
a member of
Penguin Putnam Inc.
200 Madison Avenue
New York, NY 10016
http://www.putnam.com

Library of Congress Cataloging-in-Publication Data

Chapman Weston, Denise.
   Playful Parenting : Turning the dilemma of discipline into
fun and games/Denise Chapman Weston and Mark S.
Weston.
      p. cm.
   Includes bibliographical references.
   ISBN 0-87477-734-8 (pa)
   1. Child rearing.   2. Parenting.   I. Weston, Mark S.
II. Title.
HQ769.C396   1993
649'.1—dc20   92-44229 CIP

   Most Tarcher/Putnam books are available at special
quantity discounts for bulk purchases for sales promotions,
premiums, fund-raising, and educational needs.
   Special books, or book excerpts, can also be created to fit
specific needs. For details, write or telephone Special Markets,
Putnam Publishing Group, 200 Madison Avenue, New York,
NY 10016. (212) 951-8891.

Published simultaneously in Canada

Cover design by Mauna Eichner
Cover photo © by Ed Malitsky

Printed in the United States of America
14 15 16 17 18 19 20

This book is printed on acid-free paper. ∞

Contents

Acknowledgments

WE ARE DEEPLY THANKFUL to the countless number of people who have "played" with us over the years:

To the very special parents who entrusted us with their difficulties. Without their involvement we would not have learned the resilient human spirit to make family life work. Especially to those families who tried out our playful parenting techniques, gave us feedback, and shared their successes (which are in this book) and failures (which are not in this book).

To the children we have worked with who have made our jobs rich and rewarding and taught us how to color outside of the lines, cheat on board games, make believe we're transported to another place and time, read a story 100 times and always learn something new. They also taught Denise how to throw a decent spiral and Mark how to play house.

To our colleagues, professors, and supervisors from the University of Arizona, Simmons College, Wes-Ros Park Mental Health Center, Cambridge Court Clinic, Gabeler Children's Hospital, Framingham Youth Guidance Center, Hayden School, South Shore Mental Health Center, The Providence Center, Boston College, Rhode Island College, Spurwink School, Rhode Island School for the Deaf, Austine School for the Deaf. They helped shape our professional development and put our play and views of the children and families into perspective.

To our friends Lauren, Dave, Cheri, Fred, Sherri, Nancy, Lynn, Bethelina, Tim, Daria, Sharon, Chrissy, Lynda and Fern for their ongoing support, advice, and encouragement.

To the "sitters club"—Colleen, Lisa, Megan, Kari, and their families, who have pinch-hit every Sunday for as long as we put pen to paper.

To Melissa and Courtney, who have cared for our children as if they were their own.

To Taunya, our "little sister," who taught us the meaning of determination and hope.

To our parents—Cliff and Audrey, Hermine and Arthur—who gave us the foundation to become our playful selves: Mr. Matinee stories, world's biggest sandbox, Clippie the Clown and his parades, Mark's award-winning Donald Duck Head, and Denise's mother's loud applause at every opportunity.

To our brothers—Donnie, Ross, Kenny, and Jerry—with whom we played and played and played during our childhood.

To our daughters, Arielle and Emily, who have shown us what playful parenting really means.

To our photographer, Ed Malitsky, whose excellent eye, playful patience, and creative ability captured families having true fun.

To Rick Benzel, our editor, whose creative talents made book writing fun and games.

To the Tarcher/Putnam group, Jeremy Tarcher, Daniel Malvin, Donna Gould, and Fred Sawyer—our thanks.

Preface

"Our first game is called, 'Well begun is half done, otherwise entitled—Let's tidy up the nursery!' . . . Shall we begin!" exclaims Mary Poppins.

The little girl says, "It is a game, isn't it?"

"Well, it depends on your point of view," continues Mary Poppins. "You see, with every job that must be done there is an element of fun. You find the fun and -SNAP- the job's a game."

"And every task you undertake . . . becomes a piece of cake . . . a lark . . . a spree . . . it's very clear to see!"

"That a spoonful of sugar helps the medicine go down . . . in the most delightful way!"

MARY POPPINS UNDERSTOOD CHILDHOOD very well. She knew the single most important aspect of effective parenting: to make growing up and confronting life's challenges palatable. Recall for a moment the enchanting tale of Mary Poppins, the British governess who enters a household with two undisciplined children. She meets the children, mystifies them with her wizardry, and then with the snap of her fingers, some ingenuity, fun, and magic she is able to get them to not only clean up their rooms but enjoy themselves in the process.

We don't profess to know Mary Poppins personally or practice her particular brand of magic, but we know the secret of her success, and we believe in the magic that exists between parents and children for tackling life's challenges. Mary Poppins' recipe calls for only one ingredient: a spoonful of sugar to help the medicine go down. We all agree it would be wonderful if there were such a simple recipe for solving your child's behavior problems. But odds are you wouldn't be reading this book, nor would we be writing it, if that were the case. Parents know full well that they need much more than a dash of sugar to get their kids to clean up after themselves, brush their teeth, or stop calling their sister or brother "diaper head."

What this book offers is different from all the other available parenting books and advice available to parents today. *Playful Parenting* puts the FUN back into the *fun*damentals of parenting. Raising children in the '90s has become a very serious, worrisome, complex, and anxiety-provoking task. We know many well-read parents who feel that if they do or say the wrong thing to their child, she will be damaged for life. They wrongly imagine seeing their sweet little girl or boy needing ongoing psychotherapy because they potty-trained too early, too late, with the wrong method, with the wrong-brand potty seat, or whatever. Many parenting books today respond to parents' anxieties by emphasizing ways to discipline and control children, and, worse, how to do everything just right. This approach not only increases anxiety, but detracts from the joy of parenting and the joy of childhood.

By contrast, this book combines sound guidance with fun, family-tested, kid-approved approaches to parenting and problem solving. You will find *Playful Parenting* to be informative and enjoyable not only for you to use with your child, but, as one eight-year-old boy claimed after using our methods for solving his sleeping problems, "This is fun!" Imagine—this child is associating working on a problem—something children usually dread—with having fun. Solving challenging childhood-behavior problems doesn't have to be a grueling chore anymore; in fact, you too will learn how to enjoy it.

Parents today often lack the time to read a book cover to cover or sort out a lot of theoretical jargon. As practicing child and family psychotherapists, we have listened to hundreds of parents complain about the lack of easy-to-use, understandable parenting resources. As parents of two young children, we knew firsthand how valuable it would be to have a book written in a style that's as simple and easy to use as a cookbook. In response to this need, we have embraced cooking and the practical, step-by-step recipe format used in cookbooks as a metaphor for parenting and solving child-behavior problems.

Cooking is a lot like problem solving. Both consist of a series of steps that lead to a goal-oriented outcome. Another reason we've used this comparison is that just as almost anyone who has set foot in a kitchen comfortably and unabashedly consults a cookbook for a good recipe or cooking tips, so too can any parent feel comfortable using *Playful Parenting* for parenting guidance and as a source of new ideas for old dilemmas.

Just as a great cookbook is kept in the kitchen to consult time and time again, *Playful Parenting* was designed to be kept in the family room. And, like a cookbook, it is organized to be used as a long-term reference, with a variety of ideas to solve your child's ever-changing but ever-present behavior problems. Unless you are blessed with flawless offspring, you will be confronted with dozens of parenting challenges until your child or children mature—perhaps the tantrums stop at age four, but at age six, getting him to bed, to brush his teeth, and to stop tormenting his sister becomes a new adventure in parenting.

We have taken everyday childhood-behavior problems that call for parental attention, and instead of presenting complicated concepts and theories, offer concise explanations and techniques, fun ideas, and playful activities in the form of recipes with easy-to-follow, step-by-step instructions for dealing with each behavior problem.

HOW TO USE THIS BOOK

Playful Parenting begins with a chapter that discusses the basics of positive discipline and outlines our philosophy and insights about parenting and how to use our specially designed methods for solving your child's behavior problem.

Chapter 2 contains what we call the Main Ingredients (parenting techniques), an up-to-date list of the best current advice on parenting and child-behavior-management. We have condensed this information so that you can easily learn how to use the procedures, apply the principles, and integrate both into your present parenting style. You can turn to this chapter and look up a technique when you need a refresher.

After reading chapters 1 and 2, which give you an overview of the book, you can go directly to the contents page, find the problem that you want to head off or solve, and turn to that chapter.

We consider chapters 3 through 16 to be the "main course." These chapters contain brief summaries of behavior problems and recipes for their solution. Because of our backgrounds as family therapists, and our strong belief in the power of family relationships, we have devoted chapter 3 to tips for strengthening family unity and improving communications and cooperation. Chapters 3 through 16 also contain Problem/ Solution Charts that describe and explain behavioral problems and offer possible solutions. The Solutions will in turn refer you to fun and helpful recipes.

In addition to problem-solving recipes, chapters 3 through 16 contain recipes for Planful Playing that include activities designed for fun and constructive play. These activities will indirectly address the behavior problem at hand while providing hours of family fun.

Chapter 17 is called "Just Desserts" because it talks about the recognition of good efforts and presents ways to set up reward programs and fun ways to praise your children.

In chapter 17 you will find, under "Reading Recipes," books that show you ways to use children's literature to address the problems discussed throughout the book. Reading is a wonderful leisure activity and a tool for sharing time, information, and nonthreatening advice with your child. It is also an opportunity to explore a problem from another person's point of view.

Every family is different. Some are highly structured; others are very spontaneous; and there are all sorts of in-betweens. Accordingly, we have designed the book so that more structured parents can read and then practice the introductory steps, then use the problem-solving (recipe) worksheet in the appendix. Less-structured parents can simply choose an activity and use it as an enriching family experience.

WHERE DID WE GET OUR RECIPES?

We are both trained as child and family therapists with a specialty in using play as a therapeutic tool. As play therapists, we use professional methods of play and play materials such as puppets, art supplies, dolls, board games, sport-related gear, and whatever office paraphernalia appeals to a child to discover what is troubling her, to help her overcome her problems and experience relief from emotional conflict. People sitting in our waiting rooms hearing shrieks of laughter and the joyful sounds of play are often perplexed as to how our clients could be having so much fun while talking about such serious problems. As do many play therapists, we believe that it is a misconception to think that solving children's problems necessitates a bleak environment, oversized chairs, and ominous talk. In fact, we've seen time and time again the power of play as a window to a child's world and an arena for family communication. We spend a good portion of our workday on our hands and knees, telling children stories, talking with puppets, coloring, painting, or throwing a ball. Needless to say, it can be exhausting, but at the same time it is also revitalizing to view the world through the excitement and freshness of a child's eye, with all his curiosity, delight in discovery, and boundless energy.

But play is just one way we communicate as psychotherapists. We also strongly believe in the power of the family and its influence as a guiding force in children's lives. As family therapists, we insist on including all members of a child's family in working through a problem. For example, Denise worked with a six-year-old child who was aggressive, overactive, and performed poorly in school although he was very bright. His parents complained that they had no control over him and were at their wits' end. In conventional, individual psychotherapy, the therapist would isolate the child (the problem), treat him with weekly sessions, and meet separately with his parents to give them guidance and support. Instead, Denise saw the entire family in her office, with the intention of treating and changing the family system. In this case the aggression and loss-of-control issues did not belong to the identified child, but were an integral component of the family culture. Change came about after Denise succeeded in getting the entire family to work together to resolve the problem at hand by using nonaggressive ways to communicate their feelings.

We favor a family approach because it relieves both child and parent of blame, while encouraging everyone to share responsibility for the problem and for correcting it. When parents and children are directly invited to take an active part in finding and carrying out a solution to their problems, all gain a sense of competence and control. We practice the philosophy that we need to create an environment whereby family members, parent and child alike, are "trained" to become the experts and skilled problem solvers of their own difficulties. This ultimately should increase their sense of confidence to influence their own lives, so that when a family leaves our office, they do not leave the skills of problem solving behind.

We are challenged as family therapists to find a language and a means of communication that adults, adolescents, and young children, sitting in the same room, can participate in. Even traditional family-therapy approaches often leave out the young child because it relies on talking as the primary mode of communication. "Talk therapy" is the most difficult type of communication for a young child to understand. By bridging play- and family-therapy approaches, we have originated our unique problem-solving process that allows children and parents to playfully communicate while participating in the therapy sessions.

Our problem-solving approach is based on five theories: (1) that of Alfred Adler and Rudolf Dreikurs, which teaches democratic parenting through the use of Encouragement and Logical Consequences, (2) Haim Ginott and Thomas Gordon's approach, which enhances communication skills and teaches parents how to respond to the underlying feelings of children, (3) family systems theory, which focuses on the relationships and dynamics of the family unit, (4) the behavioral approach, which emphasizes shaping or correcting behavior through positive and negative reinforcement, and (5) the basic premise behind play therapy, which holds that play is the best vehicle for communication and problem solving.

The teachings of Adler and Dreikurs as well as the theories derived from our family systems training are the foundation of our problem-solving method. These parenting methods encourage individuality and family cooperation without blind obedience. They also promote the concept of choice, invite children to make decisions within parental-defined parameters, and hold them accountable for these decisions. The primary focus of our method is on *interactive family problem solving*, the "All for one and one for all" teamwork approach.

We proudly admit that the most challenging test of our skills and emotions has been as parents of two young girls. Like all parents, we are human and fallible. Often we've both felt mystified, intimidated, and stumped by our children's behavior. Recently, Mark related a humorous example of one of our many "We're-not-perfect-parents-either" experiences. While waiting in line to have a check approved at the supermarket, he was forced to play referee between our girls, who were fighting over ownership of Dad's wallet. Mark was struggling to take it back so that he could give the checkout clerk the needed information. After many pulls and tugs from the battleground below, and a series of mundane questions from the clerk, the clerk asked, "What's your occupation?" Finally, taking the wallet out of the teeth of one child and the hands of the other, he exclaimed, in a louder voice than planned, "I'm a child psychologist!" Mark says he can still recall his embarrassment at the clerk's disbelieving stare as our children's screams and tantrums echoed in stereo throughout the store. So we can empathize and understand how difficult parenting can be, and how all the parenting advice and elaborately conceived techniques do not magically turn adults into perfect parents. There is no such thing.

We have written this book to help parents and children work through their common, everyday dilemmas. However, it is also an excellent resource for planning family activities that reinforce family values, build self-esteem, and stimulate creativity.

Although we have written this book for you, the parent, the methods, techniques, and problem-solving activities are designed to be kid-friendly. Just as we try in our family-therapy sessions to include children in the process of working with their families to understand and cope with the problems at hand, we have designed this book so that the concepts and problem-solving activities will appeal to children.

Use *Playful Parenting* like a cookbook. Bend back the pages where your favorite recipes are found. Put bookmarks between the pages of recipes you want to try in the future. We hope we can restore the fun to parenting and help strengthen your family's ability to face life's challenges. There are so many unexpected opportunities in our lives for teaching, playing, sharing, and loving our children. Perhaps this book can at least mold some of those moments. Let's get cooking.

A family doing steps 1–5 and playfully problem solving

CHAPTER 1

Introduction

OUR METHOD FOR COOKING UP positive behavior involves a five-step procedure or "recipe" that provides parents and children with a goal-oriented problem-solving process. By combining play, family systems concepts, and problem-solving theories, we have developed an approach that guides the entire family toward solving the problem(s) at hand. The five steps are as follows:

1. State and define the problem.

2. Identify skills and solutions.

3. Establish mutually agreed-upon goals.

4. Practice and play: practice these skills and reach goals through fun activities.

5. Review and recognize efforts.

We'll examine these one by one in a moment.

When a family learns to solve problems together, they share the responsibility for change. Each member feels supported and safe bringing up and discussing any difficulties. Family problem-solving gives members the opportunity to understand what the problem is and formulate objectives and solutions together. This process reinforces family unity and creates a spirit of cooperation and equality among members by respecting each person's unique contribution. By listening to and exchanging ideas, thoughts, and feelings with their children, parents also create an environment that encourages children to become invested and involved. By inviting a child to participate in the process of solving his or her own problem, an adult reaffirms his trust in, personal regard for, and overall belief in the child's ability to control behavior and work out difficulties. This affirmation increases the child's confidence in his ability to positively influence problem situations. The entire process produces more effective and lasting solutions because solutions are based not only on the knowledge and experience of parents but also on that of the children. By using this method, everyone mobilizes to attack the issue, rather than each other, and solutions work because everyone has a part in creating an answer to the problem.

To be capable of accepting this role, children need the most basic of life skills—communication—including ways to honestly and effectively share thoughts and feelings and ways to actively listen and understand the feelings of others. The five-step recipe process used throughout the book relies heavily on creating good communication, the cornerstone to successful parenting and family functioning.

THE USE OF CONSEQUENCES AND REWARDS AND PRIVILEGES

Many of our problem-solving recipes include the use of charts, rewards, and behavior management (shaping behavior through positive and negative consequences). The use of rewards for motivating children to change their behavior has been written about and practiced for decades. Some parents see rewards—objects, gifts, special outings—as a form of bribery. Although this may be true, we feel that giving children rewards and privileges for changing inappropriate behaviors into more appropriate ones is analogous to giving an adult a paycheck for going to work. The process of problem solving is very hard work for both adults and children and deserves some kind of compensation or recognition. We designed the last chapter, "Just Desserts," to reinforce the fact that any attempt to solve problems, like trying spinach for the first time, warrants a pleasurable ending, reward, or slice of chocolate cake.

FUN FOR FAMILIES

Every recipe and problem-solving activity chosen for this book is based on assuring a high-level quality experience for both parent and child. Unique to this "cookbook" is the main ingredient of fun. Because talking about, understanding, and solving personal problems is always difficult and demanding work, it is no wonder that so many people, especially children, do not like facing their problems. It is also unreasonable to expect a child to think, reason, or communicate like an adult.

This is where our play-therapy expertise comes into "play." We know through our experience that there is no better way to "talk" to a child than to "play" with her. The language of play is nonthreatening to a child and comfortably encourages him to communicate his thoughts and feelings, learn about social roles and responsibilities, confront obstacles in life, and employ skills to solve everyday difficulties. When a child comes into our office nervous, anxious, and uncertain of what is going to happen, he is comforted by the sight of dozens of toys, games, dolls, balls, drawings by other children, and other assorted "playables" in the room. After a few sessions of coloring, game-board playing, ball throwing, and other creative play adventures, a child quickly learns that going to "therapy" ("ther-a-play" as one nine-year-old girl calls it) to work through problems is "kinda fun!"

We share our play ideas with parents to reinforce the importance of relating to their child through play. One of the cherished pleasures of being a parent is having permission to be playful and indulge in the foolishness, silliness, and free-spirited recreation of play. This interchange between adult and child strengthens family bonds and binds relationships with fun and laughter.

Despite the play-oriented focus of our approach, this book is not about all play and no work. Families will be guided through the problem-solving steps while shaping a satisfying shared time together. Both parents and children often feel overwhelmed by a child's behavior problems when neither one knows where or how to begin to address them. The problem-solving process we use in each recipe makes understanding what to do more manageable by dividing it into workable and well-defined steps. The specially conceived play activities recommended in each behavior-problem chapter create quality time while solving areas of concern in your family. Best of all, by adding the "element of fun," these solution activities take the bitterness out of solving problems. With practice, we are sure our process will become second nature to you and your child, helping your family join forces and embrace a problem by becoming a cooperative team of skilled problem solvers.

The five-step method can also be used to prevent future problems in your family. By adopting the problem-solving steps so that they are proactive rather than reactive, you can use this activity to engage your family in learning experiences that will strengthen skills and anticipate or prevent future difficulties.

Above all, our process teaches your child not only how to deal with everyday situations, but also how to manage more difficult ones. When a child has practice and experience using a step-by-step problem-solving approach, he or she is better prepared to take on and find solutions to the more complicated and demanding problems that are sure to turn up as a child, teenager, or adult. We believe that teaching problem-solving skills to children should be a required academic course.

Our "recipe" process is clearly described, step by step, on the following pages. The description of each step includes the purpose of the step, an explanation and examples of how to specifically perform the step, and suggestions for playful activities that reinforce and explain the step to your child. We have also included a problem-solving or "recipe" worksheet that brings the five steps together and will further guide your family through the process. You will find this in the appendix.

STEP 1: STATE AND DEFINE THE PROBLEM

This step begins the problem-solving process. In step 1, each family member will express his or her own perception of the problem by explaining the problem as he or she sees it and stating the facts without assigning blame. *Step 1 is a process of sharing information without instructing or giving advice.*

There are several reasons why this step in problem solving is so valuable. First, each family member's feelings, beliefs, and perceptions are recognized and valued as important. Second, it teaches children how to describe their feelings rather than negatively acting them out. For a young child, learning to verbally express feelings and thoughts about a problem is a skill that takes time and practice. This first step in the problem-solving process gives you and your child the structure for practicing and learning this skill. Third, parents and children learn to tolerate different perspectives and appreciate diversity of feelings and understandings. When parents allow for a difference in perceptions, children learn that there exists more than one way to describe situations and solve problems. Finally, respecting and accepting each other's ideas and feelings as unique and valuable creates an environment in which one's self-worth is nourished.

Step 1 has two parts: problem description and problem integration. Problem description is an uninterrupted opportunity for each family member to express his or her point of view while others listen. Problem integration is the process of incorporating all the viewpoints into a common family understanding of the problem. Here is an example of how a family with a problem with messiness might do step 1. First, the children would be invited to share their opinions of the problem. Let's say that the daughter, Sherri, complains that her mom nags her constantly to pick up her things, and Tim, the son, doesn't like the way his father rushes him to clean things up. Next, the parents would share their perceptions of the problem. After each member expresses him or herself (problem description), the family needs to be able to agree on an explanation of the problem that includes each person's description (problem integration). In this case the parent of this family might summarize as follows: "Mom and Dad believe the kids in this family don't pick up after themselves. Sherri feels that Mom nags her too much about picking up her things; Tim thinks that Dad doesn't give him enough time to put things away; but we all agree that this house gets messy because picking up after ourselves is a problem." This statement shows that all feelings and opinions were accounted for and the actual problem was described without blaming or discounting anyone.

Here are a few suggestions and ideas to help make step 1 clearer to your child and easier to implement.

1. Find a common thread among all the different perceptions and join together to commiserate with each other instead of com-

Playful ways to teach step 1:

Brainstorming:
Tape a 3-by-3-foot sheet of paper to a wall. Have each family member take turns drawing pictures and/or writing on it what he or she thinks the problem is or looks like. Leave the center blank. At the end of the activity the entire family should agree on and collectively draw or write a description of what the family problem is.

plaining about each other. In other words, all should agree about the injustice of the problem.

2. Examine your actions and reactions to be sure they show acceptance and thoughtful regard for each person's description of the problem. It is important that all feelings and perceptions be accepted even if the misbehavior that is being explored is not acceptable. Express your beliefs as your point of view and not necessarily as the "problem." (See Effective Listening and "I" Messages in chapter 2 for techniques in verbalizing your thoughts and listening to those of others.)

3. Take a moment to examine your child's motives and understandings so you can comprehend what he is hoping to gain. Understanding your child's intentions gives you a stronger sense of what he is trying to accomplish and furthers your chances of reaching his and your family's goals. (See the Problem/Solution Charts in each chapter for additional insights.)

4. Try to respond to your child not just from an adult perspective but from the quite different one of the child. Think back to your own childhood to help you empathize with your child's feelings and point of view. Perhaps you can share a story of your own struggles as a child that shows you understand what it is your child is telling you. You can use puppets, drawings, and Role-Play to help him verbalize his thoughts and feelings. We will go into more details on these play techniques in chapter 2.

5. Be optimistic and convey to your child that you believe that the problem is solvable. Keep focused on the here and now, and don't dredge up ancient history as evidence of the problem or give too many examples—it might turn into a lecture. Stay to the point. Be clear and simple.

Step 1 begins the problem-solving process by fully examining each family member's thoughts, feelings, and opinions regarding a specific problem or situation. Both parents and children are given the opportunity to express themselves, listen to others, and finally participate in the process of integrating their perceptions with those of each family member.

STEP 2: IDENTIFY SKILLS AND SOLUTIONS

Step 2 makes use of each family member's natural endowments, strengths, skills, talents, attributes, and special abilities, and capitalizes on them to develop the foundation for your solution to the problem. Focusing on what a person can do (skills) rather than what he or she cannot do (be-

What does Thelma think?
This activity gives your family an extra voice and a nonthreatening way to encourage members to think of alternative ways to define the problem. Thelma is an adopted rag doll who sits quietly at family meetings, propped in a chair, and listens to the problem being discussed. At any time she can be asked, "What do you think the problem is, Thelma?" Encourage your child to answer for Thelma.

Playful ways to teach step 2 to your child:

Skill Builders:
Using Post-Its or blank stickers and the list of over 450 skills children have on page 265, have your family think of as many skills, talents, and attributes as possible that pertain to each family member and write them on the stickers. Cover each person from head to toe with the stickers. Write down your findings for future use.

Skillution revolution:
Teach your child how to wipe out a problem with a skill by combining the "brainstorming" and "skill builders" activities. Take a "skill sticker" and stick or place it on top of a problem written on the paper from the brainstorming activity. Show her that by turning her skills into solutions she can solve many problems simply by using talents she already has.

havior problems) gives each member a sense of control and the confidence to explore alternative ways (solutions) of doing something. We fondly call this concept *skillutions* and use this word with children to help them understand that skills can be solutions, and solutions are always skills.

The skillution—the method of using your child's skills and strengths as a problem-solving tool—is a threefold process. First, help him recall past accomplishments. Second, help him identify what personal skills or strengths he drew upon to achieve that accomplishment. Third, help him understand how those skills and strengths can be used as part of the solution for the current problem. By defining your child's talents, special attributes, and known capabilities as skillutions, he will recognize that he already has the potential to solve the specific problem on which you want him to work. By concentrating on what your child can do, you are communicating to him that you believe he is capable of solving his behavior problem. Once you identify current skills and past accomplishments, he will feel more confident and capable of joining you in your efforts to confront the problem.

Here are some examples of how you can turn a skill into a solution. Let's say your child's problem is that she does not pick up after herself. You might say, "You did a great job memorizing your times tables for last week's math test. You are very good at remembering things and this skill will certainly make you a pro at remembering to pick up your things before you go to bed." For a child who is afraid of the dark you might say, "You are a terrific swimmer and sure are brave and courageous when it comes to diving into the water. This means that you have the skills to be brave and courageous when you have to 'dive' into the dark."

In order to do this portion of the problem-solving recipe, you will need to take the time to explore all of your child's unique and special abilities, anything from being good at sports to being kind or even skilled at gently petting his dog. Take a few days to make notes of all the things your child does that could be seen as positive traits or skills. Ask yourself, "What can he do with his mind, his body, his feelings that is constructive?" Take a closer look at talents, hobbies, appearance, smile, clothing selection, heck, even his agile fingers, which can manipulate his Nintendo game with incredible speed. We have included in the appendix over 450 skills and capabilities children may possess, to help you develop a list for your child. When parents notice and point out what children do well, children usually want to continue doing this behavior or even make attempts at doing it better.

This step is organized around the principle that once children identify the skills that have enabled them to excel in particular situations, they can learn to apply these skills (skillutions) to less-successful areas of their life. While your short-term goal may be to solve the problem at hand, this step will help your child develop skills and behaviors which will enable him or her to successfully overcome other obstacles throughout life.

STEP 3: MUTUALLY AGREE UPON GOALS

Step 3 of the problem-solving process will help your family formally develop a mutually agreed-upon goal. This goal is stated or written in such a way that it combines the integrated definition of the problem (step 1) with skillutions (step 2) to come up with a goal (step 3).

For example, if you were consulting this book because your son Jake has a bedtime problem, in step 1 you and Jake may have defined the problem something like this: "It takes Jake too long to get in bed after he's been told, and this results in a lot of yelling and crying." In step 2 you and he may have come up with between six to eight skills (quickness, listening skills . . .) that Jake possesses which will apply to this problem. With the information from steps 1 and 2 you will now use step 3 to create a goal such as, "Jake has agreed that his difficulty was going to bed when he was told. He is good at moving quickly, listening to his baseball coach, and telling time. His goal is to use his quickness, good listening skills, and time-telling expertise to get himself to bed on time."

All humans seem to be goal-oriented. Whether it is an infant crying out to be fed or an investor keeping a watchful eye on the stock market, our behavior is usually purposeful and with a definite objective in mind. When we formulate goals, we are able to see a clear direction and defined objective. Focusing on objectives, and on the behaviors needed to reach them, outlines for children what their goal is and how they are going to get there. Setting up attainable goals can be extremely rewarding and reinforcing because as each successive objective is reached, you can all relish your accomplishments. It is terribly important to remember that the message is not about defining success as winning or losing, but about the quality of effort you and your child put forth toward reaching your agreed-upon goals.

Here are a few tips for coming up with a family goal for your child's behavior problem:

1. Keep an open mind to your child's suggestions for a goal, even if it is not exactly or even remotely how you would have worded it.

2. Make sure your goals are *realistic, attainable,* and *simple.*

3. You may have more success setting up several smaller goals that result in eventually reaching the larger one. For example, in solv-

Playful ways to teach step 3:

The Goalie Game:
Cover a kid-size hockey stick with the "skill stickers" from the Skill Builders activity on page 6. Tape family problems onto several plastic hockey pucks. Now try to use your "skill stick" to hit your "problem pucks" into a "goal" (net). Have your child identify what skills she is using on the stick to reach her goal.

Goal Book:
Make a personal goal book for each family member—have each person write or draw pictures of life goals in a booklet. Include both short-term and long-term goals.

ing a messy bedroom you might start off with goals such as, "Put clothes away." Then you would add, "Put clothes and toys away . . ." And so on. This makes the goal much more manageable.

4. Stick to your goal and do not wander too far from your original objective. This helps your child focus his energy instead of spreading it out on vague and undetermined issues.

Playful ways to teach step 4:

Practice by playing:
Come up with fun hobbies every-one in your family would be good at learning such as juggling or playing the harmonica. Spend a few hours trying to reach a goal (juggling two balls, playing a simple tune) during a practice session together. Emphasize to your child how it takes practice and time to learn a new skill.

Your family may find it helpful if you set up your goals in the form of a contract. The problem-solving (recipe) worksheet included in the appendix helps your entire family feel as though they are literally signing an agreement establishing their commitment to solving the problem. This also ensures that each member understands the problem-solving process from start to finish.

Step 3 helps your family combine problem definition with solutions for that problem, to come up with clear objectives and goals. This step also obtains a commitment from your child to strive for positive changes and provides the needed practice in defining purpose for his behavior and how that is related to reaching his goals.

STEP 4: PRACTICE AND PLAY

Now you've made it to the fun part. In this step you and your family will select and implement one of the intriguing play activities that best addresses your problem and will help you reach your agreed-upon goal. Now that your family has identified the problem and the way to solve it, this step will help you put all of your hard work into action.

The instinctive method children use for solving problems and mastering difficulties is *play*. Play is the all-encompassing business of childhood—in it, children take charge of their world, sort out misconceptions, and re-create life experiences. For example, consider the child who is terrified of monsters he believes are lurking at night in the shadows of his bedroom. During the day, this same child draws monsters, pretends he is slaying them and even makes believe he is a monster. Without realizing it, he is using various modalities of play to explore, to problem-solve, and, eventually to overcome his terrors. He can do the same thing with his behavior problems.

Remember: being confronted with one's shortcomings or problems can be difficult and serious business. With this in mind we have designed each activity to not only address the problem behavior but also to exercise your child's imagination, entice his interest in participating and reinforce his self-worth, family values and interpersonal relationships.

As practicing play therapists we have learned firsthand what elementary school teachers have known for decades: children are more likely to absorb new ways of behaving if they are actively involved in a hands-on process of learning or solving their own problem. The play activities suggested in step 4 of each recipe are designed to entice and challenge your child to try new experiences and playful ways to work through his feelings.

Let's face it. Kids as well as adults need gimmicks to arouse their curiosity and capture their attention. The activities we developed are based on sound problem-solving techniques and not just on their entertainment value. We have chosen activities that appeal to children and adults alike because solving problems can be better accomplished with parental involvement. Simply doing the activity together with your child strengthens your relationship because you are spending quality time together. In doing so, you are communicating to her that you enjoy doing things together regardless of the purpose of the activity.

The following hints will maximize the pleasure and value of these activities:

1. Be sure to set aside enough uninterrupted time to enjoy yourselves and not feel pressured to complete the activity.

2. Take a few moments during the activity to watch your child's reactions. This may give you a better understanding of the thoughts, feelings, and perceptions that constitute his complex world.

3. Don't set unrealistic expectations for yourself or your child by saying that you expect him to solve his problem completely after performing the activity.

4. Most important, put on your play clothes, sneakers, or knee pads— and have fun.

This step is clearly defined as the practice portion or "mix and bake" stage of the recipe. It allows your child the chance to experiment with new ways of behaving, and, through the fun activity, to master her difficulties.

STEP 5: REVIEW AND RECOGNIZE EFFORTS

Step 5 is the most neglected step in problem solving. It asks your family to *integrate* all that you have accomplished and to *evaluate* your progress toward reaching the goal. You should take the time to assess your achievements and acknowledge your successes. After completing all four steps, step 5 will help you decide whether or not you have attained the goal and what to do next.

Focus on the accomplishments, improvements, intentions, and overall efforts of *all* family members. This is not the time to criticize your

Playful ways to teach step 5:

Instant replay:
Video-record your family eating dinner, playing in the park, and/or doing one of the activities in this book. Watch the tape together and model for your child how to review and recognize negative and positive behaviors. See who can come up with the most observations and comments.

child's efforts or failures in trying to reach a goal. It takes time, practice, and experience to cook up a good recipe, and it is no different in testing out new behaviors for old problems.

Step 5 also helps you recognize that families do not always meet their goals the first time they try—this is normal and to be expected. Problem solving requires that old behaviors are put under the microscope and new ones are tested. As a result, there can often be complications, ones that may not have been anticipated. These unforeseeable complications make solving a problem on the first try difficult. However, our view is that even failure is great! Parents often respond as if we were nuts: "What? You don't *want* us to solve this problem?" Of course we want you to solve your problems—but not just for today; we'd like to see it vanish forever. Since solving a problem takes time and experience, the more time and experience you invest trying and retrying new ways of confronting a problem, the more the solution and skills will become second nature to you and your child. Expecting immediate results and improvements is unrealistic. Look for a gradual change, and be satisfied with each small step made toward reaching a goal. Your child may partially solve a problem on the first try and then, without realizing it, begin to apply the newly acquired skills to this and other problem situations, exchanging old, destructive behaviors for productive ones. Both you and your child may even be delightfully surprised that when he solves one problem, others of a similar nature seem to automatically improve or even disappear.

When reviewing your efforts, look back at what worked and didn't work. Generally, when problem solving fails, it is not that the *person* has failed, but that a breakdown in the *process* has occurred. Perhaps the match between the problem, person, and activity for solving that problem wasn't quite right. If your chocolate bundt cake tastes like a dried-up brick or is flat as a pancake, it doesn't mean you are a lousy cook. It suggests rather that you may have omitted an ingredient or that you misunderstood the recipe. You may need to review your recipe a second or even third time, verify the ingredients, and try again. With time, your bundt cake will float in the air and taste like it came out of Julia Child's kitchen.

If your child has not been able to solve his problem completely, point out whatever progress has been made and learn to reassess the problem, the skills used, and the goal you are striving for. Have him evaluate whether or not the goal is too difficult or if he needs to think of more skillutions to the problem. At this point you might want him to consider revisions and either try the recipe again or choose another.

On the other hand, you may have been fortunate and successfully solved the problem. Don't stop there. Talk with your child about the successes attained and the goals achieved. Evaluate how the problem was solved and how each family member contributed to the victory. Above all, share praise liberally and nurture your child's confidence by saying that this proves that he is capable of mastering other problems when they arise.

A WORD TO THE WISE PARENT

Once you understand the problem-solving steps described in this book, you are ready to take on any family challenge that comes your way. Our intention is not just to teach you and your child how to solve common, everyday behavior problems, but to give you a method, a recipe, for dealing with any undesirable situation.

We are confident that the recipes offered in this book will decrease your child's behavior problems while increasing her self-esteem and your family's connectedness. However, we want to "caution the cook." Good recipes often turn sour if the cook's expectations are not in line with the realities of the product. Similarly, either or both the parents' and the children's goals and expectations may not be entirely realistic. There are several reasons for this.

First, basing your success at solving problems solely on your child's efforts not only undermines your ability to influence her, but it places the burden of solving the problem squarely on her shoulders. Parenting is a two-way process that requires you and your child working things out together.

Second, developmental limitations or issues and maturational stages may complicate things. It is especially important to review both of these areas to help you establish realistic, developmentally appropriate goals for what is expected of your child at a given age.

Third, you need to believe in what you are doing and be confident that it will work. We all need to see ourselves and our children as capable individuals with potential to grow and to change for the better.

Lastly, give yourself a break: don't expect miracles. Parenting is hard, uncertain work, and you have permission to make mistakes. Neither you nor your child is perfect; it is the minor victories and sincere efforts that accurately reflect your abilities as a parent.

WHEN TO SEEK PROFESSIONAL HELP

Neither the 5-step problem-solving process, nor the activities are intended to replace professional help. If your child's problems do not improve, if his/her behavior substantially worsens, or if you feel overwhelmed or troubled by the situation, we recommend you seek professional advice and counseling. See page 262 for assistance in locating professional help.

Speech! Speech!
After your family does an activity in this book or participates in any activity together, have each person give a short speech about what he or she thought or felt about it. Encourage your child to discuss goals, accomplishments, and improvements needed. Make it humorous by applauding and cheering at the beginning and at the end of the speeches.

Effective listening . . . the main ingredient to good communication

CHAPTER 2

The Main Ingredients

IMAGINE TRYING TO PREPARE Chicken Piccata without knowing the ingredients and portions needed for making such a complex entrée. You would most likely find yourself mixing spices and food items by instinct, aroma, and taste. Depending on your cooking background and skill, your family might end up with a dish resembling Chicken Piccata—or something more like Chicken Peculiar. Whether or not you come close to estimating the ingredients needed, it would have been far easier and less frustrating if you had had a clear, comprehendible list of ingredients. Parenting, like cooking, is a complicated, difficult process that can be joyous or miserable depending on a parent's training and knowledge of specific parenting techniques (ingredients).

We have devoted this chapter to parenting techniques—the main ingredients of enjoyable and successful parenting. While many parents can more or less stumble through eighteen-plus years of raising their children without reading one parenting book or taking a single parenting class, it is much better to have a repertoire of techniques to draw on.

The parenting techniques contained in this chapter were carefully selected and developed by us as the most practical and sound ones available today. They were chosen from three types of positive discipline methods: limit setting, avoiding power struggles, and developing good communication.

POSITIVE DISCIPLINE

All of these techniques recognize that misbehavior in children is a normal episodic event of childhood and that the word "discipline" means "instruction" rather than "arbitrary punishment."

Misbehavior should not automatically label a child as "bad." To the contrary, we believe that most childish misbehavior has a necessary, positive function. Children learn through trial and error. In order to grow up, to become mature, independent adults, they need the freedom to experiment, just like a scientist. For example, when seven-year-old Sarah refuses to brush her teeth for three days, she is exerting her independence. There is no doubt that Sarah is misbehaving, pushing her parents to the limit. However, this trivial sort of mutiny is a normal maturational process in childhood. Sarah needs to test her skills and abilities to make decisions. As much as her parents dislike the opposing views and behaviors of their child, Sarah must at times go against authority in order to exercise her independence and build her self-confidence. There is no better environment in which to take risks and test new and different ways of behaving than in the safe, unconditionally loving, and ever-accepting home of your family.

We also believe that the word "discipline" does not mean yelling, demeaning, spanking, or intimidating a child. Rather, discipline should be viewed as a planned response to a child's behavior.

LIMIT SETTING

Limit setting is the practice of consistently yet lovingly establishing rules, guidelines, and directions for appropriate behaviors as well as explaining the consequences of misbehavior. Setting limits for and with your child does not mean limiting her experience of the world. On the contrary, when parents define the line between right and wrong behavior, they increase their child's sense of predictability and security, making the child's world safer to explore.

Techniques discussed in this chapter such as the Think Chair; Natural and Logical Consequences; Prepare, Plan, Prevent; Family Council; and Your Choice will help give your child needed direction, and, ultimately, the ability to set limits for himself and control his behavior on his own. The Five C's will help you (1) learn how to establish rules that your child can easily understand and that are developmentally appropriate, (2) encourage your child's participation in setting limits, which ensures that the rules are clear, workable, and anticipated, and (3) teach you how to fairly and consistently enforce consequences for misbehavior without being overly punitive.

If the boundaries and the consequences of behavior are clear and predictable, your child will find it easier to make decisions about what to do and what not to do. When setting limits with your child, it is important to consider her age and her ability to comprehend the rules. A four-year-old will probably have more difficulty managing the urge to throw a tantrum than a seven-year-old.

Including your child in the rule-making process motivates her to make sure those limits are upheld. You can expect your child to test new limits; this testing is a necessary and positive aspect of growing, learning, and developing autonomy. Limit setting will be most effective when, over time, your child integrates the rules and guidelines for appropriate behavior into his personal thinking, thereby moving the locus of control from the external (parental rules) to the internal (personal values and awareness).

AVOIDING POWER STRUGGLES

Power struggles are the unavoidable result of two or more persons with differing agenda colliding head-on. Parents often lock horns with their children over messy rooms, taking out the trash, and doing homework. Struggles such as these are time-consuming and energy-wasting and usually result in tears, anger, and unmade beds. A parent's goals and agenda are inevitably different from those of a child. A parent's priority might be to straighten the house before guests arrive, while the child is single-mindedly focused on finding his lost ninja warrior, even if it means tearing apart every closet and toy box in the house.

Avoiding battles with your child has an important purpose: getting her to wrestle with the problem rather than with you! This makes good sense when you consider that parents do battle with their children when they sense that their control is being threatened and they need to regain it. "Stop what you are doing right now and get to bed!" actually means "Stop doing what *you* want and do what *I* want!" Children see these situations as opportunities to assert their independence, and eventually learn better ways to manage you than controlling their own behavior. The best way to avoid World War III in your home is to arm yourself with techniques that offer ways to constructively resolve differences, avoid battles, and give both you and your child a sense of control. T.A.P, S.T.A.R., Ignoring, and Distraction, described later in this chapter, offer excellent ways to bring peace to the battlefields of your homefront and lay the groundwork for responsible problem solving.

DEVELOPING COMMUNICATION

Communication is to parenting what reading and directions are to following a recipe. Mutual understanding will develop only when both parents and child communicate clearly their feelings, experiences, and perceptions.

There is a wealth of information available regarding ways of improving communication with your child. We have selected some of the best "talking techniques" and described them for you in this chapter. Communication techniques such as "I" Messages and Effective Listening are useful in improving talking and listening skills between you and your child. Others, such as Encouragement and Positive Reframing, Try, Try Again, Modeling, Empathy, and Mutual Respect, focus on developing better styles of communication through developing self-confidence and enhancing your child's and your own abilities to express thoughts and feelings. We have also included two techniques that complement the list of communication techniques. These ingredients are called Spices of

Life (humor, loving, and affection) and Planful Playing (Role Playing and playing with your child). These techniques reinforce our philosophy that "talking" is not always the best way to get through to your kids. Humor and playing are two of the most important (and most neglected) ways of communicating with your child: they are the child's natural language.

THE MIX OF INGREDIENTS

The following seventeen ingredients are explained in a straightforward, easy-to-follow manner. Remember, though, that no single technique is effective in all cases. Becoming familiar with all the available parenting techniques is helpful, so we suggest you read through all seventeen and choose those that best suit your personal parenting style. Of course, it is not possible for you to use all the ingredients (techniques) at one time, so test out a few and see which fit your taste.

Throughout the book we suggest a few techniques described in this chapter to further help you solve the problem at hand. The names of the techniques will be highlighted in bold type (for example, **encouragement**) so that you can easily recognize them. You can then use this chapter as a handy reference for looking up a definition of a specific technique when using a problem-solving recipe.

We have not only described what the technique is, but also offer realistic ways to use it and to explain it to your child. You will find these suggestions in the margins. We hope that these main ingredients for preventing and problem-solving difficulties with your child help to create an atmosphere in your home in which communication prevails, power struggles decrease, and limits provide security.

EFFECTIVE LISTENING

Effective Listening is a communication technique by which you convey your willingness to allow feelings to be expressed without lecturing or judging. It consists of listening with your eyes, ears, and heart, with interest and approval, to your child's thoughts and feelings. This is not to say that you are expected to approve of misbehavior. On the contrary, this approach communicates to your child that his thoughts and feelings are valued by you, but that his bad behavior is not acceptable.

One effective way of listening while conversing with your child is to be a sportscaster to her thoughts and feelings: you do a play-by-play account of what she is saying. For example, if she opposes her bedtimes and screams, "No fair! Why can't I stay up later?" you refrain from saying, "Because I said so!" and say instead, "I understand that you feel it's unfair to go to bed right now . . ." By reflecting back to your child what you have just heard, you are helping her label and identify feelings she is expressing, while at the same time communicating to her that you are listening, thus opening the door for future discussions.

You may find this technique very difficult when your child is having a tantrum or if his requests are unreasonable. But try to keep in mind that when you Empathically listen, with your defenses down, with an open mind, and with consideration for his feelings, you are showing him how to take part in a two-way conversation. When the time comes for you to reply, he will probably be more prepared to listen.

Children seek the attention of their parents or parent, and thrive on being heard. Sometimes merely a familiar gesture or a predictable phrase indicating that you "know" what he is thinking or feeling will comfort your child by giving him the reassuring feeling that you really want to understand him. Of course there will be many times when you will be at a total loss to comprehend what is going on inside your son's or daughter's head. But by asking nonthreatening and gentle questions, you demonstrate your willingness to take the time and energy to understand him, thus showing you care about his thoughts and feelings, opening up channels of communication.

"Sit down next to me and tell me why you're so upset."

"I hear you saying that you're not tired at eight-thirty."

"I want to make sure I heard you correctly. You said . . ."

"I guess you're too angry to talk right now."

"I understand your feelings, but I can't accept that behavior."

ENCOURAGEMENT AND POSITIVE REFRAMING

"I love it when you two play so nicely together—it makes me smile!"

"You are really a terrific kid!"

"You must be proud of yourself."

"Wow! You put down that vase so gently."

"Nice job!"

"That's great! You only ate half of that sugary cookie!"

(To your spouse, grandparent) "Did you know that Rick didn't suck his thumb for four hours straight?"

Encouragement and Positive Reframing are processes by which you focus on your child's assets, strengths, and positive intentions to help him build confidence and enthusiasm for personal growth. These techniques express your unconditional belief in your child and thereby lay the foundation for his "I can do it!" attitude. Further, by focusing on the positive rather than on negative misbehavior, you communicate to him what you value and what you will respond to.

Positive Reframing and suggestive Encouragement can help your child renew hope in meeting his goals, feel good about himself, and continuously fuel his internal supply of motivation to strive to do his best. These techniques are especially useful in promoting and increasing your child's capacity for self-appraisal.

Encouragement and Positive Reframing are closely related and often used together. In essence, you practice them by sincerely and accurately painting a positive picture of your child's efforts and abilities. With practice, you can pinpoint and favorably describe the positive elements in any situation no matter how bleak it may appear. Choose comments that help your child appreciate her intrinsic satisfaction of her performance or behavior. For example, asking self-evaluating questions such as "Aren't you proud of yourself for studying well before the test?" or making encouraging comments such as "You sure know how to make dishes sparkle!" can boost self-confidence instantly. With self-confidence, your child will have faith in his abilities to confront everyday challenges and create positive outcomes.

Some children have difficulty accepting encouraging comments directly, but can equally benefit by overhearing them. "Did you know that Emily swam the length of the pool today?" Another method especially helpful for interrupting a negative situation and refocusing undesirable behaviors is to review special moments: "I remember when you . . ." This is a way you can help your child launch himself into a better frame of reference.

Keep in mind that this ingredient not only highlights the positives for your child, but identifies for you what makes him or her unique. Most important, Encouragement creates an atmosphere of faith, trust, and confidence. While it is easy to give Encouragement when your child is doing well, it is difficult to be positive when he is not at his best. However, this is when it is needed most.

FAMILY COUNCIL

The Family Council is a regularly scheduled meeting involving all family members. It is a time for each member to discuss relevant family issues and concerns, air grievances, and share appreciation for things well done. This special meeting enhances the problem-solving "recipes" in this book because it supports the notion that all members of a family have a role in creating a problem-solving atmosphere of cooperation and mutual respect. The meetings are scheduled weekly and follow a structured format that allows for members to share their concerns, solve problems, recognize accomplishments, and make family plans.

Here are a few tips for starting and running a Family Council:

1. Meetings should be regularly scheduled and operate under rules agreed upon in advance. Rules such as not yelling, not blaming others, and not speaking out of turn need to be clear and consistently enforced.

2. Although meetings are originally set up by parents, all members should share in the responsibility for running and contributing to them. Rotate the jobs of chairperson, secretary, and maybe even sergeant-at-arms.

3. Meeting topics should not only include solving problems, assigning chores, and reviewing family responsibilities, but should also encourage members to express their appreciation for each other and plan fun family activities.

4. Avoid criticizing or disregarding members' ideas or suggestions so that everyone involved feels safe expressing his or her thoughts and feelings.

The Family Council is analogous to the "kitchen" in our book. It gives you the time, place, and structure to carry out the "recipe" (five-step problem-solving process) for setting up goals and resolving family difficulties. If you are at a loss as how to actually run this meeting, follow the steps each recipe suggests, and your family will have a clear structure to follow.

Family Council supports family unity, builds a democratic team spirit, and supports each member's sense of self-worth. Just being heard on a regular weekly basis is comforting, especially when busy family routines leave little time for listening and talking with each other.

"The chore chart needs to be revised. Let's call a family meeting on Saturday at eleven."

"Today's family meeting will cover homework, Dad's late work nights, and what we want to do this weekend."

"Remember the rules: no yelling, speaking out of turn, or blaming others."

"First Jesse speaks, then Mom, Jamie, and finally Dad."

THE FIVE C'S FOR RULE MAKING

CORRECTING-CORRECTLY, CLARITY, COOPERATION, COMPROMISE, CONSISTENCY

"I was embarrassed today when you screamed very loudly at the restaurant. I don't like your screaming behavior." (Correcting-correctly)

"Screaming is not allowed in restaurants. If you are going to continue this I will not allow you to come out with me. Please tell me what I said." (Clarity)

"When we went to the store recently I never heard you scream once. Let's work together to help you act like this more often." (Cooperation)

"If you start using a screaming voice then I'll give you a warning. If you continue screaming you can't come with me until you have better control over your screaming behavior." (Compromise)

This parent would then follow up with this rule. (Consistency)

The Five C's is a parenting technique that can help you establish limits or rules in your home while at the same time assisting you in avoiding struggles with your child. This technique is actually a simple and easy-to-remember structure that helps you correct your child's unwanted behavior and then reinforces what your expectations are for the future. Each C word is a part of a process which includes your child in establishing rules: Correcting-correctly, Clarity, Cooperation, Compromise, and, finally, Consistency. By memorizing these five C words, you can establish a routine that both guides and encourages your child to follow behavior limits and your expectations.

Each C word has a specific purpose in the rule-making process, and they are described as follows:

Correcting-correctly means that when you are pointing out your child's inappropriate behavior that demands a limit, you must focus on criticizing the *behavior* instead of the *child* ("I didn't like your screaming behavior at the bank" rather than "You were a bad boy at the bank"). This will reduce his anxiety and defensiveness and lessen the possibility of damaging his self-esteem.

Clarity is exactly what you would think: being clear, to the point, and understood. This means seeking eye contact with your child, and keeping your statement simple. Check with her to make sure she understood you by having her explain to you what you said.

Seeking Cooperation means collaborating and interacting with your child by enlisting her help in following the rules and changing negative behaviors into positive ones. By merely asking your child for her help in following the rules and pointing out times when she was able to cooperate with you in the past, you are showing your faith in her and inviting her to be a part of the process.

Some rules are going to be flexible and some will not. For those that are, allow your child to negotiate a mutually satisfying arrangement: both of you Compromise. The best way to avoid a power struggle is to show your child that although you are serious about your expectations, her opinions are welcomed and you are willing to compromise.

Finally, rules and limits can be followed by your child only if you follow them yourself. Consistency shows her that you mean what you say, and say what you mean. Children actually welcome Consistency in limit setting because it makes their world predictable.

Once you get the hang of it, you can also use this technique to establish rules Preventively—before going to the store or to a friend's house.

"I" MESSAGES

An "I" Message is a nonjudgmental form of communication in which an individual conveys her or his feelings about a situation without accusing or blaming another person.

The person who is feeling discomfort with another's behavior is the *owner* of the problem, as opposed to the owner of the behavior. This does not mean that the owner should assume responsibility for that problem, rather that she is responsible for sharing her thoughts and feelings about how a specific behavior is causing her discomfort. When using an "I" Message, the owner of the problem is able to express her thoughts and feelings in a nonaccusatory manner. As a result, the owner of the behavior may be more willing to listen and confront the problem. When parents use "I" Messages to describe how their child's behavior affects them, the statement also conveys the message that parents are human too and have feelings, needs, and limits.

When using this technique with your child, follow these three easy steps: First, *label* the behavior or activity that is causing you discomfort. Second, *describe* the effect it has on you. Third, *share* with your child how you feel about it. For example, you might say to your child, who is being careless while eating, "When you wipe mashed potatoes on my jacket, it stains it and I feel angry."

Think about how you respond to statements in which you are directly blamed for your behavior problem or you are told, "You better, you will, or you are . . . " Your first reaction is probably "Not me!" You naturally become protective of yourself, especially when you feel attacked or directly confronted with your weaknesses and misdeeds. On the other hand, when a problem is brought to your attention in a way such that the other person owns a portion of the problem (expressing her feelings regarding the problem), you are less likely to feel judged and conversely more likely to listen. You then would invest more energy in making an effort to change rather than argue your position.

While it may seem useless and awkward at first, over time you will find that "I" Messages will become a more natural part of your communicating style. You will also see that because the message focuses on the Consequences that behavior creates, rather than pointing a finger at your child and/or giving undue attention to the behavior itself, defenses are lowered, thereby giving way to further discussion and problem-solving explorations.

"It makes me feel wonderful when you say 'thank you' and 'please.'"

"I don't like loud voices in public—it embarrasses me."

"It seems like I'm always picking up toys and games off the floor. I sure feel tired."

"I felt frustrated when you fell back to sleep after I woke you two times this morning."

IGNORING AND DISTRACTION

(At the doctor's office) "Oh, look! They have that neat book you like so much. Let's read it together."

(After Jim teased Sally) "Sally, I bet you can ignore Jim's teasing and help me plan dinner."

(Annie is misbehaving while you are trying to leave your home) "Annie, you always seem to be able to find missing shoes around here. Do you think you can use your secret powers and locate your brother's shoes?"

(Your kids are fighting) "Gee, I think I'll take a look in the newspaper and see if there are any fun things to do this weekend."

Ignoring and Distraction are techniques that are used when your goal is to avoid drawing attention to a particular behavior. Ignoring by definition means deliberately withholding attention from a child or situation. Distraction is a method of diverting your misbehaving child's attention to a more acceptable alternative. Both techniques work best with behaviors that have not been strongly established and are minor such as sibling squabbles, temper tantrums, and annoying habits. It makes sense that if you consistently ignore your child's temper outbursts he will see that you are not interested in attending to him when he is acting this way.

The most effective way to Ignore, with the hope of eventually eliminating an unwanted behavior, is to turn away, not respond verbally or nonverbally, and definitely do not show signs of losing control. Impress on your child that the newspaper article is far more interesting to you than getting involved in "Daddy, tell Mr. Stupid to leave me alone!" More serious, possibly dangerous behaviors should obviously not be Ignored: turning your back on physically aggressive acts is certainly not recommended.

Distraction is an age-old tool for getting children to focus on other, more enjoyable circumstances, rather than concentrating on the negative conditions that they are currently experiencing. Try telling your screaming child to look at the pretty picture on the doctor's wall while she is being stuck with a needle.

Your first step in using Distraction is to identify the behavioral clues such as tiredness or crankiness that indicate that your child is beginning to show signs of deterioration. Your second step is to interrupt her impending loss of control and refocus her energy and attention toward more positive and productive behaviors. You can do this by offering her something fun to do. This means, however, that you need a backup list of ideas that could be used to persuade your child to take her mind off her weakening behavior control. This not only averts her energy to more positive endeavors but also allows her to feel more in control of the outcome of her actions.

MODELING

Parental Modeling is a lifelong process of teaching your child appropriate behavior and respected values through personal demonstration. Modeling is a full-time job, and one that we are not always aware we are doing. While the engineer is quick to take pride in his son's behavior when he constructs a Lego building, he cannot understand why this same child gets upset when it does not turn out perfectly. This parent easily recognizes that the positive traits that have brought him success are already visible in his son. However, he may be unaware of how his own intolerance for imperfection has also been adopted by his son. Children learn to perform and develop personal traits by observing and emulating others, most often their parents.

Parental Modeling is the simplest and most effective teaching tool for strengthening positive behavior and correcting inappropriate behavior. It is an active blueprint for your child's behavior. While Modeling correct behavior may appear to be simple, consistent and practical use of this technique can be difficult because we are human and make mistakes. Fortunately, our children learn as much from our mistakes and the way we handle errors as they learn from our more noble behaviors.

Modeling requires no special training or extraordinary skill. It does, however, demand that you pay attention to the messages that your behavior communicates to your child. There are essentially two ways parents Model these messages to their children. The first is more a way of life than a parenting technique. It entails taking stock of your beliefs and values and determining how well your behavior parallels them. Punctuality, saying thank you, helping others, and standing up for what you believe are some common examples of how parents can express their values through the way they live and act.

The second is a practiced method by which a parent identifies problem behaviors and then planfully demonstrates (Models) how those behaviors can be successfully performed. For instance, if your child has difficulty making new friends, you might take her along with you when you go out to introduce yourself to a new person on the block. By doing this you will teach her how to introduce herself to a new person and how to extend friendship to others.

Modeling is one of the main ingredients of effective parenting that can either stand alone or be successfully combined with other techniques.

"I'm going to sit over here and cool down so I won't yell and scream."

(To a child who doesn't wash her hair enough) "I love to wash my hair and make it squeaky clean. Do you think it looks shiny after I wash it?"

(To a child who doesn't eat vegetables) "These carrots are crunchy, and they taste great dipped in a little salad dressing."

(Sharing problem) To your spouse or friend: "Would you like to share my soda? I love sharing things with you."

MUTUAL RESPECT AND EMPATHY

"You seem very unhappy about this and I understand that it makes you angry."

"Why don't you give me a few suggestions?"

"How would you like to have your hair cut this time?"

"How do you feel about that idea?"

"Wow—I can see why you got so scared!"

Mutual Respect is a technique that is effective in helping your child to build self-respect and personal regard for herself and others. It requires that one consider others as equals—not necessarily in regard to knowledge, maturity, or experience, but with regard to feelings and ideas. Empathy, the ability to understand another's experience, is an interpersonal skill necessary for building healthy relationships. Parents can teach their children much about Mutual Respect and Empathy by simply demonstrating respect and understanding for them, their feelings, thoughts, and experiences. Shared consideration for each other builds trust and strengthens the parent/child relationship.

Mutual Respect is conveyed to your child by many seemingly inconsequential things you do and don't do. You are not respecting your child when you talk down to him, purposely embarrass him, laugh at his efforts, or look through his private belongings without asking permission. You are conveying respect by allowing your child to within appropriate limits choose his own manner of dress, hair style, friends, and hobbies, thus telling him that you esteem and value his taste and individuality. Respect is also conveyed through other, more subtle actions such as not rushing to the rescue when she is independently trying to solve a math problem, repair a broken toy, or construct a Lego skyscraper, but, instead, being available to help with her requests. In each of these examples, you will communicate respect and belief in your child's capabilities, rights, and uniqueness. Teaching respect in this manner will accomplish what most parents wish for: respect from their children.

Empathy, like Mutual Respect, is best taught through practice. A parent who can empathize communicates his understanding, compassion, and sensitivity for his child's perspective. In order to do so, a parent must first imagine himself in his child's place or predicament and then share his perceptions of that experience with his child. In doing this, you communicate your sensitivity to his situation and Model for him a way to understand and articulate his feelings. Empathizing with your child will help him explore, with you, his emotions and behaviors, and eventually teach him how to use Empathy himself in developing healthy relationships with others.

NATURAL AND LOGICAL CONSEQUENCES

This technique is a means for responding to undesirable behaviors in a way that makes sense to children and adults alike. Simply put, this technique focuses upon consequences that are either Natural (leaving a bicycle on the driveway, resulting in it being run over—not purposely, of course) or Logical (leaving one's bicycle in the driveway results in its being put away, and your child is prohibited from using it for a period of time). These two types of consequences for inappropriate actions teach your child the cause-and-effect relationship between her behavior and responses to that behavior. The value of both Natural and Logical Consequences is that your child will learn self-discipline through his personal experiences rather than your personal demands.

To use this technique apply this basic rule: *When your child misbehaves, you provide undesirable consequences that logically or naturally fit the misbehavior.* Instead of punishing your child for his misdeed, the consequence does it for you. For example, if your child has not been turning in his homework on time, the Natural Consequence would be a lower grade and the Logical Consequence would be to schedule more homework time and less playtime. This approach holds him responsible for his behavior, forces him to be accountable for his decisions, and affords him the opportunity to learn from a series of events rather than by complying with the authoritative demands of others.

In order for this technique to teach your child self-regulation, you will need to be consistent and to follow through with the consequences you provide. Implementing Logical and Natural Consequences for misbehavior can be accomplished by using the following four guidelines:

First, when the behavior problem occurs, apply either the Logical or Natural Consequences most fitting for the specific misbehavior.

Second, try your best to inform your child of his misbehavior and its consequence without being angry or smug.

Third, as you follow through with the consequence, reassure your child that he will have an opportunity to try again and solve the problem.

Fourth, if the behavior is repeated, either apply the same consequence or come up with another that fits naturally or logically.

Throughout this process, try not to get into a struggle over the consequence itself, and avoid having the hidden motive of controlling your child, for this defeats the purpose of letting your child struggle with his own problem. Be patient! It takes time for a child to understand and experience the effects that either Logical or Natural Consequences impose upon him and his future.

"The consequence for breaking your sister's toy is that you will have to replace it and pay for it out of your allowance."

"Because the dishes were done poorly, you'll have to do them again."

"If you don't clean your fish water, it will get dirty and eventually the fish will die." (Natural Consequence)

"What do you think the consequence is for not respecting your teacher?"

PLANFUL PLAYING: ROLE PLAY, JOINING IN

This fun- and child-oriented technique is derived from the experiences, successes, and enjoyment that playing with children has brought us as parents and play therapists.

There are three types of Planful Playing: joining-in-play, planned play, and Role Playing. All three reach the same goal of redirecting and teaching your child better behavior in a fun, nonthreatening manner.

To use joining-in-play, utilize times when your child is inviting you to "play" with her to explore issues relevant to meeting everyday challenges. Dollhouse play, coloring, and make-believe play can uncover many important aspects of your child's thinking and give you opportunities to introduce new problem-solving techniques. You might join your child's play scene and interject a few new ways to resolve conflict between two angry stuffed animals. Help him learn how to put a frightened doll to bed or how to skillfully confront big ugly monsters. In each of these examples you are learning much about your child's interpersonal conflicts and assisting her in overcoming them.

Planful Playing is a technique in which you create fun situations that Encourage your child to playfully examine ways to improve his behavior. Play "Beat the Clock," an amusing game of "Can you pick up your toys before the big hand reaches the twelve?" This should attract your child's interest and challenge him to compete against the clock rather than competing for control with you—a great way to divert a power struggle. One method of playfully and humorously getting your message across is, rather than nagging or threatening your child with "for the last time . . . ," sing out requests in your finest operatic voice. Or pin funny notes onto misplaced items: "Help, I'm lost! Please take me to my hamper home with the rest of my stinky friends."

Role Playing is a dramatic technique in which two or more persons act out an assigned role. It is an excellent way to engage your child in practicing problem solving and involve him in looking at himself from another point of view. You can Role Play with your child either a specific problem he recently had or a situation he could encounter. When Role Playing, have him practice his new skills and test out ways he might solve a problem by acting out the situation. Ask your child to play a role other than his own so he can experience the situation from another perspective.

Through any three of these safe mediums, parents can engage their children in confronting fears and exploring personal difficulties.

"Let's practice solving an argument. You pretend to be playing by yourself and I'll come and bother you."

"Let's draw a picture together of what makes us sad."

A sign taped to your forehead says, BEWARE! MOM'S GOT A BIG HEADACHE! PICK UP YOUR STUFF BEFORE SHE EXPLODES!

"Oh no! The floor turned into hot coals. Everything on it will burn to pieces if we don't pick it up fast!"

"Looks like Hillary needs us to tickle her tantrums out before she starts screaming and crying."

PREPARE, PLAN, PREVENT

Just as a skilled business manager makes lists, writes appointments in his daily calendar, and predicts possible problems, a good family manager must do the same. By planning your own and your child's day and preparing her to handle events that may be stressful or difficult, you can prevent a possible disaster. By designing structured activities, daily rituals, and organized routines, you can eliminate some of life's recurring problems.

Thinking and planning your day does not mean eliminating spontaneity or rigidly marching your child through a set of tasks in order that you can both retire at exactly 2100 hours. Routines give your child a sense of stability and clear expectations of what is going to happen next. Children often have difficulty regulating emotions when transitions and changes occur unexpectedly. They find comfort in orderly routines and predictable activities because this outlines for them what to anticipate and when to expect it.

There are several ways parents can prevent unwanted behavior problems by developing family rituals and efficient routines. Try structuring your sixteen-hour day in manageable units or prearranged blocks of time. Think ahead about possible trouble spots: periods of the day during which you cannot be flexible and ones that may be especially stressful for either you or your child. For example, if you know that your child tends to be irritable or impatient at the end of the day, prearrange that block of time to focus on what she finds interesting and fun. If your child's mood and tolerance for adult-oriented activities is greater in the early morning, this would be the best time to plan outings to the store or the dry cleaner.

Prepare your child for the day's happenings by explaining to him what he can expect to encounter in the next six hours: "First, we'll go to the bank and then to the supermarket and then we'll visit your friends at the playground." You may even specifically describe each activity: "When we're at the bank, we'll have to stand in line quietly." Daily or weekly family rituals such as bedtime routines and Friday-evening dinner at Joe's Pizza enhance your child's ability to manage his behaviors because they provide predictable and familiar opportunities to plan his actions, prepare for changes, and prevent himself from misbehaving.

"First we're going to the bank, then to the supermarket, and finally to the park."

"Remember your goals, and if you act nicely at Aunt Linda's, you almost have enough stars to get your reward."

"What can we bring with us to keep you busy while we visit?"

"Let's see how good your memory is today. If you can tell me our schedule from start to finish we'll end our day with a special surprise."

SPICES OF LIFE: LOVING AND HUMOR

"I love having you around. You're so special!"

"I love every inch of you . . . This little toe . . . this little finger . . ."

"Time for a family hug. Let's huddle."

"I think something died in the bathroom—or maybe Jackie forgot to flush the toilet again." (An example of humor, of course)

"Whew. What a tough day we had. You're still my special little boy no matter what you do."

This technique lumps together some important ingredients of living that make up a family's heart, soul, and spirit. Loving, nurturing, Affection, physical contact, and Humor are just a few Spices of Life we all need in order to feel secure and happy. Without them our ability to take on daily challenges is greatly weakened.

We would like to stress that loving and nurturing your child should never be used as a way to get him to do something. These emotions should be unconditional—it is unnecessary and potentially destructive to withhold them even if you are doing it in the name of discipline. It is the way in which you convey these natural emotions that Spices Up your family's ability to function at its best.

Love, cherish, and accept your child simply because he is! It is important that your child know that he doesn't have to be good to be loved. This gives him the message that you may not always love his behavior, but you will always love *him*. This knowledge will better enable your child to take risks, test problem-solving skills, and examine behavior without worrying whether his efforts will be accepted or rejected.

Physical and emotional affection are extremely important spices. Verbal and nonverbal expressions show your child that your support and feelings of fondness are everlasting. Saying, "I love you!", hugging, kissing, and affectionately playing with your child's hair (especially when he is not anticipating it), tells him just how special and important he is to you.

Another important spice is Humor. When parents can see the lighter side of the problem, they defuse tension and restore perspective by enabling their children to feel less threatened in examining their difficulties.

It is important not to make a joke out of your child: it is not funny to be sacrificed for the sake of a good laugh. Make sure your humor matches the humor of the child. Help her to see that enjoying and finding pleasure in the silliness of a situation helps in accepting the fact that humans make errors and imperfection is a part of life. You may not think it's amusing that your child hasn't cleaned her room for so long that a misplaced grape has turned into a raisin or the beginnings of a fruitful wine, but with a twist of humor and a nonconfrontive approach, your child's messy room and fermenting grape can bring you laughter and a scrapbook memory for years to come—not to mention perhaps his commitment to keeping his room a bit cleaner.

S.T.A.R. (STOP THINK ACT RIGHT)

S.T.A.R. (Stop Think Act Right) is a "self-talk" technique for children that teaches self-appraisal and self-control. This fun and easy-to-remember acronym can teach your child to slow down, review misbehavior, and consider his next step. Children do not naturally know how to stop themselves from acting incorrectly; in order for a child to control impulsiveness, emotional outbursts, habitual responses, and thoughtless conduct, he must learn to listen to his inner voice, which talks him through a productive process. This internally motivated process is the key to self-discipline.

We have found that the playful word S.T.A.R. is a simple and easy-to-use method for teaching children the three-step process of self-control: (1) Stopping, (2) Thinking, and then (3) Acting correctly (Right) or responsibly. First you will need to help your child stop all activity and *think* rather than *act:* turn off his arms and legs and turn on his brain. Second, help him think about the object of his actions, consider whether this behavior will help him achieve what he wants, weigh his options, and make a decision regarding the best course of action. Third, encourage him to test his decisions and find out for himself if they bring him closer to his goal.

Let's say that your child has difficulty controlling his anger and from time to time hits others. Once you have taught your child how to use this technique, you can ask her to be a S.T.A.R. and stop and think before she strikes out with her fists. This word then becomes an easy and fun reminder of a better way to behave. You may even want to use S.T.A.R. in a playful way by involving your child in a full-day game of pasting star stickers on her every time she stops a negative behavior and engages in a more positive action. She could eventually be covered with stars for a hard day's work.

You can turn this technique around and encourage your child to evaluate a situation in which he misbehaved. S.T.A.R. spelled backwards is R.A.T.S.: Review Actions and Try Some more. This catchy expression will give both you and your child a simple structure to follow in examining a problem behavior. It is difficult for anyone, adult or child, to take a critical look at himself, and saying "R.A.T.S.!" to your child following his misbehavior breaks the tension and resistance to reviewing actions and exploring alternative ways he might have acted.

"Remember, when we get to the party we want you to be a S.T.A.R. We know you can do it!"

"Whoa—hit the brakes! Let's slow things down and think about what kind of behavior is right at the library."

"Now that you've stopped to think about your next move, what do you think is the best way to go about it?"

"You took control and stopped yourself before throwing that at your brother. What a S.T.A.R.!"

"R.A.T.S.! You lost control again. Remember, everyone makes mistakes. You can try again."

T.A.P. (THINK AND PREVENT)

(To yourself) "Boy, he's really pushing my buttons—I'm losing control. I better walk away."

"Jeff, I'm very upset and disappointed. Please start cleaning up this mess. And I'm going to walk over there and take a deep breath."

(To yourself) "If I start screaming too, we'll both look and feel like lunatics."

T.A.P. is a method for managing anger. It is based on a technique called "self-talk"—the running commentary or internal voice we "hear" in our minds throughout the day. A parent can use T.A.P. (Think And Prevent) to stop spiraling negative events and give himself or herself an opportunity to have an internal conversation about alternative ways of expressing angry thoughts and feelings.

This technique suggests that you actually tap yourself on the leg or arm when you feel the first signals of anger. This very helpful signal to yourself concretely structures your thoughts and actions so that unplanned words and reactions to anger do not escape.

All humans need opportunities to express anger and release tension. However, the way it is expressed can either bring parent and child closer together or push them further apart. Our children's annoying and irritating behaviors emotionally challenge us by igniting an automatic sequence of angry responses. In order to control anger, parents need to turn themselves off so that they have a moment to think about how to better handle their feelings. By giving yourself a light tap on the leg, you can turn off, like a light switch, your overly emotional responses and turn on your power to control and prevent unwanted reactions to your child's behavior. This helps you break the cycle of events that usually follows when you lose control and act excessively punitive (and later experience guilt). T.A.P. gives you the chance to take a time-out and think about other ways of expressing your feelings.

T.A.P. works best if you TAP into your knowledge bank of previously successful experiences of handling your anger correctly. Develop a vocabulary for angry feelings so that you can rely on those verbal expressions to take over instead of an explosion of words that have no value or purpose. Here are three simple steps for using T.A.P.:

1. When you feel the first signs of parental meltdown, give yourself a tap and disengage from the situation.

2. Once you are unplugged from the challenge your child is presenting, plug into your own self-talk methods of controlling your anger by saying to yourself, "I can be calm," or, "Getting too angry is a waste of energy!"

3. Return to your child with a renewed charge of self-control and calmly express your feelings.

Your child will benefit by observing your use of this technique. He will learn that self-control is important to you—something you work hard to achieve.

THE THINK CHAIR

The Think Chair is another name for a well-known behavioral technique called "time-out." We call it the Think Chair or think space because we want to give children the message that it is a time to regain control and think about a better way to behave. This method of quickly interrupting and removing your child from the scene stops his unwanted behavior from continuing and then directs him to sit in a previously chosen place to think about his actions. This immediate and brief intervention breaks the pattern of misbehavior.

This technique has a dual benefit for you and your child. It gives both of you a concrete procedure to follow, specifics in dealing with escalating behaviors, and, literally, a space in which to cool off and recover control. The Think Chair is most effective in correcting persistent behaviors that are impulsive, hostile, aggressive, and overly emotional. Here are a few suggestions in using the Think Chair or think space:

1. Pick a quiet, low-stimulation place in your home where your child is not likely to be distracted by the TV or nearby toys.

2. When explaining to your child what the Think Chair is, be sure to indicate what behaviors will get him a front-row seat.

3. When the time comes to use the Think Chair, tell your child in twenty words or less in no more than ten seconds why he needs to go to the Think Chair and what he should think about. There is no reason to go on with lengthy descriptions of why he is going to be there—this only invites a power struggle or an opportunity for your child to bargain his way out.

4. Always indicate how long he must stay in the Think Chair. A good rule to follow is one minute for each year of age.

5. Use a timer with a bell so that your child has no reason to ask you if her time is up, thus eliminating your need to attend to her. You are also giving her some control over the situation by being in charge of the timer.

6. When the bell rings, ask your child to explain her thoughts. If she expresses adequate and age-appropriate understanding of her misbehavior, she can leave the Think Chair; if not, she may need to sit through another session of thinking.

7. Don't speak to and/or lecture your child while she is in the Think Chair. She should see that she needs time to think for herself and that you will not give her attention for her inappropriate behavior.

"This will be your special place to sit and cool off when you're acting out of control and unsafe."

"Wow, you are really having a hard time listening. You need to spend two minutes in the Think Chair."

"Hitting is not okay in this family. Sit in the Think Chair for five minutes and think about your actions."

"You did it! Five whole minutes in the chair. Now that you're calm, can you tell me why you had to sit in the Think Chair?"

TRY, TRY AGAIN

"Try again—you can do it!"

"I think it's great that you tried."

"Oh, well—I know you meant to finish first. But you sure looked great out there."

"That's okay, we all make mistakes. No one's perfect."

Try, Try Again gives family members the permission to mess up and labels mistakes as aids to learning. This supportive approach applies to all because we are all imperfect and make mistakes. By exclaiming, "It's okay, try again!", you are telling your child that it's normal to fumble through situations, and that it is positive efforts that you really admire and appreciate. This technique emphasizes the importance of realizing that successful problem-solving comes from patiently enduring human error while waiting for newly employed strategies to work. Giving your child a learner's leeway and the opportunity to make mistakes is the kind of parental perseverance needed in allowing him to try out new behaviors.

Children need to know that mistakes are not failures, nor are they "bad." They need to separate the deed from the doer and feel supported by their parents regardless of their failed attempts to improve their behavior. In addition, they need to see that being able to accomplish something new can be done only by trial and error. Problem solving is a process of two steps forward, one step back, which enables us to develop an accurate sense of right and wrong, mature thinking, good judgment, and reasoning skills.

Keep your expectations and goals for your child reasonable and developmentally appropriate. This will lead to a situation in which she will have the opportunity to meet her goals and experience success. Showing your joy in her efforts and praising her attempts to change negative behaviors is more important than focusing on whether or not she reached her goals. Being accepting of your child, no matter how she performs, helps define for her that it is the behavior you are not happy with and not her. Further, you will communicate to your child that she is good enough without reaching perfection. When you unconditionally accept your child's efforts and inadequacies, you bring her closer to being able to develop the courage to cope with the everyday challenges of living.

Try, Try Again informs your child that it is improvement, not perfection, that is important in solving problems. It is demanding and unrealistic to expect a child to meet high standards of excellence when he is attempting to make behavioral changes. Your child will feel more motivated if he understands that you recognize his efforts toward making improvements as the actual success.

YOUR CHOICE

This parenting technique is based on a process of offering choices rather than commanding or directing your child to do or not do something. This approach will foster your child's confidence—his sense that he is in control of his destiny and is capable of making decisions that ultimately will get him what he wants. For example, a parent might say, "You can either continue fighting with each other and stay home or else end this argument and we'll all go to the movies—your choice." When you offer your child reasonable choices and outcomes for each choice, it becomes easier for him to pause and think about making a good decision. Giving choices promotes your child's participation in solving the problem, shaping the outcome of her situation, and assuming responsibility for the results of her behavior.

By giving your child an age-appropriate opportunity for control, you are saying, "I respect your ability to make good choices." A child who feels encouraged and empowered to participate in the decision-making process will focus his energies on himself rather than struggling with his parents.

Here are a few important things to keep in mind when using this technique:

1. Don't offer a choice you may regret or have difficulty following through with.

2. Be sure to accept your child's decision and refrain from exerting pressure to make the "right" choice.

3. When laying out the choices and possible outcomes for each, focus on how your child will be affected—not the person handing out the choices. This encourages your child to own the behavior and view the decision as his own. It is important that the consequence given for a choice be logically related to the behavior you are trying to correct. (See Logical and Natural Consequences.)

4. Finally, if your child refuses to participate, inform him that you will make the decision for him. Engaging your child in the decision-making process around minor issues like getting to bed, doing his homework, and being on time for dinner gives him the invaluable practice he'll need when he is confronted with the prospect of making Choices among his peers—significant Choices such as joining a group of bad kids or even taking drugs.

In summary, Your Choice can give your child an opportunity to further his skills in constructive problem-solving, critical decision-making, weighing options, predicting outcomes, and ultimately taking responsibility for his life. Don't forget: giving Choices keeps your child struggling with the *problem* rather than with *you.*

"Would you like to wear the yellow shirt or the purple one with these pants?"

"What would you like to eat for dinner tomorrow? Help me decide."

"Todd, you have two choices. Get into your pajamas in five minutes or lose fifteen minutes of television time. Your choice."

"Your choice—you can stop whining and we can play longer, or go on whining and we leave right now."

Recipe #1: The Family Emblem

CHAPTER 3

Family Unity

IT'S DINNERTIME AT THE McDonald family. Mom finishes preparing her Slim Fast Shake and retires to the study to finish her report for tomorrow's work meeting. Eight-year-old Brad disconnects himself from the Nintendo game to make a well-rounded meal of microwave cheeseburger and toasted Pop-Tarts. Eleven-year-old Shirley once again pushes aside her incompleted homework, along with her five-year-old sister, Elaine, who is pleading to go with her, to meet her friends at the Mall. Shortly after, as a fight erupts between Brad and Elaine over the prized position on the couch, Dad walks in and yells, "Where is everyone? And what's for dinner?"

Call it a family, pack, tribe, or clan; today's family is challenged by dual careers, disintegrating social supports, divorce and remarriage, and deteriorating values. Attempting to teach children the rules of life without a family atmosphere of guidance, support, and values is like trying to cook without a kitchen. We believe that in a thriving family not only should the members get along well with one another, they should also encourage each other's accomplishments, balance independence with support, use clear and understandable communication, and work together to successfully solve problems.

We have dedicated this chapter to family unity: the most important ingredient in cooking up family happiness and success. We strongly advocate the development of democratic family functioning, an approach that invites and encourages children to think for themselves, make thoughtful decisions, participate in family planning, and learn responsibility by sharing it. This chapter asks that you identify and review your family's parenting and child-management recipes, including those from your own childhood, and if necessary replace them with ones founded on democratic values.

Family Connections

Dual Careers

Divorce

PROBLEMS

Our society emphasizes individual as opposed to group needs. This reduces the role of the family and creates for many persons, adults and children, a sense of disconnectedness. Many problems have thus resulted, including:

Isolation

Not feeling that you belong or are closely connected with those with whom you live.

Not feeling useful; that your contribution is needed in the family.

Feeling alone with your problems, achievements, interests, and hobbies.

Communication

Sensing that strained, underdeveloped, or dysfunctional communication among family members is preventing information from being shared or even heard.

An atmosphere in which the traditions of culture, nationality, religion, and race are not taught or respected.

A lack of unity in which children are not given the opportunity to learn, and practice with others, problem-solving skills such as how to peacefully resolve conflicts, negotiate, compromise, and understand the point of view of other persons.

Isolation

A sense of belonging or having membership in his/her family contributes to your child's belief that he is worthwhile and valuable. (Recipes 1, 2, 3, 4, 5)

Help your child see that her contributions, such as household responsibilities and participation in family decisions, are an integral component of the family's (thus the child's) success and happiness. Identify each member's special talents and integrate them into the family situations and family functioning. (Recipes 2, 4, 25)

Communication

Support each member's interests, no matter how divergent, parents and children alike. Do this by trying out one another's hobbies, sports, and interests, and by attending events, games, and shows, or concerts together. Rally the entire family to get behind an individual member's problem rather than labeling the member as a problem to the family. Recognize accomplishments of individuals, no matter how large or small. Create family ceremonies in celebration of success. (Recipes 2, 5.2, 42, 44.5, 55.14, 60.4)

When cooperation and problem solving become a family norm, not only will your children be practiced at working with others toward a common goal, they will also develop more positive self-concepts and feel more capable and responsible. (Recipes 4, 18.3, 48.6, 57, 58, 59)

☆ *Family Emblem* ☆

This recipe defines family culture and uniqueness while strengthening each member's sense of belonging.

Step 1
State and define the problem

Discuss with your child or children how some families have problems and do not have a special sense of understanding and connection with their history, culture, and traditions. Use words and examples your child will understand to discuss and appreciate your family's uniqueness.

Step 2
Identify skills and solutions

Explore each individual member's as well as combined family skills and attributes that contribute to your specialness. Come up with at least one talent that each member has that reinforces the overall spirit of the entire family. For example, if one child has a great throwing arm, another is a good organizer and team leader, and you are an especially skilled runner, your family has the beginnings of a great baseball team. Use this opportunity to share stories and memorable events in your family's history that highlight these special skills and unique attributes of grandparents, relatives, and ancestors.

Step 3
Mutually agree upon goals

Family Goal: "I will use my special skills to gain respect for and pride in our family of origin."

Step 4
Practice and play

This activity does three important things. First, it helps your family become familiar with its past. Second, it identifies each individual's unique contributions to the family. Third, it unites and builds family pride. Design a family emblem that will become your family trademark. This emblem could resemble a coat of arms or be an original design. It is imperative that all family members work together democratically to decide on the design.

There are several ways your family can do this. One would be to research your family surname and the meaning behind it. Another would be to interview relatives and older family members to come up with a design that recognizes past accomplishments or something that has been passed down from generation to generation. You might want to research your nationality. Your design could include a picture of a flag or symbol from your ethnic origin. Elaborate on each individual's personal accomplishments or talents and integrate it into the design. You can simply photograph or draw a picture of your family. Or make an emblem that is divided in two parts, one representing your heritage, culture, ethnic ties, and one identifying present family accomplishments. Once you have come up with a design, your family can take pride in your creation by exhibiting it on T-shirts, jackets, coffee mugs, key chains, hats, or the welcome mat to your home. You can put your family emblem on stationery. Show off your family emblem by drawing your design on a piece of rectangular material and hanging it on a pole—a personalized flag. How about painting your family emblem on the front door of your home? One family we know made a totem pole out of large cylinder ice cream containers (you can find these at your local ice cream shop). Each person designed his or her own container, a replica of himself or herself, and then the family put all the containers together to make an eight-foot-tall totem pole.

Take a moment to appreciate your family's hard work in designing your special family emblem. Recognize the special feelings, the pride, and the new understanding each member gets from working together, researching your heritage, and exploring personal contributions to the family unit.

Step 5
Review and recognize efforts

☆ *Family Rituals* ☆

This recipe reinforces communication, unity, and playfulness.

Step 1
State and define the problem

Without ceremonies, traditions, and rituals, children miss out on an important ingredient of family unity. Explore with your child or children problems that arise from lack of common bonds, not spending special time together, and lack of fun and laughter.

Step 2
Identify skills and solutions

Recognize each family member's admired traits and special attributes: "John is a great baseball player" and "Sherry has a wonderful sense of humor." Explain how their knowledge and skills can sometimes shape who they are and what they are known for. Every family has special traditions and norms of behavior that are established from unstated rules, attitudes, communication styles, repeated events, and common experiences. Come up with a few unique family interests or rituals that are characteristic of your family such as "We all love camping" or "We go out for Chinese food every Sunday."

Step 3
Mutually agree upon goals

Family Goal: "I will use my special skills to enjoy our family's unique and special rituals."

Step 4
Practice and play

In this recipe you will be inventing your own family ritual: anything from putting aside one night a week to do something special together to an unusual family story told every year at Christmastime. This activity is not a one-time event. The purpose of creating a family ritual is to establish a special routine, a yearly, weekly, or daily activity that characteristically and distinctively is your family's. A ritual gives everyone a special and sometimes exclusive practice that binds the family together. Both of us have fond feelings for family rituals. In Mark's family, his father would make up and tell an ongoing nightly adventure story to him and his brothers at bedtime and during long car trips. To this day, Denise's family routinely performs a magical act of hanging spoons on their noses when they gather at restaurants, holiday events, and even at elegant weddings; it has become a trademark. Depending on what your family style and comfort level is, institute a ritual that meets your needs. Get your family involved in the planning and invention of the ritual. Here are several ideas for family rituals:

- Choose a weekly activity in which all family members come together; a special night out at Joe's Pizza or Saturday afternoon at the matinee, or Sunday mystery trips to new places.

- Think up a secret handshake, hand signal, or expression that only your immediate family knows about.

- Create an unusual family recipe. This secret concoction is to be named after your family and made by them for parties, holidays, dinners, picnics or special events.

- Make a family scrap album honoring special events, school achievements, vacations, birthdays, and the changing looks of its members. Bring out the album once a month to add new information and to reminisce.

- Take a yearly vacation that is planned and organized by the whole family.

- Have a **family council** meeting (see Family Council, page 19) or plan a weekly hour to discuss plans, grievances, chores, and accomplishments.

- Make a family time capsule in which your family collects items that signify the year's events and achievements. Place them in a box or a jar to be opened years or decades later. Make it a yearly ritual to collect the items and put them in the container. You may want to close up one time capsule and open a new one every few years.

When participating in or remembering your family rituals, talk about how it brings you all together and acknowledge the pleasure it gives you.

Step 5
Review and recognize efforts

☆ *Common Threads* ☆

RECIPE # 3
Serves: All ages

This recipe is for separated or divorced families.

Step 1
State and define the problem

In today's society, divorce affects almost one-half of American families, shattering the structure and the ties among members, pitting parents against each other in adversarial legal processes, and often trapping children in the middle. Unfortunately, as parents attempt to remedy an intolerable situation by separating from each other, children almost inevitably lose their sense of security and family solidarity. Take the time to discuss with your child her concerns and feelings stemming from the divorce or separation. Talk about the problems it has created. Use techniques such as **"I" messages** and **effective listening** to provide a safe and inviting atmosphere to discuss these often overwhelming feelings.

Step 2
Identify skills and solutions

It takes time, skill, and good communication for a child to endure divorce and successfully work through the ongoing challenge of weekends at Daddy's, new stepparents, and often parents who are continually in conflict. Point out your child's personal strengths and capabilities that will enable him to get through the divorce. Qualities such as cooperativeness, optimism, ability to express emotions and to get along with new people will help your child or children cope with the breakup of the family.

Step 3
Mutually agree upon goals

Goal: "I will use my special skills to feel connected with my family even though we may not be living under the same roof."

Step 4
Practice and play

There is no simple recipe or ingredient that resolves the intense emotions, sense of loss, and conflict caused by divorce. The healing process takes years and tremendous effort by both children and parents. The activities we are suggesting focus on creating a sense of unity and common threads among separated members. Children need to feel connected with some sort of family unit, even if it is not a traditional one. By having your family participate in the following activities, you can show them how they are still a part of a family.

The Family Quilt. Using scraps from old clothing from each family member (including grandparents, relatives, and/or new family members—stepparents, stepsiblings, etc.), make a family quilt for and with your child. While cutting and sewing the pieces together, talk with her about how the separated pieces of cloth represent each person, and how, although you may be separate, you still have common threads that bind you together.

Picture Collage. Using the above concept, select photographs of family members or draw pictures to make a family picture collage. Add to the collage pictures from the past, present, and future that symbolically represent the changes your family has experienced since the divorce.

Family Calendar. Make a family calendar by taking or using twelve photos that symbolically represent your family. This could be a picture of each member, of where a parent lives, or of activities or events enjoyed with each separate parent. Make a pictorial calendar by enlarging each of the twelve pictures and use these pictures as the photo for each month. You can order a calendar with blank picture spaces for each month from Create a Calendar, 330 Oakhurst Lane, Colorado Springs, CO 80906. Use the calendar to indicate days a child will be with one parent or the other. Mark down where she is spending the holiday, special events she will be attending, and general information that will help her understand what is happening throughout the year. This activity is especially important in giving your child a sense of order, control, and predictability in an often confusing family structure. (See Prepare, Plan, Prevent, page 27.) Explain to your child that the divorce makes things different now, but just like their special calendar, your love and attention will continue all throughout the year.

The Divorce Workbook. Make a divorce book with your family that helps your child or children understand the processes, feelings, and changes the divorce has or will have on your family. You can use a book called *The Divorce Workbook. A Guide for Kids and Families,* by Sally B. Ives (Waterfront Books, 1992), which is actually a write-in workbook that encourages children to write and draw pictures of what they are thinking and feeling about the divorce.

Once you and your child have finished the project, ask her to look back at her accomplishments and new understandings. She will, hopefully, take out of this experience a feeling of family cohesiveness and continuity in the midst of the separations and changes. Be sure to remind your child that she is responsible only for feeling safe and loved in the family—she is not responsible for the divorce and/or separation.

Step 5
Review and recognize efforts

☆ *The Family Business* ☆

RECIPE # 4

Serves: 5–12 years

A recipe for dual-career parenting.

Step 1
State and define the problem

Create an open discussion that focuses on your child's feelings and understandings of having working parents. Take this opportunity to share with him your own feelings and thoughts about working outside of the home. Use **effective listening, empathy,** and **mutual respect** when listening to your child's perspective.

Step 2
Identify skills and solutions

Label and identify your child's skills and capabilities that are specifically related to dealing with working parents. Use examples of situations when he was able to adjust to a day-care situation or wait at home for a parent. Point out times when he helped out at home or took on responsibilities that improved the overall functioning of the family.

Step 3
Mutually agree upon goals

Goal: "I will use my special skills to help my family 'work' better together."

Step 4
Practice and play

The basic premise for this activity is very simple, but its symbolic value and message are not to be overlooked. Children learn through experience. What better way for a child to understand and appreciate why his parents need to work than to establish a business of his own? You may want to first help your child appreciate what a family business entails. Many farms and other family-owned businesses invite others to come to their home or establishment for a working vacation. Your family can experience waking early in the morning to collect eggs, milk cows, and even clean the barn on a working family farm or ranch. For more information on working vacations, try *Ranch Vacations,* by Gene Kilgore (John Muir, 1989) or contact you state's office of tourism.

To start your own family business, ask your child to first choose a business that interests him: a lemonade stand, recycling bottles and cans, dog walking, lawnmowing, etc. *Jobs for Kids,* by Carol Barkin and Elizabeth James (Lothrop, 1990), has a terrific list of job ideas as well as ways to get the business started.

Have your child develop and run the business, from sending out flyers to collecting and budgeting his money. Parental involvement is crucial for the success of this activity. As your child develops his business, he will need guidance and advice from the working experts (his parents). Take on some of the responsibilities so that you can be directly involved. You can help balance the budget or solve other difficulties by having a **family council** meeting. Every parenting technique (ingredient) must be considered in helping your child understand the complexity of this activity. Concentrate on **encouragement, mutual respect, logical** and **natural consequences,** and **prepare, plan, prevent.**

There are many benefits to this activity. It teaches children a sense of responsibility and acquaints them with some of the reasons for working: goal achievement, personal growth, and meeting people. Their hard work will probably pay off in the form of a reward: money. This activity also shows your child the importance of sharing responsibilities to make a family work: if one person does not do his or her job, the family business could suffer.

You can help make this exciting for a child by making personalized business cards or stationery for him. Supply him with office equipment, a briefcase, and perhaps his own checking account. Children love these real-life playthings. They can contribute to the success of their business. Most important, this activity will make going to work a family event rather than something that takes time away from the family.

This is a long-range project that takes commitment and support from all family members. Help your child review his progress and incorporate these new experiences into a new understanding of what working is all about. In acknowledging your child's business success, try to keep the focus off the monetary rewards and instead recognize the positive feelings he gets from completing the job and meeting his goals.

Step 5
Review and recognize efforts

☆ *Planful Playing in a Pinch* ☆

Hot tips and quick recipes that enhance family unity.

5.1   *Family Reunion.* Family reunions are perfect for bringing generations of relatives together to celebrate nothing other than the family. This activity, from start to finish, will allow your child to get to know her extended family while helping everyone to feel close and a part of an important group of people. Children must be involved in the entire process: everything from designing invitations to planning activities, cooking the meal, and the follow-up to this special day or weekend. Have your child become familiar with the relatives in her immediate and extended family. Using a family tree or the book *Do People Grow on Family Trees? Genealogy for Kids and Other Beginners,* by Ira Wolfman (Workman Publishing, 1991), explain how cousins, aunts, grandparents, etc., are related to one another. On the special day, be sure to take plenty of pictures. Encourage family members to consider making this a yearly event. You may suggest to your child that she keep the family spirit alive by making a quarterly newsletter that includes pictures, accounts of the reunion, information about upcoming events, and interesting family news.

5.2   *Family Hall of Fame.* Select a hallway in your home that will become your family's Hall of Fame. Talk with your children about the accomplishments, talents, and successes of persons in your immediate and extended family. Draw or take a picture of individuals and note his or her accomplishments under the picture. Go back in your family history and try to discover hidden talents and achievements of your ancestors. Be sure to include pictures and accomplishments of your child in the Hall of Fame. Add on new Hall of Famers as your family accomplishments grow. Ask your children to take visiting friends and family through the Hall of Fame on a guided tour.

5.3   *The Family Band.* Dust off the guitar, clean off the piano: your family might soon become the new musical sensation. Have each family member pick an instrument to learn and play. It can be as simple as the harmonica, the tambourine, or the kazoo, or it can be more complicated, like guitars and drums. Each member should learn to play a different instrument so that when you all get together you have the makings of a band. Practice together and tape-record your own music. Write your own lyrics or songs that are family oriented and have humorous undertones. Be the entertainment at family gatherings and neighborhood events.

5.4   *"Hello, You've Reached . . ." Phone Message.* Invent and come up with a message for your family answering machine that includes every member. Have each member, even housepets, take part in the recording. One family we know has incredible holiday messages, including weird, scary voices on Halloween, jingle-bells music in the background for Christmas, April Fool's jokes on April 1st.

Family Greeting Cards. Design and have printed your own family greeting cards. You can either use pictures of your family or specially designed drawings for the front of the cards. Make them for holidays, birthdays, thank-you, or get-well occasions. Try to include all family members in the design and creation. *5.5*

The Secret Recipe. Invent with your child a special dish that is your family's secret recipe. Keep the list of ingredients a secret that only immediate family members will know. Name your dish and bring it to get-togethers and special events. *5.6*

The Family Board Game. Involve the whole family in inventing and creating a board game that is uniquely yours. Borrow game pieces such as dice and spinners from defunct board games and come up with an exciting adventure on a piece of poster board in which players must reach a goal. *5.7*

The Workbox. This box will help your child use imaginative play to work through issues she may have concerning your career involvement. Make a special toy box for your child that invites her to make believe she is at work. Fill the box with old briefcases, calculators, office materials, dress-up clothes, and other items used in a working environment. Be sure to include items that reflect your child's interest in what she wants to be when she grows up. Add play objects that are from your own work environment. *5.8*

(See page 252 for a list of reading recipes related to family unity.)

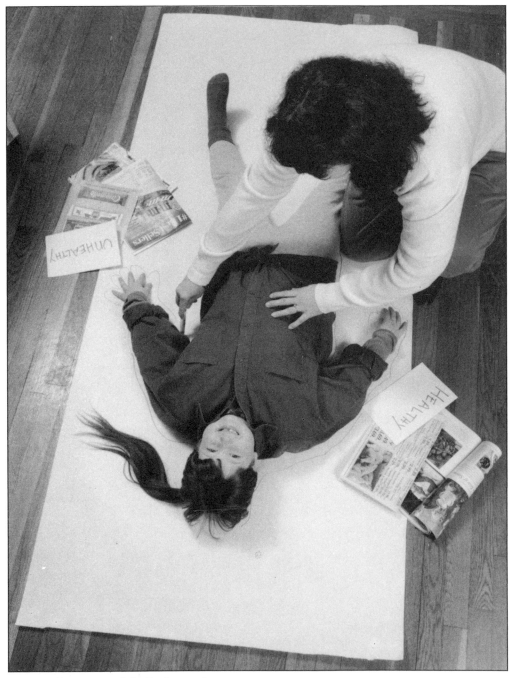

Recipe #7: My Healthy Body

CHAPTER 4

Body-Related Problems

WE REALIZE THAT THERE is nothing humorous about

- Having to put the cookies under lock and key and later finding your child's secret stash under a pile of dirty clothing.

- Having to drag your nine-year-old into the bath to scrape off a week's worth of dirt.

- Waking to the aroma of last night's urine rather than freshly brewed coffee.

Poor Eating Habits

Hygiene

Wetting/Soiling

Both you and your child deserve and need some relief from the tension that events like these present. We also realize that in order to begin the process of change, children need nonthreatening and understandable ways to approach these behaviors and the unpleasantries that go with them. We have grouped the three problem areas—eating problems (overeating and undereating), wetting and soiling, and hygiene—because they have a single theme: children often try to control parents or situations through noncontrol of their bodies (elimination, hygiene, and eating). In addition, each of these problems is evidence of psychological distress that could be related to low self-esteem, poor body perception, environmental stressors, or lack of education.

This chapter contains several fun activities that will educate you and your child while providing a refreshing **distraction** from the strain that these types of problems cause. Each activity focuses on your child's capabilities and the positive experiences of being in control of his or her body.

PROBLEMS

Overeating

Overeating is a learned behavior, frequently originating in the bad examples set by older siblings, relatives, others, and parents, and made worse by lack of education about what constitutes a healthy diet and sensible exercise.

Eating provides children and adults alike temporary respite from boredom, loneliness, or other emotional conflict.

Overeating can cause poor body image and low self-esteem.

Overeating may be used by the child as a method to gain attention and to engage his or her parents in power struggles.

Picky Eating and Junk Food

Every child has normal age- and stage-related food dislikes, peculiarities, and tastes. The refusal of a young child to eat certain foods or even entire meals may be an indication of her attempt to assert her independence. Parents who push food and force consumption create another arena for unproductive child/parent power struggles.

The problem of junk-food diets is often the result of poor education about what a healthy diet consists of. Children are overexposed to junk food by their peers, the media, and the family, and are often ignorant of snack foods that are just as tasty but healthier.

Hygiene

Poor hygiene may be indicative of a delay in social development; the child may be unaware of how he appears to others, and as a result has paid little attention to your efforts to teach him about hygiene and grooming.

A child who has a poor self-image, who doesn't take pride in or feel good about his body or appearance, may make no effort to improve his hygiene, believing that it will not help him socially.

Wetting and Soiling

It may be the result of underdeveloped or inadequate sphincter-muscle control due to medical factors or inactivity.

The child who has a tendency to become intensely involved in play may not want to stop playing to respond to toileting needs. Nocturnal bedwetting may be the result of a physical condition or a small bladder.

These behaviors are sometimes an expression of the child's anger, frustration, or defiance.

Wetting and soiling may be a result of developmental immaturity combined with negative or inadequate toilet-training practices. Pressure during toilet training to achieve control before the child is mature enough may create fear or anxiety about the process and cause it to be a temporary developmental accomplishment that will later be lost.

Wetting and soiling is often caused by emotional stress: new situations in which your child is anxious or uncertain, or new challenges such as a new baby in the family.

Overeating

Teach your child about healthy diet and eating habits. Take her comparison shopping, whether at home in the family cupboard or at the supermarket. Together make low-calorie, high-nutrition meals. (Recipes 7, 8, 13.1, 13.3)

Teach self-control and responsible eating habits through **modeling** but have reasonable expectations. (Recipes 7, 8, 13.1)

Involve your entire family in exercise on a regular basis. Vary the type and location to keep it entertaining and fresh. (Recipe 9)

Help your child become involved in socially and emotionally rewarding groups (Boy/Girl Scouts) and activities (sports or hobbies) that combat boredom and loneliness (Recipes 66, 67)

Give your child the opportunity to socialize with other children who also have difficulty with overeating. Explore with your child other possible stressors that might cause emotional distress.

Increase your child's appreciation of herself, her body, and her health. This will motivate her to eat better and lose weight. (Recipes 49, 50, 53, 55.1 through 55.14)

Refrain from engaging in arguments with your child over food restrictions. The energy expended is often wasted, and distracts attention from the problem (see Ignoring and Distraction, page 22).

Picky Eating and Junk Food

Most picky eating is not a problem and is best dealt with by being **ignored.** Consult your pediatrician for specific concerns. Try planning and cooking meals together with your child. Eat in new and adventurous settings such as your child's tree house or next to a campfire. (Recipes 13.2, 13.3)

Within limits, allow your child to make decisions about what he eats. Explore and offer alternatives to junk food. (Recipe 13.3)

Hygiene

Make learning about hygiene fun and interesting, not just another lecture. Plan an outing together with your child to purchase all the necessary tools and products for good hygiene. Let her know that you associate good hygiene with maturity, freedom, and the right to privileges. (Recipes 10, 13.4, 13.5, 13.6, 13.7) Talk with your child regarding his feelings about himself, his body, and his general appearance. (Recipes 6, 36)

Wetting and Soiling

Help your child recognize the physical sensation of needing to go. Practice specific exercises to increase control of the sphincter muscle. Consult your pediatrician. (Recipes 11, 12, 13.9)

Use motivational activities that emphasize your child's partnership in overcoming this problem. (Recipes 11, 12, 13.8, 13.9)

Teach each toilet functioning in a nonthreatening, nonpressured way. Avoid power struggles and do not become overly punitive or overly concerned with immediate success. (Recipes 11, 12)

Help your child share control and responsibility by having him help you wash his undergarments or bedsheets, but be sure to do this in a nonpunitive and matter-of-fact way. Refrain from expressing anger or embarrassing your child as a means of manipulating him into controlling his body functions. (Recipes 11, 12)

Explore with your child the events in her life that she could be worried or feeling bad about. (Recipes 11, 34, 64.8)

51

☆ *Body Pride* ☆

This recipe encourages children to take pride in and appreciate their bodies.

Step 1
State and define the problem

Depending on which body-related difficulty (overeating, hygiene, or wetting and soiling) your child is experiencing, discuss how this problem may be a sign of dislike of his body. **Encourage** him to talk about his negative feelings toward his body. Explore how this may make it difficult to solve the problem.

Step 2
Identify skills and solutions

In step 2, you and your child will identify the wonderful and special things about his body. Help your child develop a healthy attitude toward his body by listing as many positive physical attributes and abilities as he has. This will help him feel good about what he can do and at the same time convey to him that his body is something to love and value.

Step 3
Mutually agree upon goals

Family Goal: "I will use my special skills to take pride in my body, believe it is special—and treat it that way!"

Step 4
Practice and play

The following activities will help your boy or girl to appreciate and take pride in his or her body. Liking her body is the first and most important step in solving problems related to your child's eating habits, hygiene, or elimination. Without confidence in, and respect and admiration for, the body your child was born with, diet, exercise, good hygiene, and proper toileting will be worthless. Here are several activities that will help your child develop a better body image.

Look at Me Scrapbook: Make a scrapbook with your child that focuses on his year-to-year accomplishments, growth, and new physical skills. Physical changes (hand size, foot size, growth in inches, etc.) can be recorded every two months. Be creative and have your child make hand and foot prints with finger paints to visually measure his growth. Log or chart in the scrapbook physical achievements such as jumping higher, running faster, or improved handwriting. Take pictures of your child to show how his appearance and body change. Encourage him to write down reasonable goals she would like to meet every two months.

My Incredible Body. Plan a full week of exploring the wonders of the human body. There are several good books on the body and its incredible abilities such as *The Magic School Bus: Inside the Human Body,* by Joanna Cole (Scholastic, 1987), and *The Body Book,* by Sara Stein (Workman, 1992). Discuss with your child how amazing her body is. Basic facts on how a body functions and heals itself astonish most children and teach them how their bodies can do amazing things. Most science or children's museums have exhibits that focus on the human body. Your child will be able to learn while having fun, and will apply this new knowledge to her own body. Use encouraging statements like "Our bodies are great—amazing—incredible!"

The Family Spa. Pretend with your child that he or she will be going to a spa for the weekend. Explain what a spa is and that both men and women go to them for refreshing new experiences. Duplicate as many spa accommodations as possible at home, and get the whole family to participate. A massage, steam bath, nature walk, healthy meal, and afternoon nap should be included in the spa weekend. Take your child to get his or her hair cut and styled and nails manicured. Go shopping and pick out a new outfit that is becoming on your child. At the end of the spa weekend, take photographs of your child's "new body image" (hair styled and wearing the new clothes, of course). If you like, make this a monthly or biannual activity and take turns with your child being the spa owner and customer. This way you can also receive massages and take naps.

Step 5
Review and recognize efforts

Absolutely do not forget this step. If you want your child to remember all that he has learned about his body and the appreciation he now has for it, he will need to incorporate this new information into his daily thinking. Using the scrapbook, photos of his "new body," or material that he has learned about the amazing human body, remind your child often how terrific his own body is.

☆ *My Healthy Body* ☆

This recipe teaches children how healthy foods make a healthy body.

Step 1 *State and define the problem*	In this step you will need to discuss with your child his thoughts and feelings related to food and eating. If your child eats excessive amounts of unhealthy foods, resulting in a weight problem, use **empathy** and **effective listening** to help her identify this as a problem she needs to overcome. Share your experiences and difficulties in selecting and eating healthy foods. It may be comforting for your child if you label the problem as a lack of "healthy food education" and tell her that everyone in the family may need to learn more about eating correctly.
Step 2 *Identify skills and solutions*	Identify skills and characteristics in your child that focus on her ability to make good choices, delay gratification, and control her actions. Traits such as patience, thinking things through, and learning new things can help your child modify her unhealthy eating habits.
Step 3 *Mutually agree upon goals*	Goal: "I will use my special skills to learn and practice healthy eating habits."
Step 4 *Practice and play*	This activity will playfully introduce to your child how the foods she eats affect her health. You will need a piece of paper large enough to accommodate a tracing of your child's body. First have your child lie flat on her back on the paper. Trace and outline her body from head to food. Cut out the drawing and give her some markers and crayons to fill in her facial features and clothing. On another piece of paper do the same thing. Next, search through and cut out of old magazines and newspapers pictures of food items that are both healthy and unhealthy. Work together to identify high-fat, high-cholesterol, and sugar-loaded items. At the same time look for healthy foods such as grains, low-fat milk products, fruits, vegetables, and proteins.

Once you have cut and collected these food items, paste the healthy ones on one side of the drawing and the unhealthy ones on the other. Discuss with your child how eating unhealthy foods may make her body feel tired and sluggish as well as causing it to gain weight from high amounts of calories and fat. **Encourage** her to see that if she chooses (**your choice**) to eat foods that are nutritional, she will have a lot of energy and good healthy feelings (**natural consequences**). The point of this activity is to visually show your child that like the cut-out pictures the foods she eats "stick" to her body and can make it healthy or unhealthy.

You can take this exercise one step further in support of a diet and food restrictions. Pin up the body collage on the wall. Explain that every time she chooses to eat a food from the healthy body she gets a point. If she chooses a food from the unhealthy body she does not get one. Decide on the number of points needed for her to choose a reward for positive eating behaviors. Use the **S.T.A.R.** technique to reinforce her control and to reward her for stopping and thinking before eating the junk foods. Be sure to **model** good eating habits yourself! You may want to participate in the activity by making your own body collage and choosing from the healthy food pictures.

Recognize your child's progress toward better eating habits. Recall times when she chose a healthy food. **Encourage** her to continue with her new good habits and praise her self-control.

Step 5
Review and recognize efforts

55

☆ *Red Light/Green Light Diet* ☆

RECIPE # 8
Serves: 4–12 years

This recipe is for children who need a fun and easily understandable diet to follow.

Step 1
State and define the problem

Getting your child to talk about his or her weight problem will be a challenge because of how sensitive and defensive she may be about obesity. Try using **empathy, mutual respect, "I" messages,** and **effective listening** to encourage your child to take a serious look at this problem that affects his social, emotional, and physical well-being. It will be comforting to him if you take the focus off him and indicate that the whole family will be working on eating problems together—"A family meal plan."

Step 2
Identify skills and solutions

Identify and describe your child's skills in the areas of self-control, motivation, following directions, and liking himself. Explain how they will help him solve his eating problems and tell him that he already has it in him to stick to a diet.

Step 3
Mutually agree upon goals

Goal: Make the goal that of eating healthy foods and improving his control, not that of losing weight. This is important because if a child feels that his success is measured by weight loss, the improvement he makes in controlling his eating habits will be overlooked. "I will use my special skills to learn how to stop eating unhealthy foods and start eating healthy ones."

Step 4
Practice and play

We were told about this fun, kid-friendly diet by a friend and colleague, Dr. Lauren Gansler, who specializes in treating eating disorders. Later, through our research we discovered that a book was recently written about this special diet: *The Stoplight Diet for Children,* by Leonard H. Epstein and Sally Squires (Little, Brown & Company, 1988). This is a program designed to change your family's eating habits and health care. It involves the whole family, thus lifting the blame from the overweight child. This diet relies on teamwork and moral support from all members.

The diet is simple and easy to understand. All foods are divided into three groups: red, yellow, and green, like the signals on a traffic light. Green foods are very low in calories and high in vitamins, minerals, and fiber, and have a low fat content. Yellow foods are the proteins, grains, milk products, and some fruits and vegetables. These foods are the mainstay of a healthy diet but are also more caloric than green foods. Red foods have little nutrition and are high in calories and fats. Whether you use the weight program in the *Stoplight Diet* or a Weight Watchers®–type program, the color-coded food categories are the strong point of the diet for children. In order to code your food (green, yellow, or red), you will need to purchase stickers in these colors. With your child, go through your kitchen and mark foods in each category. Next, make meal plans for the whole family that include appropriate amounts of "colored" foods from each category. Absolutely have your child participate in the meal planning. The program will become a language that your family can use. For example, "You get to choose two yellow foods and as many green foods as you like." Use **modeling** as a reinforcer: "I'm going to eat only one red food today." Use **encouraging** words when your child chooses, on his own, to eat a limited amount of yellow foods or red foods by saying, "All right! You chose a green food instead of a red one—that's great!" **S.T.A.R.** is also an excellent way to help your child stop and think before eating a red food. Note: We always suggest getting your doctor's approval for *any* diet plan you decide to use with your child.

Whether or not your child has lost weight is not the issue. If he went through the process and did his best to follow it, he's a winner. Load on the praise for his efforts. Check out other recipes in this chapter to help him improve his body image, exercise levels, and nutritional awareness.

Step 5
Review and recognize efforts

☆ *Stretch and Bend/One and Two* ☆

RECIPE # 9
Serves: All ages

This recipe establishes a healthy exercise routine.

Step 1
State and define the problem

Get the family together to talk about the importance of physical exercise. You may want to **spice up** your conversation by giving humorous examples of lazy, physically inactive people. Do a little skit or **role-play,** showing how useless our bodies become without exercise. Ask your child how lack of exercise might become a problem for her.

Step 2
Identify skills and solutions

In this step, make a list of all your child's general physical talents and athletic skills such as being a great baseball player or dancer, or specific ones like jumping high or running fast. Identify and make a list of your own physical talents.

Step 3
Mutually agree upon goals

Goal: "I will use my special skills to exercise and challenge my body so that I will grow healthy and strong." This is a goal that can easily be shared by all family members.

Step 4
Practice and play

Pull out those sweat suits; it's time to make those muscles ache. In our television and video-game-infected society, exercise is, unfortunately, usually the last on the list of fun activities to do with your family. However, parents who **model** and promote physically active life-styles will usually have physically active children. Here are a few fun, family-oriented physical-fitness activities that will get all of you moving and grooving together:

The Family Activity. Try to select a sport or physical activity that the entire family can participate in. Softball, skiing, tennis, Rollerblading, and dancing are terrific fitness activities for everyone. We suggest that you don't just perform the activity once in a blue moon but regularly. Make it a family project by taking lessons, subscribing to related magazines, and taking your kids to watch the experts in the field. For example, if you choose tennis as your family sport, play it weekly with your child, join a tennis club, buy tennis magazines, and go to pro events. **Encourage** each family member to pick his or her favorite star athlete and follow this person's career. Your family activity doesn't have to be a traditional sport: try tap dancing, jumping rope, or Rollerblading, but do it often and do it together.

The Aerobic Video. Move over, Jane Fonda—we've got a video that will knock your (gym) socks off. For this activity you will need a video recorder and a VCR. Your family will be making a workout or aerobic tape to be used on a weekly or twice-weekly basis. Begin by choosing exercises your child will enjoy doing. The exercise tape should be made in three parts: warmup, aerobics, and cooldown. Choose activities that fit these three categories. You may want to review with your child exercise tapes currently available in video stores to get ideas and gain a better understanding of how a workout video is assembled. Design it to suit your child's age and abilities: three-to-four-year-olds can tolerate about fifteen minutes of hopping and ball bouncing, and an eleven-year-old can last thirty minutes to one hour. Include physical activities such as jumping rope and dancing in the tape that highlight your children's talents. Select music and dialogue that your child will understand and enjoy. You can make your workout video by taping your family dancing, jumping, stretching, and skipping to a planned routine. Now your family has something very healthy to put into the VCR. Be sure to use it at least weekly.

Indoor Play Centers. New indoor play centers for children are popping up all over the country. They are filled with physically challenging slides, bouncing mats, ropes, and tunnels. A great and playful way to get your child to exercise. Discovery Zone L.P. is our favorite. You can call 1-312-616-3800 to locate a Discovery Zone near you.

Talk with your child about the good physical feelings he gets out of exercising. Have each family member describe the rewards he or she gets from working out, and comment on new muscle firmness or other positive physical changes. You may want to use **natural** and **logical consequences** in a positive way to explain the cause-and-effect relationship between exercise and healthy bodies.

Step 5
Review and recognize efforts

59

✩ *Hygiene Hip Hop* ✩

RECIPE #10
Serves: 3–10 years

This recipe teaches children good hygienic practices and general grooming.

Step 1
State and define the problem

Invite your child to share her thoughts concerning hygiene, and use **effective listening** to show that you understand what she is saying. Use **"I" messages** to express your thoughts regarding hygiene.

Step 2
Identify skills and solutions

Point out your child's skills in task completion (puts a puzzle together nicely) and good memory (knows all the words to a song). Explain how these skills will help him remember all the things he needs to do daily to be clean and healthy. Also, give examples of times when he did a good job bathing and how terrific she looked.

Step 3
Mutually agree upon goals

Family Goal: "I will use my special skills to practice the three B's of good hygiene: Bathe, Brush, and Be clean."

Step 4
Practice and play

Children who do not practice good hygiene often have not learned these skills and do not value taking care of themselves. Some simply do not take the time to properly wash themselves, while others do not want to wash due to fear of water, dislike of their body, or simply in opposition to parental demands. Parents need to teach and **model** the skills for good hygiene.

This activity is designed to help your child develop a clean, healthy life-style while having fun. Children can use the refusal to wash as a weapon against their parents. This activity recognizes that trait but at the same time is intriguing and promotes independence: your child devotes her energies to cleaning herself rather than battling with you.

First you will need to make a hygiene kit for your son or daughter. The kit can be modified to appeal to either younger or older children. Purchase a container (a colorful bucket for younger children and an attractive travel case for older ones) and fill it with a toothbrush, face cloth, soap, shampoo, powder, lotion, comb, and hairbrush. You may want to personalize the kit by putting your child's name on the container or the items in it. You can be creative and put in special goodies such as a designer toothbrush (recipe 13.5) and fancy soaps. For younger children, design and cut sponges into the shape of hands, feet, face, and body to visually remind them of the body parts they need to wash.

Once you and your child have completed the kit, together you will invent a song that rhythmically reminds your child of the steps needed to keep her body clean. Be sure to come up with a Rap or Rhyme song that includes all the procedures of daily hygiene. Use all the items in your child's hygiene kit in your song. Put the Hygiene Hip Hop song to music so she can sing out the cleaning routine to a familiar tune. Here is an example of the beginning of a Rap song that an eight-year-old boy used to solve his bathing problems:

To be real clean,
I've got a nightly routine.
I'll show you what I mean.
You got to use your toothbrush,
Be sure not to rush;
Brush your hair well,
It will look real swell;
Don't forget to wash your face,
So your mother will get off your case;
I really must admit you got to wash those armpits.

Kids love to mix humor with the steps for cleaning their body. **Model** the cleaning procedure for your child by taking part in singing the song. If your child still gets into a struggle with you over washing and bathing, try giving him a **choice** between bathing now or later. You can even squeeze a parenting technique into the Rap song itself because—"If you don't clean well, The **natural consequence** is that you smell!"

Recognize your child's hygienic improvements. Have her identify how her cleaning habits have or have not changed. Ask him if he has reached his goal. You may want to **try, try again** and invent a new song, or try another recipe if your child continues to resist bathing.

Step 5
Review and recognize efforts

61

☆ *Forests and Hockey Pucks* ☆

R E C I P E   # 1 1
Serves 3–8 years

This recipe motivates children to stop wetting or soiling.

Step 1
State and define the problem

You should select this recipe if your child's difficulty has to do with elimination. This first step may be hard for your child because you are asking him to talk about a very embarrassing subject. Draw from several parenting techniques such as **"I" messages, effective listening,** and **empathy** to create a comfortable environment for your child to discuss this issue. Explain that it's not his fault and that some children take longer to develop skills in bladder/bowel control than others. Take care *not* to ridicule or shame your child into working on this problem. He is probably unhappy and upset with himself and needs a good dose of **encouragement** and **positive reframing** to feel more in control and self-confident.

Step 2
Identify skills and solutions

Perhaps your child is saying, "I can't control my body because I'm a baby," or, "I don't care." Parents should express their wholehearted belief that their boy or girl is mature enough to control his or her body. Make a list of the skills, talents, and special abilities your child has that make him capable, strong, or mature such as patience, perseverance, and strong muscles.

Step 3
Mutually agree upon goals

Goal: Come up with a goal that solves the identified problem such as bedwetting, soiling, or wet pants during the day. It could sound like this: "I will use my special skills to learn how to stop wetting my bed and feel good about myself."

Step 4
Practice and play

Charts and reward systems work very well for elimination problems. This activity is a behavioral technique that requires you to chart your child's progress for seven days and then reward her. Charts and rewards work best for children who need external motivation to make necessary changes: more than just the internal feeling of personal success. This activity is most successful for children who do not need to be retrained or require medical intervention. For better results, use this recipe in combination with My Instruction Book and other recipes in this chapter.

For Bedwetting and Daytime Wetting. Begin by drawing a landscape of a forest. Next draw and cut out a sun with seven removable rays of sunlight. Draw and cut out seven large raindrops. Now you are ready to chart your child's dry and wet days.

For Children Who Soil Themselves. Draw a picture of a hockey player and goal and make seven removable hockey pucks. This interesting scene will help you chart your child's progress for ending his soiling problems. If you need assistance in designing these charts, use pictures of a forest from a *National Geographic* or any environmental magazine or use a sports magazine and paste pictures onto a large sheet of paper. Explain to your child that the rays of sunlight represent dry days and the raindrops are wet days. Hockey pucks in the goal are days in which he does not soil himself; out of the goal are accidents or incidents of soiling.

Each day your child does not wet his bed or his pants, put on a ray of sun. Place a puck in the goal to represent days he makes a bowel movement in the toilet. Let your child have a role in managing the chart by having him place the rays, raindrops, and pucks on the chart himself. Decide with your child how many successful days he will need and what the reward would be for reaching his goal. The reward is given for a desired number of rays of sunlight or pucks in the hockey net.

Applaud your child's accomplishments and verbally reward her for meeting her goal. If she has not been able to meet the goal, **try, try again.** Be patient and have respect for the process of changing old behaviors.

Step 5
Review and recognize efforts

☆ *My Instruction Book* ☆

R E C I P E   # 1 2

Serves: 4–8 years

This recipe teaches children a step-by-step procedure for solving elimination problems.

Step 1
State and define the problem

Begin by explaining to your child that learning how to solve his wetting or soiling problem is really hard to do by himself and you would like to help him. Empathize and comfort him by letting him know that many other children have the same problem and there are ways in which he can solve it. Invite him to talk about his problem. It may be helpful if you describe a few situations in which he wet or soiled his pants and he seemingly had no control over the "accident." (Perhaps he was absorbed in play, or asleep, or was anxious, nervous, or frightened.) This demonstrates to your child that you understand that this problem is often not his fault and alleviates negative feelings he may have about himself.

Step 2
Identify skills and solutions

Choose several skills and talents your child possesses that will help him see that he can follow directions, learn new things, and has a capable and strong body.

Step 3
Mutually agree upon goals

Goal: "I will use my special skills to be able to stop wetting or soiling my pants or bed."

Step 4
Practice and play

This makes relearning toileting a fun and understandable process. Along with your child, you will be making an "instruction manual" on how to go to the bathroom. First take a closer look at the problem and investigate what the cause may be. Use the Problem/Solution Chart on pages 50–51 to help you explore reasons behind his elimination problems. Ask yourself if it is medical (weak sphincter muscles, small bladder, or constipation), emotional (anxieties, fears, poor self-concept), developmental (immaturity, new baby in the home), oppositional behavior (to get back at a parent, another way to say no), or simply inadequate education (did not learn the process of controlling her toileting functions). This information will help you in writing your toileting instruction manual because it clarifies for you and your child the important steps he will need to take in order to correct the problem. Next, explain to your child that you will help him reach his goal by together making a special instruction manual for toileting. Show him a few examples of how an instruction manual is written and drawn. Make sure your example has good pictures. Using paper, crayons, markers, and creativity, you are ready to make your instruction manual. The steps described below are for children between four and seven.

Step A Draw or take a picture of your child's body in a bathing suit and identify body parts, using your child's language (peepee, bum, etc.).

Step B Draw or take a picture of your child pretending to be wet or soiled and ask her to draw how she feels next to the picture. On the following page, draw a picture of your child dry and clean, with corresponding feelings. Use this opportunity to explore her thoughts about either feeling dry or being wet or soiled.

Step C Draw or take a picture of your toilet and bathroom at home, complete with toilet paper and toilet flusher.

Step D The drawing or picture for this step will differ for each child's unique problem. This is where you will use information you have worked on earlier (causes). Draw a few pictures showing your child struggling with the problem and then solving it. For example, if your child's problem is caused by lack of sphincter control (the muscle that controls the flow of urine), have him draw a picture of himself practicing sphincter exercises (see Retention Olympics in Planful Playing on page 67).

Step E Draw a picture of your child looking as if he wants to go to the bathroom.

Step F Draw a picture of him sitting on the toilet, wiping and flushing.

Step G Draw a picture of your child contented, happy, and feeling successful. Note: If you take pictures of your child rather than drawing them you will be giving her "playful practice" doing each of the steps while modeling for the camera.

Read through the manual often and/or make the instruction booklet a part of his daily routine. If your child tries to use the manual, praise him for his efforts. **Encourage** your child to **try, try again** because toilet learning is a process of success and accidents. You may want to combine this recipe with Forests and Hockey Pucks (page 62).

Step 5
Review and recognize efforts

☆ *Planful Playing in a Pinch* ☆

RECIPE #13

Hot tips and quick recipes for solving body-related problems.

OVEREATING/UNDEREATING

13.1 *Place Mat Messages.* Using a single colored plastic place mat, have your child use permanent markers or oil-based paint to paint messages, pictures, and sayings that will remind her of what her goal is for eating. Encourage her to be funny and help her to design the place mat to meet her individual needs. You can also cut out pictures of healthy food items from a magazine and press them between two pieces of waxed paper. Offer her the place mat at all meals. Parents can make one for themselves to show that everyone has important things to remember when it comes to eating.

13.2 *Feasting for the Fussy.* Make eating a creative, fun, and enticing event by inventing new places and ways to eat. Have a picnic in the backyard. Gather the whole family and eat in the tree house, have a smorgasbord, use large wooden utensils instead of silverware, or use no silverware at all. Cut raw veggies into strips and have your child think of interesting sauces he can dip them in such as peanut butter, honey mustard, or raspberry jam. Take the boredom out of eating and make it fun.

13.3 *Restaurant Menu and Family Dining.* Using a computer or handlettering, have your child design, give a name to, and create a restaurant menu for breakfast, lunch, and dinner. Have your child study other menus (you might collect a few from your favorite restaurant) and make up a healthy list of foods on the menu. The menu is presented daily for the family to choose from. Several nights a week plan and cook special healthy meals together, pretending to go out to a fancy restaurant. Play up the restaurant theme and use candles, nice tablecloths, and perhaps even a waitress. Give tips, of course!

HYGIENE

13.4 *Soap and Shower-Curtain Art.* Have your child carve anything from animals to strange people out of cheap bars of soap. Using a single-colored shower curtain, have him use *washable* paint and design different sceneries. Make hand puppets out of washcloths. Encourage your child to put on a bathing-beauty puppet show. He can use the newly painted shower curtain as a backdrop, and his puppets and bars of soap as the main performers.

13.5 *Designer Toothbrush.* Using craft paint, design and paint seven toothbrushes with your child and have him decorate each one in a special and unique way for every day of the week. Or you can simply paint one toothbrush and put his name on it.

Poster-Child Clean: Have your child clean and beautify herself to her heart's desire. Take a picture and have it enlarged to poster size. Put it in the room as a daily reminder of how attractive she looks when she is clean. You can be humorous and have your child take a picture of herself when she is incredibly dirty. Now you have a before-and-after shot to hang side-by-side.   *13.6*

Clean and Happy Potato Head: Use those famous Potato Heads made by PlaySkool to remind your child of each part of his body that needs to be cleaned. Every morning or evening go through the process of sticking on each part of Mr. Potato Head's body to indicate what part of his body has been cleaned.   *13.7*

WETTING/SOILING

Designer Underwear: Using fabric paint and a few pairs of new underwear, design with your child special designer underwear. Make them fun and creative. Write the word EMPTY or DRY on the back of the underwear. Your child may not want to ruin his or her new designer underwear after putting so much energy into creating them. For nighttime wetting, have your child decorate his bedsheets.   *13.8*

Retention Olympics. Make an Olympic sport out of exercising and strengthening your child's sphincter muscle. Once she has learned how to squeeze her sphincter muscle to control (stop and start) the flow of urine into the toilet, you can make an Olympic event out of the number of times she stops the flow. Record her progress and **encourage** her to beat her latest record. (See page 253 for a list of reading recipes for body-related problems.)   *13.9*

Recipe #18: Stomp Your Feet

CHAPTER 5

Destructive and Antisocial Behaviors

IN WALKS LEE WITH his new jeans torn clear up to his knee and leftovers of someone's lunch in his hair. "Not another fight?" gasps Father. "Uh-huh!" says Lee. "He deserved it, that's the last time that bleep bleep calls me a ———" Before Lee can blink, Father grasps him by the arm and inches from his face yells, "Watch your mouth, young man. Where the hell did you pick up such a nasty way of talking and behaving?"

Antisocial behaviors such as lying, stealing, aggression, teasing, swearing, and destructiveness differ from many of the other problems in that they not only cause discord between parent and child but may also bring the child into conflict with society. Paradoxically, our society fosters the development of these unwanted behaviors by favoring competition over cooperation, narcissism over altruism, and aggressive role models and solutions over nonviolent peacemaking and negotiation. Despite this obvious and powerful social influence, parents can guide and teach their children effective ways to control and vent anger, providing an alternative to these antisocial behaviors. In addition, children can learn to make good use of rather than misuse power. Our recipes will teach your child self-control, constructive ways to express himself or herself, peaceful problem-solving, and appreciation of and respect for others.

Lying

Stealing

Teasing

Swearing

Aggression

There are four types of aggressive behavior: provoked or reactive behavior (in self-defense), unprovoked (need to dominate others), aggressive outbursts (impulsive and explosive; out of control), and oppositional types of behavior, which are defiant and in opposition to authority figures.

Most aggression is a misuse of power. A child who feels he has no control over a situation or himself will use aggression to feel more powerful and more in control. This child tends to be impulsive, immature, and inarticulate when expressing his feelings.

When children do not know other constructive ways to express anger, they will communicate their feelings by hitting, breaking things, and hurting others.

Television and movies glamorize and **model** violence as a way of solving problems, thus encouraging aggression in our children. Our society rewards aggression by associating it with winning, especially in organized sports for children such as football and Little League baseball.

A child who is self-centered and developmentally immature is more likely to use aggression, force, or coercion rather than persuasion or negotiation to get what he needs or believes he needs.

Aggression breeds aggression—if a child is handled aggressively by adults, she learns to manage her own problems that way.

Lying

During the preschool years, children have difficulty distinguishing fantasy from reality; what may be first thought of as lying may be active and colorful imagination.

School-age children lie to deny wrongdoing or to avoid getting in trouble or being punished. They also lie to demean others, to gain an advantage, or to be loyal to their friends.

Most children lie in self-defense or to get out of a predicament. Dishonesty is often the result of your child's feeling that he has no other way to reach his goal other than lying.

Lying is a learned behavior. Children figure out how and when to do it by observing their parents, siblings, and peers who practice stretching the truth.

Stealing

Stealing is often an indication that something is lacking in your child's life. He may be stealing to gain needed attention, counter perceived or real deprivation, or as a result of peer pressure and a need to be accepted.

A child may steal due to immaturity and the inability to delay gratification. For example, a boy who sees a pack of

gum at the checkout counter and whose parents say no may be unable to control his impulse to put it in his pocket.

Stealing incidents peak at around the ages of five to eight and decrease as the child matures and moral consciousness develops more fully.

Teasing and Swearing

Children often swear to gain attention, shock people, relieve tension, communicate defiance, or gain peer acceptance.

Like stealing, lying, and aggression, teasing and swearing are in part caused by a lack of respect for others. People who

feel inadequate and powerless may tease, mock, or put others down in order to feel better about themselves.

Teasing and swearing are often learned from parents, siblings, peers, and others.

Help your child to feel more powerful and more in control of situations and himself by giving him opportunities to make decisions and express his opinion. **Encourage** him or her to develop personal power (self-control) rather than trying to use power over others. (Recipes 14, 15, 18.1, 18.5, 26, 36, 37, 39, 40.1, 40.2, 40.4, 68)

Allow your child to disagree or challenge you from time to time. This will give him an opportunity to feel powerful and able without hitting or destroying things. (Recipes 15, 18.1, 18.2, 18.3)

Give other physical alternatives for handling aggressive feelings such as taking a fast walk, hitting a pillow, stamping feet, or squeezing clay. (Recipes 18.4, 30, 31, 32, 34, 35.1, 35.3, 38)

Limit his or her exposure to aggressive role models and highly competitive environments. Limit viewing of violent TV shows and movies. (Recipes 15, 70 through 74)

Teach and model pro-social alternatives to aggression such as assertiveness and give the child appropriate ways—words and practice—to express anger verbally. (Recipes 15, 18.1, 30, 31, 32, 34)

Teach the child to respect the bodies and personal rights of others and help him to appreciate his belongings and the belongings of others. (Recipes 16, 59, 69.11)

Lying

In order to deal with young children who lie or tell exaggerated stories, simply distinguish the truth from a lie by saying, "You mean to say you *wish* it could have been that way." Let your child know the difference between his imagination and reality and that imagining is a fun game to play but it is not reality. (Recipes 17, 18.8)

Your child needs to feel that you are willing to listen to the truth even when it is upsetting for you to hear. Prove to him that when he has misbehaved or gotten into trouble or mischief it is more profitable to tell the truth than be caught lying. (See Effective Listening, page 18.)

Help your child explore every means to reach a goal or meet a need without lying; when he feels he has exhausted all possibilities, teach him to ask for help rather than lying. (Recipes 17, 65)

During these critical and impressionable years, be especially aware of your own white lies and what they communicate to your child. (Recipe 17)

Stealing

Avoid sermons and lectures; instead take the time to listen to what is missing from your child's life that has caused him to feel he needs to take from others. Treat the problem of stealing as a mistake that can be corrected. **Encourage** him to make independent decisions about his behavior. (Recipes 14, 15)

Explain the difference between borrowing and simply taking something from someone else who wouldn't notice. (Recipes 48.6, 48.7)

If you caught your child stealing, first have him (1) return the item that was stolen to the person it was taken from, (2) apologize to the person, and (3) do something in the way of restitution for having caused her trouble and betraying her trust. (Recipe 14)

Teasing and Swearing

If your child uses a "bad word," try not to laugh or look shocked. Check first to see if he knows what the word means by allowing him or asking him to give you a definition. If it is incorrect, explain to him the correct definition. This approach takes the power out of the word because you do not become shocked or upset. (Recipes 17, 18.9, 18.10)

Teach your child that while humor is a wonderful and useful skill, teasing is not considered funny; it hurts others and may eventually backfire. (Recipes 16, 48.9)

Set guidelines of what is considered funny and not funny in your family. Be sure to do as you say. Practice what you are asking your children to practice yourself. (Recipes 16, 48.9)

☆ *Restitution, Repair, and Rethink* ☆

RECIPE #14

Serves: 4–12 years

This recipe teaches children to take responsibility for the results of their actions.

Step 1
State and define the problem

Discuss with your child your perceptions of his misbehavior. Whether it is hitting, breaking things, teasing, bullying, or stealing, share with him your values and respect for property and for others. Use this opportunity to establish family rules regarding his antisocial behavior (See The Five C's for Rule Making, page 20). Take the time to understand why your child may be acting in an antisocial manner. Try **effective listening** when hearing your child's perception of the problem.

Step 2
Identify skills and solutions

Give as many examples as needed to remind and impress your child with his positive social behavior. Identify skills that center around sharing, sensitivity, being sorry, giving, caring, and good moral judgment. Do a **role play** with your child, showing his ability to have empathy and respect for others as well as appreciation for objects.

Step 3
Mutually agree upon goals

Goal: "I will use my special skills to learn how to take responsibility for my wrongful behavior and to make amends for my misdeeds."

Step 4
Practice and play

When a child is antisocial, a parent's first impulse is to lecture the culprit to boredom about right and wrong and decency. A better solution is to see the problem as a misbehavior your child can correct. The logic behind the Restitution Exercises is that the **consequence** for hitting, stealing, and destroying is to pay back for your misbehavior. As simple as it might sound to correct by making restitution, motivating children to do it is another thing. With this in mind, we devised the following restitution activities with a little spice and playfulness to make "giving back" more palatable for your child. The objective of restitution is to teach your child to accept responsibility for his actions, take ownership of his problem, have respect for others, and realize he can make amends for his wrongdoing.

The Fund-Raiser (for destroying property). Explain to your child that his negative behavior requires him to pay back for breaking something or destroying property. Suggest that he give a fund-raiser such as a car wash to raise money to pay for his destructive actions. Encourage him to think of other honest ways to raise money. He could collect cans and bottles and return them for a deposit or he could put on a fund-raiser talent show and charge a small fee. Even a walk-a-thon is appropriate. Help him make a donation sheet that requires him to get signatures from family members and relatives who gave a certain amount of money for every block he walks. Whichever fund-raising event he chooses, be sure to label his actions as restitution for destroying property. After he collects the money for his hard work, have him ceremoniously give the money to the "owner" of the destroyed property or object. Encourage him to express how he felt when he was destructive and now how he feels when he is being constructive.

Let's Make a Deal—Don't Steal. If your son has stolen something from a store, not only have him apologize and return the item, but have him do something to benefit the store owner. We suggest that you have your child make a colorful poster encouraging other children not to steal. Have him donate this to the store owner. Or suggest that he volunteer time to the store owner or manager. Be sure to ask him how it felt to give back.

The Formal Apology. If your child has hit or hurt another person, have him make a nice apology card or letter to the victim. If you have access to the parents of the child receiving the note, ask their help in thinking of something your child could do to make amends. Older children may enjoy taking out a small ad in the local newspaper to announce their apology to the hurt child. One boy we know decorated the teased child's locker at school with his formal apology.

It is important that you take the time to review what your child has done to make amends for his antisocial behavior. Pour on the praise and express your delight in his restitutive actions. This recipe works best when combined with others in the chapter. This specific activity focuses on after-the-fact solution while the others are more preventive.

Step 5
Review and recognize efforts

☆ *A Piece of Peace* ☆

RECIPE # 1 5
Serves: 5–12 years

This recipe teaches peacemaking skills for resolving conflict and decreasing aggression.

Step 1
State and define the problem

Ask your child to explain the difference between aggressive (hurting others) behavior and peaceful (being nice) behavior. Show your interest in her perception of the differences by carefully listening to her. Explore problematic behaviors in your home that fall under the definition of hurtful or aggressive. Share your perceptions of violence and peace and come up with a mutually agreed-on definition for both.

Step 2
Identify skills and solutions

List your child's skills, traits, and attributes that indicate she can cooperate, share, care, negotiate, compromise, and think before she acts (**S.T.A.R.**). Come up with several examples of when your child was willing to work out differences in a nonviolent manner.

Step 3
Mutually agree upon goals

Goal: "I will use my special skills to help us become a more peaceful family and for me to be a nonviolent person."

Step 4
Practice and play

As discussed in the Problem/Solution Chart on pages 70–71, learning how to deal with aggressive impulses and angry feelings takes skill, education, and experience. You as a parent can take the first steps toward creating an atmosphere of peace in your family. When you educate and focus your child on the skills of peacemaking, he will begin to see how these skills can be applied not just to his family but to the world around him.

Start your peaceful endeavors by reading *Learning the Skills of Peacemaking,* by Naomi Drew (Jalmar Press, 1987). It gives dozens of suggestions and activities for helping elementary-school-age children build skills in cooperation and conflict resolution. Next explain to your child that the entire family is going to learn how to be more peaceful. *Peace,* by Carole MacKenthun and Paulinus Dwyer (Good Apple, 1986), is an excellent work on the subject. Next explore ways how your family can become skilled peacemakers by incorporating the following activities into its life-style:

Be a United Nations Family. Talk with your family about the purpose of the UN. Turn **family council** meetings into personalized UN family meetings to resolve conflicts peacefully.

Make a Peaceful-Hero Poster. Read and learn about peaceful heroes of the past or present such as Martin Luther King, Gandhi, or Mother Teresa. Create a poster describing what a peacemaker is, using expressions such as "cares about and accepts others," "patient," "forgiving," "compromising," "finds nonviolent solutions," "keeps trying even when discouraged." Display this poster in your home along with the images of peaceful heroes.

Learn About Peace Education. Send away for a Peace Education kit, published by the U.S. Committee for UNICEF, United Nations, New York, NY 10017. Use the material to inspire your child to join this organization or other peace-oriented groups so that your family can share its peacemaking skills.

Teach Skills in Negotiation and Peaceful Resolution. Educate your child about how to handle angry feelings through the use of **"I" messages** and **effective listening.**

Be a S.T.A.R. See recipe 39, S.T.A.R. Man/Woman. Encourage your child to seek internal peace by using techniques such as **S.T.A.R.** to learn how to stop and think before he acts aggressively. Consider other recipes such as The T-N-T Corner (#31), The Cool, Calm and In-Control Clubhouse (#37), The Feeling Box (#34), and The Relaxation Center (#38) to give your family ways to calm down and vent frustration.

Celebrate Peace. Have a peace party to celebrate honorable efforts to achieve peace in your family. Broaden your goals and celebrate peace in our nation. Talk about how peaceful feelings can be special in your child's social life.

Review your family efforts to develop peacemaking skills. Explore how these skills can help establish peaceful relationships with others outside of the home.

Step 5
Review and recognize efforts

☆ No Kidding and Only ☆ Clowning Around

RECIPE #16

Serves: 6–12 years

This recipe helps children develop appropriate ways to be humorous while decreasing teasing and bullying.

Step 1
State and define the problem

Talk with your child about the seriousness of teasing or bullying. Use **effective listening** and **empathy** in listening to her perception of the problem. Use **role play** and take turns being the aggressor. Ask your child how it feels to be the victim. Explain that you understand that she may be trying to get attention and laughter by teasing, but this behavior is unacceptable to you and needs to be stopped.

Step 2
Identify skills and solutions

Point out characteristics in your child that exemplify both a desirable way of treating people (complimenting, saying sorry, helping a younger person) and skills for making people laugh that are proper (telling a good joke, slapstick body language). Ask him to come up with examples of these leadership qualities and indications of a good sense of humor in himself or others.

Step 3
Mutually agree upon goals

Goal: "I will use my special skills to learn ways to be a good friend, make people laugh without hurting anyone, and be a good leader."

Step 4
Practice and play

Make way Jay Leno and Bozo the Clown—here is your future competition! This activity will give your child clear guidelines for using **humor** to get attention, while nurturing his power over himself and not others. Often children who tease and bully are overcompensating for weak, insecure feelings within themselves. Their antisocial behavior can be easily corrected by developing a more positive self-image (see chapter 12, "Self-Concept Problems") and by using humor to appropriately get attention, instead of teasing, bullying, or hurting feelings.

Explain to your child that, as discovered in step 2, he has the potential to get the attention of others and to make them laugh: **Positive reframing.** Using one or two of his role models, talk about how they make people laugh by telling good jokes, funny stories, and using silly body language. Talk about how this type of humor is a skill that has to be learned. Suggest that you are going to help him develop his humor skills by learning how to "clown around" or by being a standup comic. Depending on your child's type of humor, **encourage** her to pick a new, funny identity, other than a teaser or a bully. Two good ideas for developing these skills are to learn how to be a clown or to prepare a show for family and friends in which your child is a standup comedian. First you will need to make a list of good humor and bad humor. A clean joke is an example of good humor, but making fun of someone's race, religion, language, or body is bad humor. Next, decide with your child what his new "funny identity" is and research, train, and practice these new **humor** techniques. Here are some suggestions. The books *Be a Clown: The Complete Guide to Instant Clowning,* by Turk Pipkin (Workman Publishing, 1989) and *The Instant Juggling Book,* by Bob Woodburn (Firefly Books, 1990) are terrific for learning how to be a clown. Go to the circus and/or interview a real clown. Check Party Services in your Yellow Pages; you may be able to find phone numbers for clowns in your area. **Spice up** the activity and help your child develop a funny routine. You will need to buy clown makeup and design a costume for him. Finally, take the show on the road. We suggest you **positively reframe** the whole teasing social situation by **encouraging** your child to do something nice for others. Maybe he can clown around at a children's hospital or a senior citizens' home.

If your child wants to take a stab at being a comedian, help her come up with a standup comedy routine. Look through children's joke books for good ideas on how he could create a skit. You can videotape her performance or do it for family and friends. Throughout this activity, **model** for your child what good humor is all about. Try to ignore silly name-calling that promotes teasing. Apply **logical consequences** and use the **think chair** for persistent teasing. Most of all, **encourage** all signs of good humor and have fun laughing with your child.

Ask your child how much more powerful he feels getting people's attention in a positive, fun manner rather than teasing, hurtful ways. Show your delight in his newly acquired humor skills to make people laugh.

Step 5
Review and recognize efforts

☆ *White, Yellow, and Red Words* ☆

RECIPE # 1 7
Serves: 4–12 years

A recipe that decreases lying and bad language.

Step 1
State and define the problem

We have combined lying and swearing in this recipe because the activity can be used for both problems. Discuss with your child the lying or swearing problem in your family. For children who lie, use **empathy** to express your understanding that many of us stretch the truth, but that lying to avoid responsibility ("I didn't do it") or to purposely demean someone is not appropriate. Explain that **mutual respect** and trust are built on honest communication. For excessive use of bad language, show your understanding that bad words may accidentally come out of his mouth when he is angry or trying to be funny ("you poopy head"). However, it is not appreciated, and everyone must learn to control himself or herself in this regard. (See The Five C's for Rule Making, page 20.)

Step 2
Identify skills and solutions

Concentrate on your child's truthful behaviors or use of good language. Ask her to identify times when she told the truth. **Positively reframe** her exaggerated storytelling as a special skill (See Planful Playing, "The Fairy Tale Book," page 81). For the child who uses bad language, simply suggest that her ability to think and say such complicated words must mean that she has an incredible vocabulary—she probably knows dozens and dozens of good words as well!

Step 3
Mutually agree upon goals

Goal: "I will use my special skills to decrease lying and/or bad language in our family."

Step 4
Practice and play

Every time your sweet, innocent child utters vulgarities or tells such a magnificent lie that you believe he or she will grow up to be a famous storyteller or a politician doesn't mean you need to label her or him as an antisocial outcast. It is rare that a child does not go through a lying or "poopy-head" phase. For preschoolers, distinguishing fact from fantasy is difficult, and swearing adds color to any child's vocabulary, usually getting instant attention. The White, Yellow, and Red Word activity will not only educate your child about how to use language properly, but will playfully guide your entire family toward more truthful, "cleaner" communication.

This activity is actually a game. To start, you will need a very large piece of paper taped onto a wall. This will become your White, Yellow, and Red Word graffiti board. With your child, write "White, Yellow, and Red, lies (or swears)" across the top of the paper. Since these problems are separate issues, do not do lying and swearing together: instead make a separate graffiti board for each. Using the following descriptions, tell your child what White, Yellow or Red lies or words are. Here is a brief outline of each category:

- White Lies are used to avoid hurting the feelings of others: "Your dress is nice" when you really think it's an eyesore, or, "I'm having a good time" when you would rather be getting your teeth drilled are two good examples.

- Yellow Lies are exaggerated stories or face-saving statements. A child will use a Yellow Lie to gain an advantage: "My parents gave me a real elephant for my birthday." Or to avoid punishment your child says, "Josh ate the cookies, not me."

- Red Lies are deliberate lies to hurt someone's feelings or take advantage of them. Fabricating a story about another child to get attention is an example of a Red Lie.

- White Swears are made-up family words that are used to verbally release tension and to express anger. "Oh, fizzleberries!" or "dinkle-muck!" are two of our favorites.

- Yellow Swears are childish words such as "poopyhead" and "do-do brains."

- Red Swears are those four-letter words we wish we had never "accidently" said in front of our children.

With the understanding of what each color designates, write down with your child all the lies or swears he uses in each category. Even do "graffiti writing" on the paper to **spice up** this part of the activity. Keep your graffiti paper of White, Yellow, and Red hanging on the wall so that your family can refer to it throughout this recipe.

Now you are ready to play the game. You will need a small box and white poker chips. Every time a family member tells the truth or sensitively uses a White Lie (swear) he or she gets the White poker chip, which is put into a small box. If a Yellow Lie (swear) is said nothing happens—no chips no attention. It is totally **ignored.** But if a Red Lie (swear) is told, two White chips are taken from the box. Decide how many White chips are needed for your family to win a prize. After a week of playing this game, count the White chips to see if you have reached your goal. Since everyone in the family participates, all must encourage White language and ignore others when they say something Yellow. Red words activate a **logical consequence**—loss of two chips. Think of all the ingredients that are built into this game for decreasing lying or swearing: **encouragement, modeling** (you play the game), **ignoring,** and **logical consequences.**

Review with your family how well you accomplished your goals and won your prizes. Be sure to praise and compliment everyone involved for their efforts. You can even use your new "colored" language to discourage lying and swearing after the game has been played. For example, for a child who fabricates and exaggerates stories, you might want to say, "That's one of the best Yellow Lies I've heard in a long time!"

Step 5
Review and recognize efforts

☆ *Planful Playing in a Pinch* ☆

Hot tips and quick recipes for solving destructive and antisocial behavior.

AGGRESSION

18.1   *You're Bugging Me.* Make dozens of little fuzzy bugs out of yarn (like a pompon) about one inch in diameter. Fill a bowl in the kitchen with the "bugs." Anytime someone in the family does something irritating to another person, the one who does the irritating is given a bug and told, "You're bugging me!" **Encourage** your child to give out bugs to let people know how he is feeling instead of becoming aggressive.

18.2   *A Day in Court.* Set up a court system with your family. Take your kids to a courthouse to show them how the process works and then decide how your family wants to proceed. Take turns being the judge. Bring up unacceptable behaviors that happened during the week. You can get as detailed as you want. Write down behaviors that occurred and send out subpoenas. Family members can bring witnesses. After hearing the matter, the judge's decision should be fair, and restitution—doing something nice for the person who is the "victim"—is the only sentencing that should be given (no punishment).

18.3   *The Great Debate.* This teaches kids how to solve their problems verbally. Pick out situations in which your child has been inappropriate and set aside time weekly to have a family debate. If the quarrel was with someone outside the family, assign a person to **role-play,** to speak for that individual. Show kids how good debates are carried out. Examples are televised political debates and college debates. Set up a debating stage. Show your child how to make a point without becoming aggressive, personally attacking someone, or using inappropriate language. End the debate in a peaceful manner in which it is clear that both sides have clearly listened and expressed valid arguments to each other, and do your best to solve the problem at hand. **"I" messages, effective listening, empathy,** and **mutual respect** are excellent ingredients to add to this activity. Establish formal debating rules before beginning. This avoids petty squabbles.

18.4   *Stomp Your Feet.* If your child needs an outlet for his aggressive energy, bubble packs will come in handy. Yes, those wonderful plastic sheets of bubble packing you wrap breakables in are terrific for foot-stomping children. Give him a few sheets and instruct him to stamp out all the bubbles or to stamp until he has stamped out all his angry feelings.

18.5   *Gentle Olympics.* Set up a "gentle Olympics" in your home or backyard. Think about games in which your child must accomplish an activity by using his gentleness to win. Olympic activities could consist of carrying an egg from one point to another, two people holding a cooked spaghetti noodle and walking side by side without breaking the noodle, or running up to a person but stopping short before contact. Make sure your child wins a gold medal for his success. Remind him of his gold-medal behaviors when he is becoming destructive or getting out of control.

Gentle Skill Games. Reinforce your child's belief that he can be gentle and 　18.6
in total control of his hands. With him, make a house of cards, working carefully and gently to stack the cards on top of one another. Create a domino race: long, curved rows of dominoes set up so that if the first standing piece is pushed over, the rest will follow. Throughout these activities, continuously comment on how gentle and controlled he is. Then, when he becomes aggressive or destructive, remind him that you saw him using his gentle skills.

The Take-Apart Box. Write the words "Take-Apart/Put-Together Box" on 　18.7
the front of a cardboard box. Fill the box with broken items like old radios and clocks, broken tools, and discarded toys. Explain to your child that every time she feels the need to take something apart, she can select an item in the box instead of destroying something valuable.

LYING

The Fairy Tale Book. Make a Fairy Tale Book out of all the grandiose lies 　18.8
and long-winded stories your child tells. Explain that each story will be recorded, and that she can draw pictures of her stories for a special Fairy Tale Book. When you catch your child in an obvious lie, take out the Fairy Tale Book and say, "That's a good one. Let's write it in the Fairy Tale Book."

SWEARING

Bad-Mouth Stickers. On blank peel-and-stick paper, draw and cut out pic- 　18.9
tures of a big mouth. Every time your child swears, stick the mouth on him. This will help him take notice when he is using inappropriate language or being rude or sassy.

Bad-Mouth Detective. Have your child become the Bad-Mouth or Bad- 　18.10
Manners Detective. Explain to her that the bad-mouth and bad-manners behaviors that she should be looking for are tattling, swearing, complaining, being verbally aggressive, or whatever. She should write these down. At the end of the day have the family gather to hear the report. The Bad-Mouth Detective should try to educate the family on ways to stop this uncalled-for behavior and not be seen as a classic tattletale. (To ensure this, do not use this information for punishment.) (See page 254 for a list of reading recipes for destructive and antisocial behaviors.)

Recipe #19: The Worry Warrior

CHAPTER 6

Fears, Anxieties, and Nervous Habits

IT HAS BEEN RAINING for weeks. Finally the sun breaks out and you've made it to the park for that long-awaited picnic. It's a perfect lunch for four, including peanut butter sandwiches, potato chips, and vintage grape juice. You have just begun to relish this sunny day with your children when it happens: a monstrous canine killer (actually a fluffy golden retriever pup) appears from behind the bushes, heading straight for your blanket at 200 miles per hour. You try to distract your six-year-old, but she notices the dog heading your way, screams for her life, leaps into the air, landing right in your dessert. After she has been cleaned up, she proceeds to bite her nails nonstop and screams every time a dog passes by that afternoon.

While situations like these are difficult and aggravating, it is important to realize that your child's fears and nervous habits often are normal reactions to developmental challenges. Some fears may become pronounced at certain ages and stages of maturation, but most will be over in the normal course of time, with experimentation and gentle **encouragement.** However, certain fears and nervous habits not overcome during childhood may continue into adulthood. One good example is the very common fear most of us have of public speaking, which is probably a leftover fear from childhood.

While children are less capable than are adults of handling their fears, they are usually more flexible, more willing to be guided to confront their fears and nervous habits. These confrontations will probably enable your child to develop skills and confidence in her own abilities, thus succeeding in overcoming her difficulties and preventing them from growing into paralyzing obstacles to fun and personal growth. The activities that we have developed and collected for this chapter are all geared toward this goal.

Fears

Adults can unintentionally instill unwarranted fears in children in order to make them obey ("The bogeyman will get you if you don't get in bed").

A child's incredibly vivid imagination can transform a small fear into a grandiose phobia. Highly reactive children who may be especially sensitive, timid, and generally anxious by nature tend to be constitutionally more prone to having difficulty with fears.

Fear instinct is necessary to human survival. It alerts us to potential dangers and provides us with an internal early-warning system for harmful situations. Many are normal and developmentally appropriate, such as stranger anxiety in infants and fear of the dark in young preschool children. Many types of fear are instinctual such as the movement we make in response to loud noises, loss of balance, or sudden motion. Specific fears such as fear of water or of animals originate from upsetting, frightening, or misunderstood experiences.

Fears can be used by a child to manipulate his or her parents and to gain attention.

Children are more prone to have problems with fears if they live in a conflictual, unpredictable, or overly authoritarian environment. These situations promote feelings of insecurity and loss of self-confidence.

Anxieties

While fear is a momentary reaction, anxiety represents a general feeling of impending doom. Anxieties are specific fears that tend to lead to general, all-encompassing feelings of apprehension and insecurity.

A child who is overanxious may withdraw from challenging activities because he feels incapable of dealing with the real or perceived dangers that he associates with those activities.

Nervous Habits

Nervous habits are behaviors that help a child cope with nervous tension and stress. They serve as immediate gratification and satisfaction of instinctual needs and tend to be automatic reactions that a child seemingly has no control over. Thumb-sucking is a common example.

Nervous habits are responses to life's normal pressures and frustrations and the body's way of providing relief from anxieties, boredom, or upsetting situations. Nervous habits become self-soothing and self-perpetuating and difficult to give up without an alternative. Most of them give a child something to do during boring moments such as watching television or riding in the car.

Fears

Never use a feared object as a disciplinary tool, dismiss your child's fears, or tell him he is a baby and should not be afraid.

Encourage your child to share with you everything she knows about her fear and its background. If you find it is based on misunderstanding or lack of information, try to educate her about the reality of the situation *without invalidating her underlying fear*. Present to your child the feared object or situation in less threatening doses so that she can become more accustomed to it and gradually master her fear. (Recipes 19, 20, 23)

Normalize your child's fears by exposing him to others who have similar problems. Use storybooks or stories of yourself as a child. Explain that all children have fears and that some fears are normal and good to have. (Recipes 19, 20, 23, and reading recipes on page 254.)

Distinguish between normal and necessary biological fears (early-warning systems) and those that are limiting your child's experience. Encourage your child's natural process of developing autonomy by helping him to shift from dependence on others to self-reliance. (Recipes 19, 20, 23, 51, 55.16, 55.17, 55.18, 55.19)

If you suspect your child's expression of fear is intended to manipulate or gain attention, try to avoid being manipulated.

Examine your child's living circumstances. Are there conflicts and problems that might give rise to fears? Provide an anxious, fearful, or overly sensitive child a safe environment where she can freely master, explore, "play out," and conquer her fears or worries. (Recipes 19, 20, 23)

Anxieties

Encourage your child to fully communicate his worries to you. Listen to his concerns and ask him questions such as, when was the first time he remembers feeling this way and when did he feel most able to handle his worries? (Recipes 19, 34, 35.8, 64.8)

Empower your child by helping him come up with a plan to approach and address the source of his anxiety. High-

light special skills he possesses that will help him feel in control and more capable of handling his worries. Examples are relaxation and problem-solving skills and successful experiences in his past in which he coped with similar challenges. (Recipes 19, 23, 38, 68)

Nervous Habits

Even if you find your child's nervous habit annoying, try to appreciate how it serves as a tension outlet. Do not become overly concerned at first; most nervous habits are neither life-threatening nor permanent. Everyone, adults and children alike, has one or two. Remember this when you are starting to become exasperated. (Recipes 21, 22, 23.10, 23.11)

Some nervous habits need to run their course and require no special attention. Too much pressure to stop the habit may cause your child to develop others as replacements. (Recipes 21, 22, 23.11)

Teach other, more mentally and physically satisfying ways to release tension such as exercise, sports, relaxation techniques, music, or art. Help your child find a socially preferable replacement (gum chewing rather than nail biting). (Recipes 21, 22, 23.10, 36, 70)

When fears, anxieties, or nervous habits that might seem in the beginning to have been normal and developmentally expected become unreasonable or overpowering, or your child experiences panic states, you should seek help from a therapist.

☆ *The Worry Warrior* ☆

RECIPE #19

Serves: 3–8 years

This recipe is for children who are overanxious and worry excessively.

Step 1
State and define the problem

As we mentioned in the Problem/Solution Chart, fears and anxieties in children can be developmentally and situationally appropriate. This recipe is for children whose fears and anxieties exceed the normal range for any given age or situation. The child becomes so anxious and worried she is unable to try new experiences, socialize, or separate from Mom and Dad. If this describes your son or daughter, this recipe will hit the spot. To begin, you will need to **encourage** your child to discuss what his fears, worries, and/or anxieties are about. If the response is the familiar "I dunno," share with him that you understand (**empathy, mutual respect, effective listening**) that worries are hard to talk about, but that you want him to become less worried. Make a list of his worries.

Step 2
Identify skills and solutions

With your child, identify and list all his skills, capabilities, talents, and "powerful" attributes. This activity relies heavily on using your child's skills and innate abilities to counteract his anxieties (see page 265 for a list of skills and capabilities in children). Focus on any skill that suggests strength, courage, the ability to cope, independence, and perseverance. If you are scraping bottom to find any of these, **positively reframe** her worries and uncertainties as the talent for being very careful and cautious.

Step 3
Mutually agree upon goals

Goal: "I will use my special skills to feel strong and capable, to try new experiences, and to battle big worries with courage."

Step 4
Practice and play

This activity will playfully guide your child through a natural process of shifting from dependence on others to dependence on himself or herself. Explain that you are going to transform her into the Worry Warrior—Conqueror of Fears and Foes! With her help, create a costume that makes her look like a superhero. A cape, wand, and mask, and a shirt with a big W on it will do. The Worry Warrior needs a backpack to keep her worry weapons in. Don't *worry;* these weapons are three-by-five index cards with a word or picture of each of your child's skills you listed in step 2. Every possible skill your child has will become a weapon against her worries.

Sit down with your child and, using the list from step 2, write, draw, or cut out and glue a photo of each of her skills on each index card. Put these cards in her backpack. Once she has her Worry Warrior outfit and backpack filled with her skills, you are ready to **planfully play** or work through her worries. **Role-play** and pretend the Worry Warrior is confronted with worry after worry—all her major fears and anxieties. Using her backpack of skills, have her pull out a weapon (skill) to fight off the worry. For example, *afraid of getting lost:* weapon—*good at finding help,* *knows the telephone number, doesn't wander away.* Play this game as often as you need. Bring her weapons, the index cards of skills, with you when you are not at home to remind her of her capabilities when she is not the Worry Warrior. This steady flow of **encouragement** will eventually teach her to use her strengths and belief in herself to overcome her anxieties.

Now that your child is aware of her own power and skills, she is better prepared to deal with anxiety-producing situations. Older children can participate in this activity by drawing a cartoon of the Worry Warrior. Frame by frame, following the above guidelines, have your child draw himself as the Worry Warrior character in the cartoon. **Encourage** him to include how he deals with his fears by using his skills.

Acknowledge your child's newly developed courage and ability. Ask him to identify the special skills of the Worry Warrior and how these skills helped him with his worries. If he hasn't reached his goal, either try a new recipe in this chapter or take a closer look at whether his anxieties are too complex and require the help of a therapist. (See page 262 for information on professional help.)

Step 5
Review and recognize efforts

☆ *Fear Week* ☆

RECIPE #20

Serves: 3–12 years

This recipe teaches children how to deal with their fear by approaching it in small steps.

Step 1
State and define the problem

In a calm, **empathic** way, support your child as she tells you about her fear. Whether it is heights, doctors, water, dogs, spiders, monsters under the bed, or the dark, tell her that you will help her learn how to conquer her fear. Find out what frightens her the most. Get as many details as you can. If your child exaggerates, gently correct her but do not laugh or joke. Respect your child's terrors and tell her how you will join forces to defeat them.

Step 2
Identify skills and solutions

Point out skills, traits, and abilities that will help her cope with her fear. Come up with positive statements such as "I am strong," "I can handle it," or "I am smart and brave." Explain that she can use these for the **"T"** in **S.T.A.R.** (See chapter 2 on how to use S.T.A.R.) Every time she encounters her fear, encourage her to be a S.T.A.R.

Step 3
Mutually agree upon goals

Goal: "I will use my special skills to be able to deal with my fear one step at a time."

Step 4
Practice and play

This activity is based on a researched and proven behavioral technique called "desensitization." Through a step-by-step encounter process, your child can learn to gradually reduce the magnitude of her fear. (Desensitization works with adults as well.) We have **positively reframed** this activity as Fear Week.

Before beginning Fear Week, your child will need to learn new ways she can cope with her fearful feelings. Show her the relaxation techniques taught in recipe 38, The Relaxation Center. Have her practice and use her self-talk techniques, skills, and positive statements listed in step 2 when confronting her fear. Find **distractions** such as music, counting numbers, or reciting a nursery rhyme to keep him or her calm and focused on something other than the fear. Throughout the week of these "fear encounters," **model** calmness, optimism, and the ability to cope. This **encouragement** is imperative. With each day of the week, her fear will be gradually and *carefully* introduced to her in small amounts. The fear will be paired with a fun activity or game to countercondition your child.

Here is a Fear Week with the "dreaded dog" as the problem.

Day 1. Read dog books and stories that are illustrated and charming. Study the books with your child and talk with her about the friendly, silly, and nonthreatening behavior the dog is displaying in the book.

Day 2. Watch TV programs and movies about dogs. Select movies such as *101 Dalmatians* that depict dogs as fun, harmless, and as man's best friend.

Day 3. Read books and see movies that show real-life pictures of dogs. Some dog books contain many puppy pictures. These are good because they are the least-threatening. If, during this process, your child becomes fearful, have her use her coping skills discussed in step 2.

Day 4. Observe dogs from a distance. Go to a dog show and sit a good distance from the action. Check out the puppies at the local pet store. Observe a neighbor's dog from a car or fenced-in yard.

Day 5. **Role-play** and practice meeting a dog. Ask an adult who has a well-trained and friendly dog that has never demonstrated aggressive behavior to participate in Dog Week. Show your child how to interact with this friendly dog and explain how she can do this.

Day 6. For the first meeting be sure to have the dog on a leash. Keep the dog at a distance (a yard or two) and introduce your child to it.

Day 7. Play with the dog. Have your child meet and play with it. Mission completed! Each of these activities should occur only under the close supervision of the dog's adult owner and the child's parent.

After your child has successfully accomplished her fear encounters, provide more experiences with the feared object and recognize, praise, and compliment her successes.

Step 5
Review and recognize efforts

☆ *"When I Grow Up"* ☆

RECIPE #21

Serves: 3–12 years

This recipe helps children eliminate their nervous habits.

Step 1
State and define the problem

Encourage your child to talk about his nervous habit. Ask when it becomes a problem for him. Use **effective listening** and **empathy** when he shares his feelings with you. Be sure to tell your child that his nervous habits will probably end when he grows up. However, if he doesn't take action now, he will have a much harder time later.

Step 2
Identify skills and solutions

In this step you may need to identify your child's special abilities and strengths that would help him gain control over his habit. Point out his skills in thinking before acting (**S.T.A.R.**) or times when he concentrates on, or is aware of, his behavior. Also focus on the positive maturational changes your child has achieved over the years. Show him that as he has grown older he has been able to eliminate some behaviors—and replace them with better and more mature ones such as giving up diapers and learning to use the toilet or sharing his feelings verbally rather than crying or tantruming.

Step 3
Mutually agree upon goals

Goal: "I will use my special skills to stop my nervous habit—eventually."

Step 4
Practice and play

Nervous habits are automatic reactions often resorted to when children are tired or idle. This activity will help them find other ways to deal with nervous energy and boredom. It will show them how to find consolation in discovering that as they grow older the habit will eventually vanish.

In this exercise your child will pretend to be interviewed as though he were an older person—an older self. This unique **role play** not only invites him to ask his older self about his feelings and thoughts concerning his nervous habit, but playfully leads him to find ways to solve the problem.

First you will need to learn a few techniques for ending nervous habits. Then share them with your daughter or son for the purpose of setting up this interview and answering questions about how the "child" solved the problem. Here are a few suggestions for the interview and for steps you might take:

1. **Ignore** the habit. This eliminates making an issue out of it that will lead to a power struggle between parent and child.

2. Use **distraction** and other alternatives. Have your child think of other satisfying behaviors he can replace the nervous habit with.

3. Restrict the habit (see Planful Playing, Habit Hut) page 94.

4. Teach relaxation skills (see recipe 38).

90

5. Use awareness training. To do this you need to chart and record the times and places your child uses his habit and explain the results to your child.

6. Set up a reward system (see chapter 17, "Just Desserts") for cutting back his habit by using an incentive.

7. Let **natural consequences** and social pressures take their course. For example, peer comments and/or ugly-looking nails could motivate children to stop biting their nails.

To begin, have your child make up a mock script of an interview between a reporter and her older self. Come up with a half dozen questions the reporter will ask that probe feelings and suggest solutions. Help your child prepare responses to the questions. Remind her of her special skills, discussed in step 2, for coping with nervous habits. Help her imagine that she is grown up by playing this game:

Have her put on an adult's overcoat, hat, and glasses. Now put her up on your shoulders. The overcoat should button over your face so that you and your child present a composite that looks about six feet tall. Now another family member should pretend to be the reporter, and using his or her script, ask the suddenly grown-up child how she once felt about her nervous habit, how she got rid of it, and how she feels about it now.

Practice the interview a few times, then use it as a skit for other family members and relatives. Perhaps videotape the interview.

When your child falls back on her nervous habit, remind her of what her older self said about the problem. Be sure to compliment her on her progress.

Step 5
Review and recognize efforts

☆ *Habits Anonymous* ☆

RECIPE #22
Serves: 4–12 years

This recipe helps children decrease or eliminate nervous habits.

Step 1
State and define the problem

In order for this recipe to function, everyone in the family will need to identify and talk about his or her nervous habits. Tension-relieving behaviors in children such as thumb-sucking, nail-biting, hair-twisting, and rocking are commonly used to reduce anxiety and deal with stress. Adults might smoke or bite their lip or nail. Since most of us have some sort of nervous habit, this step would be a good time to admit your own nervous habit or habits and **model** for your child how to talk about and deal with the problem.

Step 2
Identify skills and solutions

Identify for your child his skills and abilities that relate to controlling himself and thinking about his actions (**S.T.A.R.**). Concentrate on skills that highlight his ability to communicate feelings and share concerns. At this point share your skills and abilities too. In fact, every family member should make a list of his or her special skills and abilities in relation to personal control and self-discipline.

Step 3
Mutually agree upon goals

Family Goal: "We will use our special skills to help everyone in our family get rid of our nervous habits."

Step 4
Practice and play

"I bite my lip," says Dad. "I suck my thumb," says his son. Welcome to Habits Anonymous, a family support group that gives your child **encouragement, empathy,** and **humor** to help him decrease or eliminate his nervous habit. Set aside a time each week for this special family meeting. In it, each person should admit his or her habit and ask for advice. Family members can ask supportive questions like, "When do you find it hardest to control your lip-biting (or thumb-sucking or finger-rapping) problem?"

Parents can **model** for their child how to admit problems and supportively question others. Take time to remind each other what your special skills are for countering the habit. Helpful advice could include using relaxation (see recipe 38) to help release nervous tension. Teach your child how to use **distraction** and alternative behaviors to compete with the habit such as chewing gum for thumb-sucking habit. Teach him how to use **S.T.A.R.** and to stop and think before he sucks his thumb. Best of all, see what kind of advice your child has for you. It may surprise you! Continue your weekly meeting as needed. **Spice it up** with some **humor** and **affection** to calm the nerves and release tension.

Step 5
Review and recognize efforts

If all is going well, and you or your child has reduced or stopped your nervous habit, throw a good-bye-habit party. Celebrate and praise each person's accomplishments. If the nervous habit continues, be patient. It may just need to run its course or you may need to **try, try again** with another recipe.

☆ *Planful Playing in a Pinch* ☆

RECIPE #23

Hot tips and quick recipes for solving fears, phobias, and anxieties in children.

FEARS/ANXIETIES

Safety Video. Children feel much more powerful and capable of handling their fears if they believe they are knowledgeable about and in control of them. By having your child write, direct, and act in a safety video that examines fears and anxieties, she can feel as though she were an expert in this area. Let your child know that the video might be used to teach other children about safety. Subject areas include water safety, traffic, strangers, animals, fire, and other life situations that worry your child. Be sure she comes up with the solutions herself. Encourage her to show the video to younger children to teach them the safety skills. 23.1

Monster Friends. Make a friendly monster with your child. You can make it doll size or human size. It doesn't matter if the monster looks scary, just be sure to remind the child that the monster is helpful and will be a good friend. Help her try to use this friendly monster to make friends with the monsters that upset her. 23.2

The Haunted House. You don't have to wait for Halloween to make this. With your child, design and decorate a room to become a Haunted House. Put scary items that commonly upset your child in it. **Encourage** her to play "friendly monster" or to play with these objects. Charge admission to family members and try to scare them with your spooky Haunted House. 23.3

My Scarecrow. Scarecrows are used by farmers to frighten away intruders (crows) and keep them from eating the crops. This stuffed person can help your child playfully "scare" away his imagined or feared intruders. This activity asks you to make a scarecrow with your child that is actually a replica of her or himself. Stuff your child's shirt, pants, and socks and add a pair of old sneakers. For the head of the scarecrow, stuff a pillowcase and draw your child's face on it. Top it off with his favorite hat. Place the scarecrow somewhere in your home where he feels it could best protect him. 23.4

Play in the Dark. Here are some fun games to play in the dark. These playfully help your child become more accustomed to the dark and to deal with his fears. The games should be played at night so that the room can be really dark. Try to use your child's bedroom so that he becomes more accustomed to being in the dark in his own room. 23.5

1. Give a large piece of paper to your child. Turn off the lights and ask her to draw pictures of a door, a house, or a person. After a few minutes turn on the light and look at the silly picture. Extend the length of time the light is off by having her draw more complicated pictures.

2. Put on a shadow show—create hand shapes and hand shadows in the dark by following the instructions in *Shadowgraphs*, by Phila Webb and Jose Corby (Running Press, 1991).

3. Turn off the lights and have your child touch and feel various objects. Have him guess what they are.

4. Glow-in-the-dark stickers on the walls and ceiling of your child's bedroom make wonderful fun in the dark.

23.6   *Louder Than Lightning.* When the storm hits your area and your child is terrified by the thunder and lightning (a normal, instinctive reaction to loud noises), play Louder Than Lightning. While waiting for the thunder after the lightning flashes, tell your child to scream louder than the lightning. Join in with her and make as much noise as possible when the thunder rumbles across your home. Use pots and pans, tambourines, and other noisy objects to combat and defeat the noise (and fear).

23.7   *Playing with Water.* Squirt guns, water balloons, pools, and creative waterslides make hot days fun while decreasing your child's fear of the water. Play games that make getting your face wet fun.

23.8   *Doctor Play.* Using a PlaySkool Doctor Kit, dolls, and stuffed animals, play and practice going to the doctor. Throughout the activity, mention how skillful the doll is in going to the doctor. Make sure the story ends with the "child"—the doll—feeling safe and happy.

23.9   *What's Up, Doc?* Some pediatricians are truly wonderful persons and do not mind an invitation to attend a special lunch with an anxious child. This is a way to give your child the experience of being with his doctor in a friendly setting with no strings (or needles) attached. A picnic lunch at the doctor's office or an ice cream outing is also a terrific way to ease your child into the office at a later date.

NERVOUS HABITS

23.10   *Thumb Puppets.* Make thumb or finger puppets by cutting the thumbs off old mittens and putting faces and clothing on them. Encourage your child to wear them as fun reminders to keep her thumbs or fingers out of her mouth.

23.11   *The Habit Hut.* Set up a special, unrewarding place in your home where your child who has annoying habits such as nail-biting or gum-cracking can indulge her "bad" habit. This is the only place she can suck her thumb, bite her nails, twist her hair, or pick her nose. When your child engages in her habit, ask her to head to the Habit Hut! (See page 254 for a list of reading recipes for anxieties, fears, and nervous habits.)

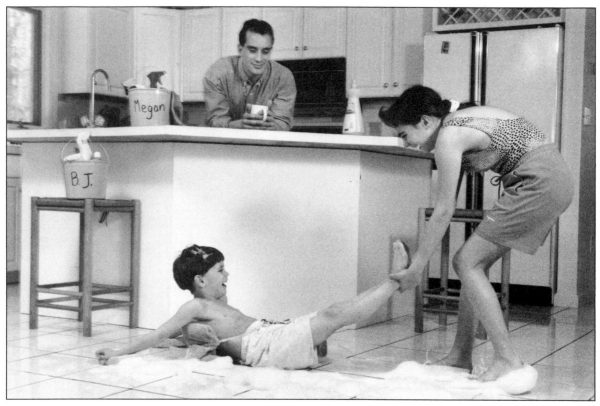

Recipe #29: Good Clean Fun

CHAPTER 7

Irresponsibility

ANNA HAS MISSED THE school bus three days straight, and her mother has promised herself for the umpteenth time that she will *not* drive her daughter to school. "Anna!" Mom screams. "Are you ready? The school bus will be here in five minutes." "In a minute, Mom . . . almost ready," Anna answers in classic style. Moments later, Mom swings open Anna's bedroom door to a horrifying sight: piles of dirty clothing fossilizing on the floor, a half-eaten Tootsie Roll glued to the dresser, her half-dressed daughter, hair uncombed and wet, cross-legged on the floor, engrossed in a video game. Just as Mom is about blow up, they both hear the school bus horn. In a fury, Mom dresses Anna, combs her hair, and pushes her, coat open and wet hair steaming in the cold air out the front door. As Mom picks up her now cold coffee, she sighs and notices Anna's unfinished homework sitting on the kitchen table.

Problems associated with irresponsible behavior often arise when children are relentlessly told by their parents what to do, when, and how to do it; or when, out of frustration, parents assume the child's responsibilities and do the child's job themselves, a misguided approach that affords the child few opportunities to develop, exercise, and integrate badly needed skills and personal standards.

The activities we have selected to discuss in this chapter are designed to strengthen your child's life skills and help her learn to assume ownership of that which rightly belongs to her: personal obligations, household responsibilities, good listening and organizational skills, her successes and mistakes.

Procrastination

Doesn't Do Chores

Messiness

Doesn't Listen

PROBLEMS

Irresponsibility

Many children are impulsive and act before considering how their choices of behavior may affect them later.

For some children irresponsibility is an inability to assume accountability and ownership of their obligations, successes, and mistakes. This is often caused by one or more of the following: (a) failure to understand what is expected, (b) disorganization—where or how to begin or how to carry through the job to completion, (c) lack of motivation, (d) difficulty in concentrating.

Some children who are oppositional refuse to accept responsibility in the belief that they are asserting their independence and autonomy. Parents interpret refusal to accept responsibility as a sign of immaturity.

A child who is pressured to manage responsibilities in excess of what he is capable of developmentally will inevitably have difficulty meeting either his or others' expectations. If this goes on too long, it will damage his belief in himself and his motivation to keep trying.

When parents come to the aid of their irresponsibly behaving child, they are unknowingly reinforcing the behavior problem and failing to encourage the child to own up to his or her behavior and its consequences.

Procrastination and Messiness

Some children who procrastinate use time as a weapon in power struggles with their parents—a means to indirectly express opposition or anger.

Procrastination may also be your child's way of avoiding unpleasant situations in which he feels uncomfortable or fears failure.

Procrastination can easily become a pattern of behavior on which your child relies and which limits her. This is a particularly difficult pattern to alter once learned and practiced.

Messiness may be your child's expression of his personality and independence, but for the long-suffering parents it might appear to be pure and simple defiance of a reasonable request for order and cleanliness. Messiness can also be caused by poorly developed organizational skills, problems in concentrating, or failure to understand instructions.

Irresponsibility

Help your child appreciate how her actions frustrate and inconvenience others. Use **empathy** and **mutual respect** to teach this. (Recipes 25, 29.2, 29.8, 47, 48.1, 48.5, 48.9)

Help your child understand the correlation between responsibility and privileges. Teach him the importance and benefits that responsibility confers: more personal power, decision-making privileges, and increased respect and autonomy. The more responsibility he assumes, the more he will be trusted with freedoms and privileges. (Recipe 26)

Offer **choices** that help structure the task from the beginning to the middle steps to the conclusion. For some, organizational skills and cleanliness are learned skills. Teach and **model** these patiently through communicating your belief in their value. (Recipes 24, 25, 26, 27, 29.9 through 29.15)

Help your child participate in the day-to-day functioning of your home and family and take pride in the results of his efforts. (Recipes 25, 46)

Be sure that your expectations fall within your child's skill level and developmental capabilities. Advice from other parents, teachers, and books on child development will be helpful.

Procrastination and Messiness

Encourage your child to express her disagreement actively through discussion and negotiation rather than passively by putting either things or you off. (See Family Council, page 19.)

Support your child in facing a dreaded task as soon as possible rather than expending the same amount of energy avoiding it. Use examples such as tooth care: taking five minutes to brush his teeth now will save him time and pain in the dentist's office. (Recipes 24, 27, 29.6, 44.3, 44.4)

As soon as you notice a developing pattern of procrastination, address it. The earlier you begin to modify this behavior, the less chance there is that it will develop into an ingrained strategy in dealing with day-to-day demands. (Recipes 24, 44.3, 44.4)

Reflect about your own personality and that of your child. Try to appreciate and find humor in the differences that exist between the two of you. Make expectations and tasks clear and unambiguous. Help your child analyze projects and structure them into more manageable steps. Be sure to look for improvement—not perfection! (Recipes 24 through 29)

☆ *What's Next . . .* ☆

This recipe teaches children how to follow directions, organize their time, and correct procrastination.

Step 1
State and define the problem

Have your child define the meaning of "getting it done on time" or "following directions." Share your own description of the problem. Give examples of times when each family member did not follow directions, procrastinated, or didn't organize his or her time well. Show how this later became a problem. Your child's perception of time-related responsibilities may be different from yours. Remember, he has different priorities than you and therefore chores, homework, catching the bus, or practicing an instrument may not be as important to him as they are to you.

Step 2
Identify skills and solutions

Give good, **encouraging** examples of when your child organized her time well, followed directions, and got a project in on time.

Step 3
Mutually agree upon goals

Goal: "I will use my special skills to be more responsible by organizing my time better and by following directions."

Step 4
Practice and play

Children who have difficulty managing their time are often seen as lazy procrastinators or as disorganized. These traits have something in common: the inability or refusal to follow a time-determined structure. The following activities teach children important memory skills such as how to record, retain, and retrieve information. They also help children break down a day's or a week's work, which will enable them to better plan and organize it. Most important, these activities teach children how to assume responsibility for their own time and personal duties.

The What's-Next Room Chart. Make a full-length room border that covers the four corners of your child's room, or make a chart out of a long sheet of contact paper and write on the border or chart with crayons or markers the hours of the day from morning to night. Try to do it in half-hour segments. Discuss the normal daily routine with your child, from waking up to going to bed. Draw pictures of each activity, cut them out, and paste them on the border in the order of the time of each event. Try to make a complete border of scheduled activities, including brushing teeth, dressing, and catching the bus, straight through bedtime story and lights off. Your child will now have a clear picture of what is next, what he is expected to do, and how much time he has to do it. On days when your child's schedule changes, peel off the activity and replace it with a new or changed one. Go through the expectations and daily routine with your child the night before by chanting out each activity as it appears on the border. This is a **playful** way to get your son or daughter to follow directions without always having to tell him what to do next.

100

The Appointment Book. Buy an appointment book or a pocket recorder. Every night, or on Sunday night, record your child's responsibilities for the next day or the next week. Go through each day, stating the time to wake up, the time to catch the bus, and the time to play. List projects that need to be done, and help your son or daughter think of a plan to do them on time. Use a few **planful playing** ideas such as "noticeable notes" or "73 hours to go" along with the appointment book or recording. You may want to schedule periods when you are available to help him with homework or with projects. If he does not follow through with the scheduled appointment times or responsibilities, let the **natural consequences** do the work for you. He will experience the effects of his laziness and procrastination—not doing a report on time results in a bad grade or a late night of cramming. Keep referring him to his schedule, or have him listen to the recorder. Let him know it is his decision to put things off, but it will make it harder for him later. Use **T.A.P.** and redirect your actions so that you don't revert to nagging or yelling when he doesn't follow through.

Anytime your child follows through on a task, checks off a completed project, or simply gets something done on time, recognize his accomplishments. These activities work well with other Recipes in this chapter. You may want to consider giving your child a reward for her efforts in following a schedule (see chapter 17, "Just Desserts," for an incentive program).

Step 5
Review and recognize efforts

☆ *The Team Chore Chart* ☆

RECIPE #25
Serves: All ages

This recipe teaches children to do their chores and take part in family responsibilities.

Step 1
State and define the problem

Use the structure of a **family council** meeting to gather your family to discuss the needs and responsibilities of your home. Take turns talking about each person's perception of family responsibilities and chores. Express your concern that without everyone's help and contributions, the family home would not run smoothly. Use your child's favorite mode of communication and consider **role playing** different situations that show what happens when someone doesn't do his or her chore.

Step 2
Identify skills and solutions

List your child's skills and accomplishments in completing tasks and following through on a commitment. Practicing, then playing for a baseball team, or rehearsing, then performing for a dance troupe, are examples. These highlight your child's ability to be a part of a group and to follow through on her commitments.

Step 3
Mutually agree upon goals

Goal: "I will use my special skills to work as a team and share responsibilities."

Step 4
Practice and play

This activity may not be new to you, for making chore charts is a part of American family history. However, this chart has a little twist: it requires all family members to do chores as if they were players on a team. Without team members doing their share, the team won't win. If everyone performs his or her team chore, the entire family wins a mutually agreed-upon reward such as a trip to a favorite restaurant or a new household item that everyone would enjoy.

We believe that responsibilities and household chores bond a child to his or her family and home, providing a sort of club membership. Participating in washing the dishes, vacuuming, clearing the table, and making beds gives a child a sense of value, self-worth, and accomplishment. This ultimately builds self-esteem and self-reliance and prepares your son or daughter for more demanding responsibilities.

The first thing to do is to make your team chore chart by deciding on daily chores that need to be done. Depending on your child's age and developmental ability, choose three to seven chores to be accomplished each week. Explain to your child that doing his chore for the day is like doing his part on a baseball, soccer, football team. Everyone has to do his or her chore to help the team win or to win the reward. Encourage your child to remind others to do their chores for the sake of the team. You may want to include a "personal chore" section in your chart that requires your child to do homework or make her bed.

When your family has accomplished its team objective, enjoy your reward! Be sure to tell your kids how great they are. You can **spice up** your praise with a family handshake or high-five at the end of a successful week. If someone doesn't do his or her job, let the pressures and **logical consequences** speak for themselves. Be sure to let your child know that he or she can **try, try again.**

Step 5
Review and recognize efforts

FAMILY CHORE CHART

Put x or sticker in square when you do your chore.

Date:

	clean dishes	set table	take out garbage	walk dog	fold laundry	clean bathroom	dust clean vacuum	total points
George	mon	tues	wed	thurs	fri	sat	sat	
Tammy	tues	wed	thur	fri	sat	mon	sat	
Suzy	wed	thur	fri	sat	mon	tue	sat	
Mom	thur	fri	sat	mon	tue	wed	sat	
Dad	fri	sat	mon	tue	wed	thur	sat	

☆ *I'm Responsible Association* ☆

This recipe helps children become more internally motivated to be responsible.

Step 1
State and define the problem

Use **effective listening** and **mutual respect** when discussing your child's perceptions of personal responsibilities. **Encourage** her to express her thoughts on the topic of being responsible for yourself and explain how this eventually increases her opportunities for more freedom and independence. Share with your child that in order to gain more **choices** and privileges in her life, she needs to be responsible and make good, thoughtful decisions for herself. Use effective listening to tune in to your child's thoughts and feelings throughout this step.

Step 2
Identify skills and solutions

Identify your child's skills, attributes, and capabilities that show mature decision-making and following through on tasks. **Positively reframe** a recent situation in which your child made efforts to reach a goal or follow through on a responsibility.

Step 3
Mutually agree upon goals

Goal: "I will use my special skills to become more responsible for myself."

Step 4
Practice and play

This activity is based on the concept that when your child takes on more responsibility for himself and his behaviors, he gains personal power and decision-making opportunities. "Personal power" is the knowledge that you are in charge of your life and that you have the ultimate responsibility for the outcome, whether it is positive or negative (**natural** or **logical consequences**). Just like the teen striving for her driver's license—the privilege of driving and controlling a car—your child will be working toward a "responsibility license" and a membership in the I'm Responsible Association with all its privileges. Set up with your child a system that gives her more freedom, **choices,** and rewards for following through on required responsibilities.

First go to chapter 17, "Just Desserts," where you will find The Level Program. This section includes a chart that you can use as a model in making a Level Program with your child. Depending on your child's age and developmental ability, chart out the responsibilities and chores required and the privileges or rewards she would receive for successful completion. You may want to use **the 5 C's** to establish which responsibilities are house rules that must be obeyed and which are more flexible. Each of the four levels progressively adds more responsibilities that coincide with more privileges. For example, on level 1, the responsibilities could be personal hygiene, getting up in the morning when told, and making the bed. The privileges would include a couple of choices such as playing a board game with a parent and/or a later bedtime. Level 4, however, would entail more demanding responsibilities, such as your son's getting up in the morning on his own. Of course, with his accomplishment, the privileges would increase correspondingly, like being able to decide on his own bedtime. As your child moves from level 1 to level 4 in the I'm Responsible Association, she can receive her "responsibility license." If she is successful at maintaining this level, the family can celebrate by throwing a party. By receiving her license she will be allowed to remain at level 4 and slowly increase her privileges week by week. Of course, if she is not successful at maintaining level 4, her license is revoked. (She can always **try, try again.**) Use parenting techniques such as **your choice, S.T.A.R., logical consequences,** and **modeling.** All of these are terrific ingredients for providing children with guidance, options, and structure in seeing an everyday procedure through to its conclusion. **T.A.P.** yourself when you feel the urge to nag or yell at your child to do a job. Instead let the chart and its privileges and/or lack of privileges do it for you.

Discuss with your child the personal power and sense of achievement she experiences in becoming more responsible. Congratulate her for her accomplishments and remind her that there is always room to **try, try again** if she is not successful at first.

Step 5
Review and recognize efforts

☆ *Doesn't Belong Box and Auction* ☆

RECIPE #27
Serves: 3–12 years

This recipe teaches children to be responsible and pick up after themselves.

Step 1
State and define the problem

Discuss with your child the importance of caring for his belongings and putting them in their proper places. Tell him how leaving things around makes them hard to find when he wants them. Ask him to explain what he understands by being responsible for his property and how it is kept clean and orderly. Share with your child that you realize it is difficult to clean up after yourself (**empathy/mutual respect**), but it is a job that has to be done. Use **the Five C's for Rule Making** to establish clear expectations you have regarding picking up after oneself.

Step 2
Identify skills and solutions

Point out your child's past accomplishments and clean-up skills. Talk about how great it is that he, not someone else, can be responsible for his things. Remind him of times when he showed responsibility for his property.

Step 3
Mutually agree upon goals

Goal: "Make this a family goal because the activity to follow involves everyone. For example, we will use our special skills to become more responsible for our belongings by putting them in their proper places."

Step 4
Practice and play

This activity teaches children how to put things away and take care of their belongings. You will need a medium-sized cardboard box, some patience, and yourself as a role model. First write "Doesn't Belong Box" on the cardboard box. Next sit down with your family and give your view of what the pick-up problem is as discussed in step 1. Explain that every time a family member uses or plays with something that needs to be put away, he or she can either put it in its proper place or in the Doesn't Belong Box. Similarly, if another family member sees an object that has not been put away, he or she can put it in the box. At the end of the day, everyone looks inside the box, sees if anything there belongs to them, removes the object, and puts it where it belongs.

The **logical consequence** of not putting away your things at the end of the day is that they will be put aside for an auction two or three days later. At the auction, the owner of the item needs to buy back his possession by offering services such as doing extra chores or emptying the box by himself. Schoolbooks and essential objects can't be auctioned; instead, just apply a logical consequence for these.

Throughout this activity use parenting techniques such as **your choice**—either put it away now, put it in the Doesn't Belong Box to put away later, or you'll lose it for a few days. Tell your child to use **S.T.A.R.** to stop, think, and remember his belongings. **Model** putting things away and using the box. **Spice up** your activity by having your child draw pictures on the box to help remind him of his responsibilities. Try to imitate a real auctioneer: "Going, going, gone to the kid with the baseball cap for his offer to wash the dishes tonight!" Keep your child's developmental age in mind when expecting him to remember his things or to decide what he needs to do in order to buy back his item. This activity works very well because it gives responsibility to the child, provides a playful reminder to pick up things, teaches logical consequences for not putting things away, and makes cleaning up as easy as throwing it into a box. Over time, you will find that you don't need a Doesn't Belong Box. Your child will become accustomed to putting things away, and will find that it's much easier to do it immediately rather than risk losing the item.

Praise your child for the times he remembers to put his belongings away. Double the praise each time he put someone else's item in the box. Compliment her for offering to perform a buy-back chore, and when she completes it.

Step 5
Review and recognize efforts

107

☆ *Dust and Treasure Hunt* ☆

RECIPE #28

Serves: 4–12 years

This recipe teaches children how to follow directions while having fun cleaning their home.

Step 1
State and define the problem

Talk with your child about the importance of cleaning her home. Use **"I" messages** and **effective listening** in trying to understand what her perception of a clean home is. You may discover that your standards are very different from hers. Come to a common understanding of what a clean home looks like.

Step 2
Identify skills and solutions

Accentuate your child's skills for following directions. Whether she plays board games well, does what her soccer coach asks, or is a whiz at "Simon Says," she has the beginnings of a pro direction-follower.

Step 3
Mutually agree upon goals

Goal: "I will use my special skills to care for our home by giving it a good cleaning."

Step 4
Practice and play

Both younger and older children can participate in this activity, which turns dreary and monotonous Saturday housecleaning into an exciting event. You and your child are going to participate in a treasure hunt. Going from room to room, your child will clean certain areas or objects according to a treasure map. At the end of this journey, she will have a little treasure to eat or to keep, and you will have a cleaner home.

Learning the process of housecleaning can be very challenging for children. This motivational game will teach your child important organizational skills and at the same time **spice up** an age-old chore. Think of areas in your home your son or daughter is capable of cleaning. Make a map of the home that indicates which items need to be cleaned from start to finish. At the end of the hunt (and parental inspection), your child will "find" the treasure (a snack, small prize, etc.). Older children will enjoy a short riddle written on paper and stuck to each object or room to be cleaned. Each riddle requires the child to figure out what needs to be cleaned next, and at the end of the treasure hunt she will receive a riddle describing her treasure.

Step 5
Review and recognize efforts

Let your child know how wonderful it feels to have a clean house. Remind her that cleaning house does not have to be seen as boring. In fact, it can be fun and exciting. When you give the house a good cleaning you never know when you will find "lost treasures" such as misplaced toys and items that fall behind beds.

☆ *Planful Playing in a Pinch* ☆

RECIPE #29

Hot tips and quick recipes for solving irresponsibility.

NOT LISTENING

No, No Beans. With a permanent marker, write the word "no" or draw an unhappy face on five white, uncooked lima beans. Let your child know that he is allowed to say, "No," "You can't make me," and/or "I don't want to" only five times a day. Carry with you five No, No Beans. Every time your child says something oppositional, says no, or refuses to do something, give him a No, No Bean. Let him know how many he has left before he runs out of beans. Inform him that once the beans are gone, he can't receive his reward. He must have one remaining. If your child goes through the day without getting a single bean, he gets a special reward.

29.1

Big Ears. A humorous way to point out to your child how often she doesn't listen to you is to draw and cut out a large pair of ears. Every time she refuses to listen, stick the ears on her. Let her know that she can stick them on you, too. This little joke may help both of you become more aware of when and how often you are not listening to each other, while lessening the tension, thereby reducing the risk of developing a power struggle.

29.2

Listening Games. One way to help develop listening skills in children is to play listening and memory games such as a simple scavenger-hunt game in your home. First make a list of items in your home that you want your child to find and bring back to you. Call out the list of items to her. She must listen carefully and bring back as many as she can remember and find. Later, when she is not listening to you, remind her of how well she knows how to play listening and memory games—which means she is skillful at listening!

29.3

Mime and Rhyme. If your child does not listen to you the first time, break the frustration with a **humorous** mime or rhyme. Go over to her and silently act out what you are asking her to respond to. Kids get a big kick out of this, and it breaks the tension. You can also try asking your children to answer you in a rhyme when you ask them to do something (just to make sure they are listening).

29.4

PROCRASTINATES

Lazy Lizards and Doing Dinosaurs. This is an activity in which you will need to either draw or locate pictures of a lizard and a dinosaur. Laminate or glue them to a hard cardboard surface, then cut them into five to ten pieces each, like a jigsaw puzzle. Every time your child is lazy or procrastinates—doesn't put things away when he is told, says wait and doesn't follow through, etc.—a piece of the Lazy Lizard puzzle is completed.

29.5

Every time he does what he is told or follows through on his responsibility, a piece of the Doing Dinosaur is completed. If the dinosaur gets completed first, he gets his reward. If the lizard gets completed first, then he does not.

29.6 *Magic Memos.* Place reminders of things your child needs to do on funny places, using Post-It notes or sticky pads. Be creative. Place reminders on pillows, in underwear drawers, or inside shoes.

29.7 *Reminder Mobile.* Using a hanger, string, and index cards, make a weekly reminder in the shape of a mobile. Change the reminders each week and let your child hang the mobile in a room as an interesting way of reminding him of the things he needs to do.

IRRESPONSIBILITY

29.8 *Parent's/Child's Day.* Choose a day when you and your child switch places: you are the child and your child is the parent. Be sure to make it fun. Let him sleep in your bed, and you sleep in his. Wake up to begin each other's day. Give him the opportunity to plan the day, but also give him a list of things that need to be done, such as laundry, housecleaning, and making the meals. Have him give you a list of things that he needs to do. At the end of the day, talk about what it is like to be each other.

29.9 *Independence Day.* Discuss with your child the reasons we celebrate the fourth of July as the day our country won independence from the "mother" country, Great Britain. Motivate your child to feel the need to be independent and responsible for himself by accomplishing certain responsible behaviors. When he is successful at this you will throw him an "Independence Day" party. Make a list of responsible behaviors you expect from your child; everything from making his bed to cleaning up after himself. When he accomplishes most of the expectations, throw a party for him, including barbecue and safe fireworks (if they are legal in your state). Remind your child that independence takes a lot of hard work—just as it did for our country 200 and more years ago.

MESSINESS

29.10 *Human Cleaning Machine.* Kids love to play in water, so why don't they like to clean? Make cleaning the floors and furniture fun. Turn your kid into a human cleaning machine. Tie large sponges on her feet and have her help you wash the floors with her sponge feet. Put old socks on her hands and have her help dust the furniture. Wrap her rear in towels and have her buff the floors. If you have two children, one child can push the other around the floor for double the fun. Put a bathing suit on your child, give her soapy water, and stick her in the shower or tub with a task in mind to clean. Put on some of your child's favorite music and make cleaning a dancing event. Make a dry-cleaning machine by having several members of your family stand in a line and do one part of the folding process (you shake the clothes, the next person folds them, the next puts them away, etc.).

Crackerjack Bed. If you have problems getting your child to make his bed, encourage him to do this chore by leaving a funny note or little prize on the sheets if it is made. Unmade beds do not get surprises.   *29.11*

How to Clean Your Room Video, or, Life-styles of the Clean and Famous. Make a video with your child on how to clean his room. Let him be the reporter who interviews people on their favorite room-cleaning ideas. Let him think of quick ways to clean and helpful hints to remember. Have him clean his room as an example of "How To . . . starring Ridley Scott." Be sure to watch the video with your child if he needs reminders of how great he is at cleaning his room and teaching others how to do the same.   *29.12*

Before and After. Let your child know that you will be taking a picture of his room at its very messiest. After a good cleaning, take a picture of it looking clean and wonderful. Blow up both of these pictures to poster size and hang them on the wall. Let him laugh and comment on the differences and how much better he feels in a clean room. Frame the pictures and put them in his room as fun reminders of what it looks like clean or dirty.   *29.13*

Special Cleaning Bucket. Put together a special cleaning bucket for your child. Put his name on it and include sponges, dusters, rags, safe cleaning supplies, and perhaps even a Dustbuster.   *29.14*

Let's Make a Deal! As much as we don't like the idea of paying our child to be responsible, children, as well as adults, know that money talks. This activity can be very useful in teaching children the realities of responsibility. Show how people look in the help-wanted sections of newspapers to find work. In the form of a classified, write out a job description, with the amount to be paid (real or token money) and "advertise" for new jobs by posting them on your family bulletin board or refrigerator. At the end of the week, your child can get his "paycheck" if the work was done properly.   *29.15*

(See page 255 for a list of reading recipes for solving irresponsibility.)

Recipe #30: Feeling Cards

CHAPTER 8

Moodiness

A DORMANT VOLCANO LIVES in your home. (Little Charles can be an angel.) Occasionally the volcano comes to life. (When four-year-old Charles doesn't get his way, he acts unnaturally to his parents.) A volcano's wild fury begins with a rumble deep within the earth. (Charles begins to turn red and shake with anger after his mother refuses to buy him candy at the supermarket.) The rumble progresses violently to blasts of lava, smoke, and steam. (Charles throws himself to the floor, kicking, screaming, arms flailing.) The lava leaves in its wake a path of destruction and despair. (Tears spill from Charles' eyes as he kicks over a carefully stacked display of Rice-A-Roni.) People run for cover, leaving their worldly possessions behind. (Mother abandons her full cart of groceries, covers her face, and drags her prized possession out the door.)

Charles' difficulty in managing his behavior is due to his inability to cope with intense feelings. We have grouped behaviors related to feelings of anger, sadness, frustration, and irritability under the heading of moodiness because they all become problematic when a child is unable to control or appropriately express his or her emotions and manage his or her mood. While emotions are a part of every child's developing personality, most young children do not easily learn how to harmoniously integrate thoughts, feelings, and actions. All children need "emotional education" to learn what it is that they are feeling (feeling signal), words and names for those feelings, and appropriate actions for expressing them.

The recipes offered in this chapter are designed to increase your child's feeling-related vocabularies and playful ways to control and express his feelings rather than be controlled by them.

Temper Tantrums

Whining

Excessive Crying/Anger

PROBLEMS

Tantrums

Angry feelings can at times become so intense that your child's thinking becomes disorganized and confused. As a result he may act impulsively and illogically, causing behavioral problems such as temper tantrums, emotional outbursts, and aggression.

Tantrums or violent outbursts of anger could be your child's attempts to solve a problem by forcing an adult to give in to his or her needs.

Children who frequently tantrum have a particularly low tolerance for frustration, change, stimulation, or simply being told "no."

Tantrums and emotional outbursts can be developmentally normal, especially during ages two to six. They result from a child's not having the capability and control necessary to modulate and express strong feelings.

Unexpressed anger and frustration can lead to emotional and physical tension that needs to be released or defused. Without the means for acceptable expression, children will eventually react with out-of-control and at times explosive rage (temper tantrums) or physical ailments such as headaches.

Whining and Excessive Crying

Similar to tantrums and emotional outbursts, whining and excessive crying are often a result of (a) a child's inability to use language to express his or her feelings, (b) low frustration tolerance or inability to delay gratification, (c) your child's efforts to manipulate and break you down so as to get what she wants, (d) an inability to perceive the steps that lead up to the point of emotional overload; a limited ability to identify or differentiate his feelings as he experiences them.

Try to **ignore** or **distract** your child rather than giving him attention for inappropriate behavior. Keep your anger under control so that both of you are not "tantruming" at the same time. (Recipes 31, 32, 33)

Do not let your child's tantrum or whining turn a "no" into a "yes." This would teach him that he can manipulate you to get his way. (Recipes 29.1, 31, 32, 33, 34)

Try to objectively collect data on what situations seem to precipitate a tantrum. Once identified, you can begin to **plan, prepare, and prevent, model** and **role-play** to help your child better cope.

Use the **think chair** to help your child collect his thoughts and regain composure. (Recipe 31)

Model ways to express angry feelings.

Create a supportive environment in your family in which feelings and their appropriate expression are unconditionally accepted. In this atmosphere children can trust their parents to pay attention to their feelings, enabling them to express themselves without risk of ridicule, criticism, or rejection. (Recipes 30, 31, 32, 33, 34, 35)

Skills for socially acceptable verbal expression of feelings can be learned through parental **modeling** and by identifying and naming "feelings states." You can also model effective expression of feeling through assertiveness rather than aggression or unproductive complaining. (Recipes 30, 34, 35)

Consider and rule out possible physical causes of your child's mood such as fatigue, hunger, or overstimulation. Plan ahead and try to avoid situations that could frustrate an overtired or overstimulated child. (Recipes 65, 68, 69.2, 69.6, 69.7)

Since the purpose of tantrums, whining, and excessive crying is often to get parental attention, it is best not to respond to these negative behaviors. Praise your child when she expresses herself appropriately. Be patient; as she matures, so will her ability to identify, understand, and communicate her feelings verbally.

Teach and use this three-step process:

1. Learn to recognize feeling signals—for example, the way our muscles tighten when we are angry.

2. Identify and name that feeling. Ask your child what feeling the signal in her body seems to indicate.

3. Discuss how to cope with that kind of feeling. Share examples from your personal experience.

Remember: The art of controlling and expressing the emotions is a lifelong process, and even adults like us still have difficulty with it. Keep in mind your child's developmental skills and his or her limitations. (Recipes 30, 31, 32, 33, 34, 35)

☆ *Feeling Cards* ☆

This recipe teaches children to name and define specific feelings.

Step 1 *State and define the problem*	Have your child name and identify as many feeling words as she can think of. Ask her to give examples of feelings by **role playing** situations when she felt sad, happy, mad, etc. Encourage her to talk about why people feel that way. Use **"I" messages** to show your child how to own and identify a feeling. **Effectively listen** to your child when he expresses a feeling and **model** how to listen to someone else's feelings.
Step 2 *Identify skills and solutions*	Recognize and describe situations when your child named and expressed his feelings appropriately, such as times when he expressed that he was sad when he lost something, or got mad when he didn't get his way.
Step 3 *Mutually agree upon goals*	Goal: "I will use my special skills to be able to better understand and express my feelings."
Step 4 *Practice and play*	Some children first learn to express feelings physically rather than verbally. Feeling Cards will teach your child a vocabulary for her feelings and effective ways to express emotions.

Using the list of feelings below, sit down with your child and select as many as you feel you need and write each of them on 3 × 5 cards. On the back side of the cards either draw a picture or paste a photograph of your child expressing that feeling. (We recommend investing in a few rolls of film and taking the pictures, rather than drawing. Your child will be more likely to make the connection between the feeling word and the way it actually looks and feels when he is expressing it.)

Now you have a deck of Feeling Cards with which to play games and identify feelings with your child. These are some of the most common ones; however most children cannot use a list this large, and a younger child will initially need only a few of these.

sad glad happy angry mad frustrated warm proud quiet shy nervous chicken scared bad lucky joyful small safe upset hassled silly alive hopeful creative stubborn loved strange funny cool beautiful encouraged uncomfortable excited confused afraid weird stupid worried insecure rotten selfish grouchy put down used sick awkward furious crazy embarrassed talkative curious clever strange unloved free sensitive ugly successful disappointed likable good strong left-out energetic hateful unimportant important hurt sorry rejected bashful smothered calm great cheerful fresh brave gross inferior worthless worthwhile depressed troubled hopeless skillful capable confident smart tearful accepting jealous judged secretive positive wonderful

Note: It is best to start with a small number of these and add more over time.

Here are a few games you can play with your Feeling Cards:

Feeling Charades. Play charades by having members of your family take turns picking a Feeling Card and then play-acting what that feeling looks like. Other family members have to try to guess what the Feeling Card is.

Flash Card Feelings. Use the deck of Feeling Cards like flash cards. Go through the feeling words you've selected from your child's list and have him or her try to guess the name of the feeling that you are showing the picture side of, or what the expression looks like if you are showing the word side.

Feeling Mix and Match. Duplicate your cards and have a mix-and-match game. Put both decks of cards on the floor with one deck showing the word side and one exposing the picture side. Try to match the expression with the word.

Right and Wrong. Play "right and wrong" by selecting a card from the feeling deck and having family members take turns showing the right way and the wrong way to express that feeling.

Invent games on your own.

To help your child integrate feelings when using these games, you should reinforce what the feeling is, what makes a person feel that way, and how to express that feeling appropriately. Use your Feeling Cards in your daily routines. When your child becomes moody and is unable to identify or appropriately express her emotion, have her go through the deck and choose a card or two that indicates her emotions. **Model** for your child when you have a specific feeling by selecting a card yourself.

Acknowledge your child's ability to identify and express feelings correctly. Express your own prideful feelings in the new "feelings" she has learned.

Step 5
Review and recognize efforts

117

☆ *The T-N-T Corner* ☆

RECIPE #31
Serves: 3–8 years

This recipe teaches children how to deal appropriately with strong and angry feelings and to decrease tantrums.

Step 1
State and define the problem

Identify for your child the tantruming behavior you want to help her improve. **Spice up** this topic by doing your own slapstick version of your child having a tantrum. Ask her to describe what she was feeling before, during, and after the tantrum. Use **empathy** to show your understanding that it may be hard for her to control her strong feelings. Let her know you respect her feelings but not her behavior.

Step 2
Identify skills and solutions

Express your confidence in your child's ability to express her anger and upset feelings in a productive way. Point out times when she appropriately and positively expressed her unhappiness over a parental command or unwanted situation. List specific skills such as patience, acceptance, and good decision-making, all of which will help your child avoid tantrums.

Step 3
Mutually agree upon goals

Goal: "I will use my special skills to express strong feelings the right way!"

Step 4
Practice and play

As mentioned, tantrums are developmentally normal expressions for children ages from two to six. Tantrums usually decrease as your child grows older, but may continue or increase if he doesn't discover alternative ways to express his anger, disagreement, or individuality. By using this activity, you can structure your response, teach acceptable ways to express opinions, and nurture his independence and your sanity.

This activity is called the T-N-T (Tantrums-N-Tirades) Corner. Basically, you specify a corner or area of your home or a place outside your home in which your child *may* have tantrums: a sort of hotel for tantruming. (Actually, this is another way to creatively use the **think chair** without calling it that.) Let your child know that she has your permission to tantrum, but only in the designated area. Show her where the T-N-T Corner is located.

You may want to **spice it up** by hanging a sign there indicating TANTRUMS ONLY! When your child begins a tantrum, suggest that she go to the T-N-T Corner or space, where she can let it rip! **Ignore** her while she is there. **The Five C's for Rule Making** will help you clarify your expectations regarding her tantrums and negative expressions of anger that will land her in the T.N.T. Corner. **T.A.P.** yourself for an extra boost of support to keep from being pulled in. As with the **think chair** procedure, if she refuses to go, apply a **natural** or **logical consequence** until she gets herself there. Carry her if need be. Once she is finished, she can leave. Ask her how she got there, how she could have prevented going there, and what alternative ways she can think of to express her strong feelings. Give her suggestions for alternatives such as using **S.T.A.R.**, saying how she feels with words like "I'm really, really mad!", and using relaxation techniques.

Combine this recipe with others to help your child think of specific methods for dealing with strong feelings other than using the tantrum corner. Reward, compliment, and praise her when she goes to the tantrum corner herself or solves her problem without using the space. **Distract** her—there is nothing that squelches a tantrum more successfully than a child thinking there is something better to do! **Model** for her how you sort out your own feelings, settle yourself down, and successfully cope with things that don't go your way. Go to the T-N-T Corner yourself when you lose your temper. Bring your T-N-T Corner or sign with you when you travel, and be sure to **prepare, plan, prevent** all the vulnerable situations for your child. (Overtired or overstimulated children obviously do not fare well at a supermarket.)

Review with your daughter the times when she used the T-N-T Corner appropriately and times when she redirected her negative behavior positively. This method requires time and patience on the part of both the parent and child.

Step 5
Review and recognize efforts

☆ The Piñata Punch ☆

RECIPE # 3 2

Serves: 3–10 years

This recipe teaches children how to control excessive anger.

Step 1
State and define the problem
Describe to your child specific examples of when he acted in an excessively angry way. Acknowledge that it is okay to have angry feelings, but it is not okay to hurt others or break things. Use **"I" messages** and **effective listening** to enlist your child's participation in sharing his perceptions of the problem. Use **empathy** and show that you understand his behavior may not be on purpose. He may have a lot of energy or just be curious and accidentally break something. Nevertheless, this has become a problem for the family and you are going to help him control himself and handle himself more appropriately. To establish rules concerning the appropriate ways to express anger, **the Five C's** will come in handy.

Step 2
Identify skills and solutions

Identify skills, traits, and positive examples of behaviors your child has that prove he can be in control of aggression or impulsivity. **Role-play** situations in which he has been challenged with a **choice** of acting aggressively or appropriately, and made the right choice.

Step 3
Mutually agree upon goals

Goal: "I will use my special skills to slow down and think about mad feelings and expressing anger the right way."

Step 4
Practice and play

The Piñata Punch is a terrific activity for teaching your child how to control his impulsive, angry, and aggressive actions such as hitting or breaking things and to use other, more constructive ways of expressing his feelings. You will need a papier-mâché piñata (found in stores that sell party supplies) and trinkets for prizes. Explain to your child that he will get a prize every time he uses his skills and does not hit, carefully handles an object, thinks before he acts and/or stops himself before breaking or damaging something. The prize is put into the piñata. Tell your child he will have the opportunity to let out all those stored-up angry feelings and physical energy at a more appropriate time. After a few days or at the end of the week, depending on his age and ability to delay gratification, he will be able to smash open the piñata and get all his rewards.

Children are not born with the instinctive knowledge of how to focus anger properly and use it for their benefit. It takes practice and effort to step aside from the fury of the moment and consider choices of not hitting or destroying something. The piñata activity teaches and motivates children to use good social judgment and to think before they act (**S.T.A.R.**). Children usually can learn the appropriate way to express anger, but often need added inspiration (a little incentive) to encourage them to express and release this anger in a constructive way. This activity also gives them the supervised opportunity to free pent-up hostility by smashing open the piñata.

Here is an example of how you might do this activity with your child. Let's say he tends to react with destructive rage when he doesn't get his way. When he expresses his anger verbally, uses **S.T.A.R.**, or redirects himself without hitting or breaking something, he receives a small prize to put in the piñata. **Positively reframe** a situation and give him another prize to put into the piñata when he acts calmly, shares, talks nicely, and so on. After three to four days, hang your piñata from the tree and let your child take as many slugs at it as he wants until it showers him with his prizes. Be sure to encourage him to verbalize what made him angry during the last four days and what would be the best way to handle that anger. You can have him tell you all the things that made him angry each time he takes a swipe at the piñata. You may want to **model** this for him. Explain that the piñata is the only item he is permitted to destroy or hit. If your child acts in an aggressive or destructive manner that calls for immediate attention, and you feel you cannot **ignore** it, use the **think chair** or **logical consequences.** Definitely do not **ignore** this behavior.

You may want to consider a small Piñata Punch party that recognizes your child's efforts to refrain from impulsive and aggressive behaviors. The activity has built-in parenting techniques such as **try, try again** and **natural** and **logical consequences:** the result of good behavior is a prize, a logical consequence. Combine this recipe with others in the chapter to help your child to channel his anger in a more constructive way.

Step 5
Review and recognize efforts

121

☆ *Whiners and Winners Rap Song* ☆

RECIPE #33

Serves: 3–10 years

This recipe encourages expression of feelings and opinions without whining.

Step 1
State and define the problem

Discuss with your child your perception of the whining problem in your family. Encourage her to share with you her perception of the same difficulty. Come to an agreement that considers everyone's opinion of what the word "whining" means and how it has become a problem for you and your child.

Step 2
Identify skills and solutions

Point out your child's abilities to ask, share opinions, express feelings, and negotiate her desires without whining. **Role-play** a situation that shows how your child used appropriate language to get what she wanted. Highlight skills such as being nice to people, accepting the opinions of others, and even the skill of using a soft, pleasant voice.

Step 3
Mutually agree upon goals

Goal: "I will use my special skills to stop my whining and find new ways to express my feelings and what I want."

Step 4
Practice and play

Whining has been described to us by some parents as similar to the grating sound of fingernails on a blackboard, and the victims often surrender and agree to the wishes of their child to avoid further torture. This of course results in the children discovering that power and avoidance of responsibility exist in tears and a high-pitched voice.

This activity can help you turn the volume down on whining through the use of the parenting techniques **planful playing** and **ignoring.** With your child, you will create a Rap and Rhythm song called "Whiners and Winners." Set to music, this song will teach her how to get her thoughts and feelings heard without whining. Your first step is to explain that you are going to write a song that rhymes (this makes learning the words easier for children) about whining behavior versus winning behaviors. The song will teach her to recognize when she is whining and when she is talking appropriately. Here is a start for children ages five and up.

Here is a song that is real fine
About a kid who likes to whine;
Her voice is hard to miss, it sounds just like this
(use a whiny voice)
   Mommy, I wanna go
   Daddy, don't say no
   I don't want to go to bed
   Give me, give or I'll turn red.
(stop using whiny voice)
But I know a kid who is no fool,
Because his voice is really cool;

He asks for things in a nice way,
and this is what he might say:
    "Mommy, I'm feeling kind of sad,
    and I'm feeling kind of mad
    that I can't stay up later or play in the elevator."

Your child will get a kick out of this type of informal education on whining. Try to memorize your song with her. Anytime she uses a whiny voice, sing out a few verses from the song in a whiny voice to indicate that she is whining. **Positively reframe** situations when she is about to whine and sing out the nonwhining portions of the song. If the whining continues, this is your key to **ignore** it. And remember: "**T.A.P.** yourself and don't give in, because if you bend to his demands she's gonna win!"

Recognize times when your child used a cool instead of a whining voice to share his feelings. Compliment his positive talking behaviors.

Step 5
Review and recognize efforts

☆ *The Feeling Box* ☆

Serves: 3–12 years

This recipe encourages appropriate expression of feelings.

Step 1
State and define the problem

Discuss with your child that feelings are important and you wholeheartedly support all of hers. Explain that there are rules for expressing feelings. Hitting, kicking, physical attacks, damaging property, and using bad language are not allowed. Ask your child to come up with as many feelings as she can. (See recipe 30 for a list of feelings.) **Role-play** the right and wrong way to express each feeling listed.

Step 2
Identify skills and solutions

Use examples of times when your child identified and/or expressed a feeling constructively, especially moments when she used self-restraint in a challenging situation that might have otherwise ended in a tantrum or whining. Have her assist you in thinking of special skills she has that could help her express feelings appropriately: "Has a bright smile when she is happy" and "Uses tissues when she cries."

Step 3
Mutually agree upon goals

Goal: "I will use my special skills to learn how to express my feelings in the right way."

Step 4
Practice and play

The Feeling Box can help your entire family identify feelings and express them in socially appropriate ways. It is a large container of objects, games, activities, and tools for identifying and expressing feelings. Family members can go to the Feeling Box when they are angry, sad, happy, moody, etc., and use the contents of the box to express their feelings. This provides structure and guidance in managing emotions. To begin, design the box for all your feeling tools. With your child, write the words FEELING BOX on it and draw pictures of people who are mad, happy, sad, etc. Next, fill your Feeling Box with these items:

Feeling Cards. Put in a deck of Feeling Cards as described in recipe 30. Direct your child to the box when he is feeling moody and needs some guidance from the Feeling Cards to pinpoint what exactly is upsetting him.

The Angry and Mad Pillow. To make an Angry and Mad Pillow, draw pictures and write feeling words on an old pillowcase to indicate emotions and behaviors related to anger (frustrated, furious, upset, etc.). Fill your pillowcase with a pillow or stuffing that is soft and won't hurt when being hit. If your child becomes angry and needs a physical outlet, tell him to get the Angry and Mad Pillow out of the box and either hit it or pillow-fight with a willing family member. **Model** for your child how to use the pillow.

Relaxation Tools. See recipe 38, The Relaxation Center. You can either put the tools in the box or make a list of what Relaxation tools are and put that list in the box. Relaxation tools are very useful for calming an anxious, overstimulated, or agitated child. Let your child know that it is much easier to express feelings when he is relaxed and in control.

I Want Attention Hat. This is a hat with a sign that has written upon it I WANT ATTENTION. Anytime your child negatively tries to get your attention (tantruming, whining, crying), teach him how to use the I Want Attention Hat. Tell him when he puts on the hat, you know he needs attention. When he puts it on, immediately praise him for getting your attention the right way and either give him attention then or at a mutually agreed-on time later.

Feeling Masks. On paper plates draw a face depicting a feeling, cut out holes for the eyes, and paste a Popsicle stick to the underside of the faceplate. Make enough to cover the range of feelings your child is capable of expressing.

A Mirror, Tissue, Some Puppets and Dolls. Use the puppets, dolls, and Feeling Masks for expressing play-acting and feelings. **Role-play** real-life situations and help your child figure out ways he can handle emotional challenges. Use these items in preparing for distressing and/or problematic events (going to a toy store and not being able to get what he wants). Have your child look in the mirror and describe what he sees (an angry face, a sad face, a happy face). The tissue is there for drying tears—an acceptable way to express feelings.

Put your Feeling Box in an accessible area in your home. Whenever your child becomes agitated, moody, whiny, or overly angry, direct him to the Feeling Box, where he can choose and express his feelings. Every object in the box has a purpose. Playfully allow your child to label and express her feelings.

Whenever the child begins to express an emotion inappropriately, give her a choice to either use the Feeling Box or expect the **consequences.** Join your child as much as you can on his trips to the box, **encourage** appropriate use of items, and **model** the correct way to express feelings. Most importantly, take emotions seriously and give a clear message to your child, who needs added support in coping and dealing with his feelings.

Congratulate your child and yourself! This is a difficult recipe to do. Coping with feelings is a lifelong process and requires a great deal of experience and practice.

Step 5
Review and recognize efforts

☆ *Planful Playing in a Pinch* ☆

RECIPE #35

Hot tips and quick recipes for solving moodiness.

35.1   *Tantrums and Anger.* Show your child what happens to angry feelings when you store them up inside and don't express them appropriately. Shake a soda can while naming situations and occasions during the day that might make a person angry. Take the top off (in an open space, of course) to show how a person explodes over little things because of all the anger and "shaking" he has felt all day. Explain how to let out anger in small, controlled steps instead. You can do this activity by pretending that you are a Volcano. Begin by showing your child how a volcano begins to rumble, shake, and spurt out lava before it explodes. Explain that these are warning signs that the volcano is becoming angry. Throughout your child's day notice when he is becoming agitated, and suggest that he is rumbling or beginning to shake. This might help him recognize when he needs to express himself appropriately rather than holding things in and exploding later.

35.2   *Whine and Dine.* Have a family dinner during which everyone whines. "I wanna napkin, pleeeeeese" and "What did you do tooooooooday" are spoken in irritating, whiny voices. Discuss at the end of the meal about how funny it was to pretend to whine. However, suggest to your child how irritating it can be if whining is done all the time.

35.3   *Tantrum or Whinier Fairy.* Say good-bye to tantrums by throwing a party. Have your child scream or whine into a box, then close it up, wrap it in party paper, add a bow, and leave it on the doorstep for the Tantrum or Whinier Fairy, who takes it to a younger child who needs it. Then have a party. (The Fairy usually leaves a present in exchange.)

35.4   *Mime Your Moods.* Using clown makeup or face paint, make your child into a mime. For this activity we suggest that you also become one. Practice expressions in a mirror. Notice how different your face looks when you are angry and when you are happy. Put on small plays and performances, using different feelings for the theme of the show.

35.5   *The Three-Penny-Feelings Opera.* Make a "feelings opera" with your child by pretending to be sad, happy, mad, or frustrated while singing a song. Try singing the alphabet sadly or with anger. This is good practice in identifying and recognizing feelings.

35.6   *Feelings Chart.* Make or purchase a Feelings Chart for your child. You can order one from the Childswork, Childsplay catalog—see page 268. Also available at many print and poster stores. Make faces with different feeling expressions out of felt and attach Velcro on the back. Write TODAY I FEEL on a large piece of white felt and hang it on your daughter's door.

Every morning, afternoon, or evening, or whenever you suggest, have her choose the facial expression that indicates how she is currently feeling and stick it on the chart.

Slow Motion. When your child gets overly excited and needs the opportunity to stop and think about how she is feeling, suggest that she tell you in slow motion. You can practice this technique and **model** how to say things that you feel angry about by telling them in slow motion. "I am—very, very—angry—that you—did not—pick up—your toys." This is good practice for everyone in your family because it teaches them to take control of their emotions and say things with thought.

Feelings Journal. Older children enjoy writing their feelings in a diary. Suggest that diaries are good for boys and girls alike. (Boys may feel more comfortable calling it a journal.) Buy a special book for your child in which, day-to-day, she can write her feelings and express her emotions. Make this book private and special. There should be no occasions on which you look through this book without your child's permission.

Here are a few "feeling journals" that can be purchased that not only give spaces for children to write or draw their feelings, but guide them through feeling explorations: *I Am Special* and *Marvelous Me* Workbooks, by Linda Schwartz (The Learning Works, 1992), *Feeling Good About Yourself,* by Debbie Pincus (Good Apple, 1990), and *My Life,* by Delia Ephron (Running Press, 1991).

(See page 256 for a list of reading recipes for solving moodiness.)

35.7

35.8

Recipe #36: Control Panel

CHAPTER 9

Overactivity

THE PATH OF DESTRUCTION was devastating. What could it have been—a tornado? A wild bull? No, none of the above. It was Stewart, who is now standing sheepishly in the corner, shaking his head back and forth, ready to mouth those all-too-familiar words, "I didn't do it." Only two minutes had lapsed since your leaving the room—how could he possibly have dismantled so many objects and made such a mess? It's all in a day's work for Stewart!

If your child seems to be unusually active and unquenchably inquisitive, this chapter is for you. The recipes in it have been designed to help parents and children learn to manage and cope with highly active, fidgety, and physically intrusive behaviors, impulsivity, short attention span, distractibility, and impatience. In developing this chapter we've drawn on our training and experience working with overactive, alert, and inquisitive children and their parents. Unfortunately, these children, who also tend to be impulsive, unresponsive to direction, and heedless of danger, cause parents and teachers worry and exhaustion. The children are likely to receive more than the average amounts of negative feedback, which is powerfully reinforcing and part of an unfortunate pattern of downward-spiraling self-worth and escalating behavior problems.

Paradoxically, the active and alert child can be very bright, full of fun, a charismatic leader and keen observer, and truly enjoyable to know. But these attributes and skills are often overshadowed by a few disheartening and negative behaviors. Your goal as parents therefore is to design learning experiences that are active, stimulating, and productive, and which aim to help the child gain control of his body and behaviors while feeling good about himself.

The recipes in this chapter will not only be helpful for children who have been diagnosed as hyperactive or attention deficit disordered, but for those who keep going and going and going—they even outlast the Energizer Bunny.

Impulsivity

Attention Deficit Disorder

Hyperactivity can be defined as a behavior that is characterized by excessive and at times incessant or frenzied movement beyond normal or tolerable limits. This behavior may more often than not be undirected (not goal-oriented), unproductive, inappropriate, and—especially—annoying to others.

The overactive child has difficulty concentrating on a single topic and difficulty screening out peripheral and generally unrelated stimuli. This child is easily distracted from an intended task, and tends to have a short attention span.

The overactive child sometimes demonstrates impulsive behavior characterized by sudden escalation—forceful or unpremeditated actions without consideration of results or consequences.

The overactive child has difficulty delaying gratification: when he wants something, he feels almost uncontrollably compelled to get it now, not later.

There is a tendency for an overactive child to follow his first impulse rather than plan his actions. He may appear to be rude and inconsiderate of others.

There is a tendency to overstep physical boundaries and intrude into the personal space of others. An overactive child may overcompensate for a felt lack of control by becoming controlling, bossy, or manipulative.

In some children, overactive behavior may mask an underlying problem of avoidance. These children often are unable to successfully stick to one task before moving to the next, and may repeatedly experience failure. This unfortunately reinforces their feeling of inadequacy and eventually leaves little motivation for them to attempt or finish a task.

Harness this energy and activity potential and redirect it into productive, high-energy situations such as sports, highly active hobbies, and even housecleaning. (Recipes 9, 29.11, 40.3, 40.4, 40.5)

Teach your child how to physically relax (using relaxation techniques) and to control her actions through "self-talk." (Recipes 36, 37, 38, 39)

Provide a calm, quiet, structured atmosphere that is predictable and familiar. (Recipes 24, 37, 38)

Design your child's work strategies to consist of several manageable parts or tasks so she can experience success (completion) at frequent and regular intervals. (Recipes 24, 40.7)

Look for and take advantage of windows of opportunity. Pay attention to your child when he is being attentive, and if at all possible don't wait until later. (Recipe 39)

These children often provide parents with an overactivity early-warning system in the form of low-level behavioral cues such as subtle changes in mannerisms, behaviors, and attentiveness. Once parents have identified these cues, both parents and child can develop plans to catch deteriorating behavior before it becomes unmanageable. Help your child tune in to his energy level throughout the day, before and following specific activities and transitional periods. Use fun and visual measurement indicators of his energy level. (Recipes 36, 37, 38, 39, 40)

Ultimately, children can learn to self-monitor their own behaviors even in a highly stimulated situation. (Recipes 36, 37, 38, 39, 40, 68)

Teach and use with your child a full repertoire of "waiting skills" such as relaxation techniques, fantasy and imagery, and distraction. (Recipes 37, 38, 40)

Practice with your children problem-solving exercises affecting everyday decisions. Help them learn the skills and value in making purposeful and planful decisions about their behavior. Also, encourage open, nondefensive ways to review and be reflective after the fact, whether the incident at hand was a positive or negative event. (Recipes 36, 37, 68, 69.2, 69.7)

Teach your child about the need for respecting the body space and privacy of others. Refer to real-life social situations and point out how activities are often dictated by the space they occupy. (Recipes 59, 69.11)

Provide occasions for your child to experience control of his body by giving him opportunities to make decisions for himself. This allows him to feel in charge of situations and reinforces his belief that he can positively affect his life. (Recipes 26, 36, 37, 38, 39, 40)

Look beyond and beneath the glaringly obvious behavior. Explore with your child her feelings about success and failure. Look closely at those subjects or activities that she seems to have the most difficulty with and structure situations to enhance the possibility for success. (Recipes 30, 34, 35.7, 39)

☆ *The Control Panel* ☆

R E C I P E   # 3 6
Serves: 3–10 years

This recipe teaches self-control for overactive children.

Step 1
State and define the problem

Talk with your child about his difficulty in controlling his energy. Ask him to identify times when he feels really excited and wants to move, move, move. If he can't verbalize his thoughts, have him do a few **role plays** with you that give a good example of this overactive behavior. Respond with **empathy** by exploring how difficult it is to control his excited and overactive behaviors.

Step 2
Identify skills and solutions

Express to your child that being active, excited, and full of energy is not a bad thing. List all positive characteristics he has because he is so active (alert, a performer, fun, a keen observer). Explain how these energy-filled skills should never be turned off, but that you would like him to have more control over himself.

Step 3
Mutually agree upon goals

Goal: "I will use my special skills to be able to control my energy and my body."

Step 4
Practice and play

This activity will help your child tune in to her own energy and make choices about what to do with it. This puts her in control of her body and ultimately helps her to develop coping skills for dealing with overactive behaviors. Begin this activity by telling her that you believe that deep within her mind and body she has the ability to control her behavior. This ability to control her body is like a control panel. You can use the example of a radio-powered car, a computer, a robot, or an airplane to explain to your child how a control panel works. If she does not turn on the control panel, she will have a difficult time controlling the speed and direction her body goes. You may want to draw or find a simple illustration depicting how the brain controls the functions of your child's body just as a control panel does for an airplane.

Ask your child to help you make a control panel of her own so that you both can practice using it to control overactive behavior. Use a piece of cardboard, markers, string, paper, levers made out of paper, buttons, and lots of creative thinking to make your child's own special controlling device. It must have a lever that controls speed, a start-and-stop button, and an emergency brake. Additional options include a **S.T.A.R.** button, a distractor reactor (a button that helps her focus, listen, and pay attention) and a "You're Great" button (instant self-praise at your child's fingertips).

Once you have finished the control panel, "plug it in" by connecting a piece of string to the panel and to your child. Have her respond as though the panel controlled her movements. Playfully test out the panel by holding it in your hands and turning it on and off, moving it fast and slow. Use the emergency button to stop action immediately. Pretend you are at the restaurant, playground, classroom, or doctor's office, and maneuver your child through each of these situations. Press the "You're Great" button every time your child responds favorably to your commands, and praise her for controlling her behavior. You can **model** and **humorously** take part in this activity by connecting the control panel to yourself and then having your child maneuver you through different situations. Have her hold the panel and take control of her body. Practice different situations and see how she does. Use the control panel in a **planful** and **preventive** way by having your child practice how she would take control of her behavior. Explain that the panel may be made out of cardboard, but it really exists within her. Show her how she can mentally use it to interrupt overactive behavior, control her actions, and think before she acts. Tell her she can pretend in her mind to slow down the behavior by using the lever. You can **encourage** your child to use her panel by making statements such as, "Press your **S.T.A.R.** button," or, "Quick, press the emergency stop button," or, "Pull down the lever and slow it down."

Recognize your child's attempts to control her overactive behavior. Remind her that you *like* her high energy—you just want her to be and feel more in control of her actions.

Step 5
Review and recognize efforts

133

☆ The Cool, Calm, and ☆ In-Control Clubhouse

RECIPE #37
Serves: 3–12 years

This recipe gives children a specific space for calming and cooling down.

Step 1
State and define the problem

Use **"I" messages** to explain your opinions to your child regarding overactive behaviors. **Encourage** him to share his perception of the same behavior. Give examples of situations when he was excessively active. Ask him to give his own examples. Determine and agree on a definition of overactive behavior.

Step 2
Identify skills and solutions

In step 1 you defined overactive behavior. In step 2 you will need to identify skills and capabilities that your child can use to help him calm down and feel in control. Playing board games calmly, listening to music quietly, and coloring are excellent types of a calm behavior. **Encourage** your child to come up with her own ideas regarding calm behavior.

Step 3
Mutually agree upon goals

Goal: "I will use my special skills to design and use a special place to calm and control my overactive behaviors."

Step 4
Practice and play

Children who are in constant motion do not purposely act this way to manipulate parents or misbehave. Children who are easily overstimulated and are compelled to play with just about anything they can get their hands on need external structure to support their self-control. Explain to your child that together you will be making a special place for her to use her skills and capabilities to control overactive behavior. (See step 2.) Use **empathy** and **mutual respect** to acknowledge that it is very difficult for her to slow down and listen to directions, so this special area of the room (family room, bedroom, living room) will become the Cool, Calm, and In-Control Clubhouse (CCC Clubhouse).

- Choose a place in a room where your child will not become distracted or overstimulated. We suggest that it be somewhere where the visual field is limited. Put a small table and chair in the space. It's best to face the chair toward a wall.

- In the CCC Clubhouse, put books, games, and crafts that support controlled behavior, quiet skills, and concentration skills. Look for activities your child would like to have in her special corner that she finds interesting but that require her to sit at a table. Examples are cards, crossword puzzles, coloring books, crayons, markers, origami (paper folding), yarn crafts (knitting, needlepoint), and puzzles.

- Put a recorder on the table with CD's or cassettes of soft, relaxing musical selections for your child to choose and play while she is in the CCC Clubhouse.

- Have relaxation tools available to her. (See recipe 38, The Relaxation Center.)
- Decorate the wall with pictures that he thinks are calming and comforting.
- Put a timer with a ringer on the table.

To use this special place with your child, you must first decide on which overactive behavior she needs to cool, calm, and control. When your child becomes overstimulated and loses control, direct her to the CCC Clubhouse and determine the time she needs to regain control. You can set up a reward system. When your child follows your directions and uses the corner, she gets a sticker. When she goes to the corner on her own, she gets two stickers and lots of **encouragement** and praise. Give her a reward for obtaining a certain number of stickers. (See chapter 17, "Just Desserts.") Use the corner yourself and **model** calming yourself down when you are upset. Although it resembles a **think chair,** we do not recommend using the clubhouse punitively. Children should identify this space as a positive place to go to calm themselves down. The CCC should be fun and enjoyable as long as they "play" within the agreed-upon guidelines. You can take your Clubhouse on the road by packing up a few activity objects from it and making a cool, calm, and controlled bag "to go." (See recipe 65, The To-Go Bag.)

The purpose of this recipe is to help your child identify overactive behaviors and to take control of them. Praise your child for using the CCC Clubhouse, and **encourage** her to **try, try again** if she was not initially successful.

Step 5
Review and recognize efforts

☆ *The Relaxation Center* ☆

RECIPE # 3 8

Serves: 3–12 years

This recipe teaches overactive children how to slow down and relax.

Step 1
State and define the problem

Using **mutual respect** and **effective listening,** explore your child's perceptions of his overactive behavior. **Encourage** him to describe why he thinks he loses control of his body. Take this time to describe the problem as you see it. Use **role playing,** picture drawings and/or puppets to explain your thoughts and feelings about your child's overactive behavior.

Step 2
Identify skills and solutions

Choose any skill, trait, or attribute your child has that helps him slow down his actions and relax. Focus on skills such as hums softly to himself, falls asleep easily, and quietly puts puzzles together.

Step 3
Mutually agree upon goals

Goal: "I will use my special skills to be more in control of my actions and learn how to calm myself down and relax."

Step 4
Practice and play

The basic idea behind this activity is to teach your child how to physically relax. By teaching these playful relaxation techniques to your child you can give him a head start toward taking control of his body and calming himself down. Here are a few "funtastic" tools and techniques that promote your child's ability to relax and slow down.

Breathing Techniques. Telling your child to take a deep breath and calm down has very little "fun" potential. **Spice up** this needed component of relaxing by playing breathing games.

- Use bubbles and have your child take deep breaths and slowly blow into the bubble wand. Instruct him to make as big a bubble as possible until he makes a world's record bubble.

- Using child-size sunglasses, tape a piece of crepe paper or soft flexible paper about four inches long onto the nose or bridge of the glasses. The piece of paper should be directly in front of his nose and fall down to his chin. Have your child put on the glasses, take a deep breath, and try to keep the paper off his face for five seconds. Make a game out of increasing the amount of time he can keep the paper off his face. Make sure he takes deep, long breaths and blows out the air as slowly as possible in order to keep the paper off his face.

- Using an inexpensive harmonica, have your child inhale and exhale to your cues. See how long he can keep the harmonica going. When he has become a master at breathing games, identify these skills as ways he can relax through breathing.

Music Relaxation Center. Make a music relaxation center for your child. This includes a soft mat to lie on, a stereo with personal headphones, and soothing music.

Picture This. You can use the Music Relaxation Center to teach your child how to calm and soothe himself through visualization and fantasy. First, look through magazines and picture books that capture peaceful environments and serenity. Second, use these peaceful places—the ocean, the sky, or a meadow full of flowers—as the scenery for his visualization. Third, make up a story that places your child in that peaceful place. Finally, select soothing music to accompany his pictures. A good book to read is *Moonbeam: A Book of Meditations for Children,* by Maureen Garth (HarperCollins, San Francisco, 1992).

Relax-to-the-Max Bath Kit. Adults have used hot, bubbly, and candlelit baths to soothe their nerves and relax their bodies. Children can find similar pleasures in taking a soothing bath. Make this bath special by creating a "Relax-to-the-Max Bath Kit" which includes bubbles, soothing music (from a battery-operated—not electric—recorder) and a night-light.

Relaxation Tape. Make your child his own personalized relaxation tape. First, review and listen to relaxation tapes available in bookstores. Using the concepts and techniques described in the tapes that you reviewed, come up with your own special tape that both you and your child relax to. Use your child's name throughout the tape. For example, "Jerry feels relaxed and light as a feather." You may want to play relaxing music in the background. Have him listen to the relaxation tape in the Music Relaxation Center or in the tub.

The Family Spa. See chapter 4, recipe 6, Body Pride, on how to get your whole family to rest and relax at "the family spa."

You may want to design an area of your home (similar to the Cool, Calm, and In-Control Clubhouse on page 134) that can be used for relaxing. Whenever your child begins to become overstimulated and frenzied, instruct him to go to the Relaxation Center and choose an activity to calm himself and his body. **Model** how to use the center by taking a few moments to listen to a Relaxation Tape, use the breathing activities, or simply lie on the mat and close your eyes.

Try not to use the relaxation techniques punitively. Your child should see this as a positive and useful way to get back in control of his body.

Step 5
Review and recognize efforts

When reviewing your child's efforts toward relaxing and calming herself, remind her that any attempt to take control of her body is considered excellent progress. Remind her that relaxation is important. It calms nerves, releases tension, and makes you healthier.

☆ S.T.A.R. Man/Woman ☆

RECIPE #39
Serves: 3–10 years

This recipe teaches children how to stop, think, and act right.

Step 1
State and define the problem

Use **empathy** and **role playing** to show your child that everyone has a problem with impulsiveness. Do a skit showing several impulsive and problematic situations that highlight what happens when you don't think before you act. Use recent situations in which either you or your child acted impulsively. Discuss the negative outcomes of such actions and then agree to correct the problem.

Step 2
Identify skills and solutions

Select skills and abilities your child has in being able to think before he acts. Any small attempt will do, such as knocking on the door before entering and looking both ways before crossing the street. Even if your child does not always accomplish these tasks—**positively reframe** the ability as a potential skill that needs a little fine-tuning. It is important to highlight the fact that he has the ability to think before he acts but just needs to identify it as a real personal skill.

Step 3
Mutually agree upon goals

Goal: "I will use my special skills to be a **S.T.A.R.:** to Stop, Think, and Act Right!"

Step 4
Practice and play

This fun activity is based on the technique titled S.T.A.R. (see page 29), which activates through play your child's ability to talk himself through his own behavior. Rather than taking action without purpose, he is taught to tell himself, first out loud and then silently, to stop, think, and then choose the appropriate action. Impulsive children act in a sudden, forceful manner. They do not consider consequences and respond often without thinking. Most significantly, they act on their first thought rather than considering alternatives before deciding what to do. This activity will help your child recognize his ability to stop and think about his actions. Further it will teach him the steps required to interrupt impulsive actions, reflect, and then take purposeful action.

Begin by teaching your child the meaning of S.T.A.R. Use **role plays** to show her exactly how to stop herself, think about her actions, and then choose the appropriate behavior. Explain that for one day she will become S.T.A.R. Woman. Throughout the day you will be looking for S.T.A.R. behaviors and you will give her a sticker in the shape of a star every time she stops, thinks, and acts right. Depending on your child's age and interest, you can make a cape for her to wear all day and use this cape to stick her S.T.A.R.s on. Some children forgo the cape but like the stickers to be stuck on their body. Older children may prefer to have their accumulating stickers put on a chart. Decide upon the number of S.T.A.R.s needed to get a special reward. The most important component of her day is to notice any efforts of thoughtful behavior and award a S.T.A.R. Systematically ignore all impulsive behavior unless it is dangerous. Make the number of S.T.A.R.s required in line with your child's capabilities. Whenever she stops and thinks just for a brief second, stick a S.T.A.R. on her and let her know that she is acting and behaving like a S.T.A.R. Woman. You can use it **playfully** and preventively by positively reframing her actions and giving her a S.T.A.R. just before she mishandles a breakable object or does something impulsive. You might even want to say, "Wow—I could tell that you were going to think about handling that vase carefully or act in a slow, calm way." Playfully practice S.T.A.R. Man or Woman for future situations. Act-out situations in which your child practices how S.T.A.R. Man or Woman would handle getting frustrated, crossing the street, and even going into a toy store.

Of course, your child will be more motivated if he can receive a reward for getting a certain number of S.T.A.R.s. Do this activity as often as he needs. You may want to give him S.T.A.R.s throughout the week even when he is not S.T.A.R. Man.

This is the most important step of this recipe. You need to look back at the day your child was **S.T.A.R.** Man and review all the thoughtful reasons he got a S.T.A.R. Encourage him to see that these S.T.A.R. behaviors are skills toward controlling impulsive actions. Express your belief that he is capable of being S.T.A.R. Man whenever he takes the time to use his skills described in step 2. Remember to teach your child to reverse S.T.A.R. to R.A.T.S. (see page 29). Assure him that even a S.T.A.R. Man can make mistakes and he can say R.A.T.S.

Step 5
Review and recognize efforts

☆ *Planful Playing in a Pinch* ☆

RECIPE #40

Hot tips and quick recipes for dealing with overactivity.

40.1   *Turtles and Rabbits Race.* Draw with your child a map of a race with a start and a finish. Be creative—and include hills and valleys. Draw and cut out a picture of a turtle and a rabbit. Discuss with your child how his impulsive or overactive behaviors are like a rabbit and how his calm and thought-out behaviors are like a turtle. Each time your child displays either of these behaviors, move the rabbit (overactive behaviors) or the turtle (calm behaviors) across the race board. If the turtle arrives at the finish before the rabbit, he gets a reward.

40.2   *The **S.T.A.R.** Statue.* Play the Stop, Think, and Act Statue Game, in which your child becomes a statue and thinks before acting impulsively. When you sense trouble coming, have her freeze, then tell you what she believes her choices to be, then go ahead and act.

40.3   *The 1-Through-10 Thermometer.* Sit down with your child and describe and draw a picture of a thermometer, using the number 1 as the lowest degree and 10 as the highest. Decide with your child what his highest and lowest activity levels are. Younger children will especially benefit from **role playing**—acting-out these behaviors so that they are made more clear as to which ones you are indicating as highly active or calm. Starting with the lowest-level activity, move up the thermometer and label each "degree" of behavior. Use the thermometer as a constant indicator to your child of which activity level he is currently behaving at and which level you want him to be at: For example, "That behavior is a seven—in restaurants it's more appropriate to be a three." Be sure to leave room for the high-level behaviors: "Let's go to the park, where we can all behave like eights!"

40.4   *Totally Losing It.* Set aside time each day, or perhaps once a week, during which your child has your okay to really "lose it." She can run, shriek, jump, chase birds, move quickly, and physically exhaust herself. This can be done in a large field, in a park, or at a gym. You can **model** for your child how to totally lose it, letting off steam yourself in these acceptable locations.

40.5   *Butter Maker.* Put your child's high energy to work. Have him make homemade butter for the family dinner. Use a container with a tight lid and fill it with whipping cream. It will take about twenty minutes of shaking to make butter. Instruct him to shake, shake, shake until the mixture is smooth and creamy. Compliment his controlled cooking skills.

40.6   *Waiting Games.* Overactive children have trouble waiting. Standing in line can be made less stressful if you plan a few waiting games.

140

Here are a few suggestions. How long can your daughter stand on one foot? How long can your son keep his eyes closed and stand on one foot? **Encourage** him to break his record (use a watch to time it). Can he say the alphabet backward? Write letters with your fingers on his back and have him guess which one it is. (This feels calming as well.) Come up with some waiting games that your child would enjoy, and remember to **prepare, plan, prevent** disasters.

Countdown to Control. Use this to help your child settle down after high-intensity play or during the transition from one activity to another. Five to ten minutes before it is time to end an activity, together with your child count down minute by minute. At each interval he must control (calm down) one body part (left arm, left leg, toes, etc.). Demonstrate, using your own body, until you and your child are ready to move on. Now your child is ready to lift off to the next event. *40.7*

Put on Your Shades. Maintaining eye contact is very difficult for overactive children. Teach your child to look you in the eyes by pretending to put on imaginary glasses that help him pay attention and look at you without becoming distracted. Have him choose a special pair of child-size glasses that he wears to help him look people in the eyes. When your child looks at you without needing his "glasses," let him know how terrific his eyes are becoming and how his glasses must be correcting the problem. *40.8*

Movement Metaphors. Using your child's favorite music, pick out songs that are fast, normal, and slow paced. Explain to him that you are going to teach him how to "feel" himself becoming "wild" and then how to slow down his actions by dancing to music. Play the songs that you selected and **model** for your child by dancing or just moving to the speed of the music. Have your child join you and dance wildly, move normally, or move slowly to the pace of the music. Ask him how it feels inside when he is wild, normal, or calm. Play a game in which he must listen carefully to the music and move or dance according to its speed. Use the title of the song to determine the activity level (fast, normal, or slow). Eventually, instead of playing the music, you can "cue" your child by using the title of the song to help him gauge his speed. Let him know that he can use these skills to help him change the level of activity by listening to the musical cues that you give him or actually "hearing" the cues in his head. *40.9*

(See page 256 for a list of reading recipes for solving overactivity.)

Recipe #41: Home Office

CHAPTER 10

School Problems

IT'S NINE O'CLOCK, YOUR son Joshua's bedtime—otherwise known as parent survival time. You're beginning your evening routine, packing his books and homework into his backpack, when a paper catches your eye that has that look—an assignment. "Not again," you hear yourself groan as you read it: a two-page report on Christopher Columbus due tomorrow! You reluctantly hand it to Josh, fully expecting another late-night battle full of tears and other unpleasantries. As you think to yourself, "Where did we go wrong?" you realize you are reviewing the chapter on Columbus and taking notes for Josh—probably the last thing you would choose to do at that moment. As you ask yourself, "Why in the world am I doing this?" you realize it is just to get it done.

Children are exciting and eager learners. They want to know everything: Why? How? and What for? They live for learning, loving, and pleasing parents and teachers. They seek mastery, control, and competence, yet many experience difficulties in school with behavior, with academic achievement, and with homework. The goal is, then, to build on your child's innate love of learning and unique skills, through **encouragement** and support.

You can help motivate your child to become an eager learner by **modeling** a desire for knowledge, exposing her to a variety of information and experiences, supporting her interests, and teaching organization and self-discipline. You, as parents, are your child's first and most important teachers.

Homework

Motivation and Academic Achievement

Learning Problems

PROBLEMS

Homework

The most commonly reported school-related problem is homework. There are a number of reasons for this problem. Among them are: (a) today's homework involves technical skills different from those that parents were taught; (b) most homework tends to be redundant and unstimulating; (c) children who have underdeveloped organizational and time-management skills tend to avoid and procrastinate, and so their frustrated, well-intentioned parents often find themselves doing the homework.

Motivation and Academic Achievement

Children who seem to be generally unmotivated and/or uninterested are usually struggling with underlying issues: (a) low self-esteem resulting in an "I can't" rather than an "I can" attitude; (b) fear of failing and exposing their inadequacy—it's safer not to try; (c) children who feel unchallenged or are bored by their studies often become disruptive and cause distractions, so they are labeled as troublemakers and unmotivated (ironically, many of these children are bright or even highly gifted); (d) the child believes that he can't live up to the standards and expectations of parents, older siblings, or peers, and (e) the child is pressured to assimilate with his or her peers, and, to avoid being called a nerd, achieves below his or her potential or assumes the role of the class clown or rebel.

Many children who have difficulties in school may be suffering from undiagnosed or unrecognized disabilities: (a) there are many kinds of learning disabilities, including visual and hearing problems, attention deficits, fine and/or gross motor-skill disorders, cognitive processing, and communication problems; (b) a child with any one of these difficulties needs and has a right to specialized services in order to benefit from a positive and fruitful learning experience; (c) due to undiagnosed problems such as the above, a child with a learning disability will feel frustrated, stupid, defeated, inadequate, and often be scapegoated by his peers.

Homework

Join your child in her homework responsibilities by assuming a "coach" role. Encourage and support her work by reading and reviewing instructions (if need be, learning the work yourself), discussing problem-solving procedures that seem to fit, and checking for accuracy, clarity, and comprehension. (Recipes 41, 44) However, refrain from doing the work yourself. A sense of ownership, pride, responsibility, and self-discipline can be had only when your child does his homework himself. (Recipe 41)

Together with your child, develop a homework/playtime schedule and help her stick to it. Develop a system for her to list/organize the work that needs to be done each day. With structure and goal orientation she will find it easier to stay focused and motivated and to complete the work in a shorter period of time. (Recipes 24, 26, 41, 44.1, 44.3, 44.4, 44.6)

Try to help your child imagine real-life applications of homework topics. Speak to his teacher, express your concerns, and offer suggestions and help. Join your school's parent-teacher organizations or the PTA. (Recipes 42, 44.5)

Motivation and Academic Achievement

Challenging but reachable goals are the hallmarks of highly motivated and successful people. Motivation and **encouragement** are the key to an "I can" attitude. (Recipes 42, 44.5)

Share a sense of excitement in learning new things with your child. In the course of a day with him or her, talk about your curiosity concerning how things work. (Recipes 42, 44.5)

Demonstrate acceptance of mistakes as an integral part of learning, and **model** your willingness to risk being wrong or not knowing, such as by asking directions when you are lost. (Recipes 53, 54)

If your child is completing her homework much too easily, feels she is inadequately challenged, or is being told that she is working below her potential, have her evaluated in order to better assess her learning abilities.

Help your child develop personal goals independent of others. Avoid comparisons with yourself, siblings, or peers. Remember: no two persons are alike. (Recipe 60.3)

Challenge stereotypes, both yours and your child's, that limit growth and potential. Support his or her individualism while keeping in mind the powerful pull to be like one's peers. For example, challenge distortions such as, "Everyone will like me if I make them laugh," or, "No one will like me if I get A's." (Recipe 43 and see chapter 15)

If you suspect, for whatever reason, that your child may have a learning disability, get an evaluation by an education specialist right away. Many parents deny their own intuition for years, despite the fact that they know their own children. Careful testing and diagnosis can determine the presence of a learning disability and can result in recommendations to help your child's learning needs. (Recipe 43)

☆ *Home Office* ☆

RECIPE # 4 1

Serves: 6–12 years

This recipe helps children do their homework.

Step 1
State and define the problem

Using **"I" messages,** discuss with your child your perception of homework problems. Specifically identify problem areas such as poorly done homework, incomplete homework, or refusal to do homework. Encourage your child to share his thoughts regarding homework and his reasons for not doing it properly. Use **empathy, mutual respect,** and **effective listening** to show your concern for his struggles to cope with homework.

Step 2
Identify skills and solutions

Encourage your child to think of as many skills, talents and/or capabilities as he can to show his perseverance, ability to complete a task, and motivation to finish. Organized sports and dance recitals are excellent ways to show your child that he has the ability to get involved in an activity, stick to it, and try his best to finish successfully. Since "homework" is actually "practice time" for learning, your child may understand that she needs to do homework to improve her academic skills just as she needs to practice throwing and catching a ball to improve her baseball skills.

Step 3
Mutually agree upon goals

Goal: "I will use my special skills to improve my study habits and create a place that makes doing my homework easier."

Step 4
Practice and play

Homework not only provides a child with an opportunity to practice and strengthen academic skills, but it also gives him experience in handling responsibility, managing his time, acquiring independence, and completing tasks. Most children today do not see the overall benefit of doing homework, mostly because it is *work* and requires self-discipline, and the ability to postpone more interesting, less taxing activities. We adults understand that work is much more enjoyable if the environment is attractive and comfortable. This activity will create a personal work space for your child that is inviting and special.

First set up a physical arrangement that defines the space as your child's personal "office" for doing homework. Be sure that the space is private and away from distractions. There must be no television nearby, and it can't be a high-traffic area. Furnish the space with office equipment that makes doing homework more appealing. Here is a list of materials that we have found particularly helpful.

- A desk with lots of drawers, files, and compartments. Fill the drawers with pencils, pens, markers, crayons, and art supplies such as glue and scissors, writing paper, colored paper, folders, index cards, etc.

146

- A wall calendar that appeals to your child.

- A children's dictionary and thesaurus can be placed nearby.

- Special touches include a cassette player, a special desk set with penholder, and perhaps even his name on a nameplate. We also found that kids really love fancy, grown-up schedule books.

Once you have decked out the office, encourage your child to go there as part of his daily homework ritual. **Model** the need to go to the office to get work done by setting up your own office for paying bills and answering correspondence. Let your child know that doing her homework is her responsibility and that you will be supportive and give her help if she needs it. Use **the Five C's** to set up rules in your family that establish your expectations for doing homework. You can promote homework responsibility by getting involved in the planning and organization of her assignments. Help her map out the week's schedule by writing assignments and times for doing homework in her schedule book. You could write in times when you will be available to help with specific assignments. That way, if she waits until midnight to do an assignment that is due the next morning, she can't expect you to come to the rescue without an "appointment." This also reinforces the **logical consequences** of avoiding responsibility for doing homework.

At first you may need to monitor or supervise your child's homework schedule and office attendance. This is not a good time to use **ignoring.** Try to give him a **choice** instead: "Do your homework now, or do it later, but *do* it." Over time, as your child becomes more self-reliant, you can phase out your supervisory role and get out of his office.

This recipe works best if you **spice it up** with a little incentive. Learning new things and completing homework is hard work and should be seen as a real job. An incentive could be as simple as bringing your hardworking child a little snack to his office a half hour or so after he begins doing his homework. Consider setting up a homework chart that records your child's efforts and is used as a part of a reward program (see chapter 17, "Just Desserts"). You can add to this chart other school-related behaviors you would like to strengthen such as good behavior in school or being on time for the bus. Make the reward something new for his office like a new set of folders, an attractive calendar, or a leather schedule book.

Using the homework space and following through on school assignments could be major accomplishments for your child. Recognize any small changes she makes toward using her office. The chart and incentive program will automatically reinforce learning improvements.

Step 5
Review and recognize efforts

☆ *Family Fun and Games* ☆

RECIPE #42
Serves: 4–12 years

This recipe teaches children that learning is a family affair, and is fun.

Step 1
State and define the problem

Describe to your child your perceptions of the purpose of school and learning. Share your opinions but stay away from lectures and sermons. Use **"I" messages, empathy,** and **effective listening** when hearing your child's point of view. Guiding the conversation toward describing school problems and lack of motivation to learn is something the entire family will need to work together on.

Step 2
Identify skills and solutions

Since this recipe requires that the entire family participate in the learning process, make a list of learning-related skills for each member. Get everyone to participate in sharing what they think they are good at learning as well as what they think the skills of others are. Use **positive reframing** to help your child see the positive in a negative situation: for example, poor at math but great at keeping score at baseball games. Use your child's hobbies and physical achievements as proof of his ability to love to learn things.

Step 3
Mutually agree upon goals

Goal: "I will use my special skills to learn new things and have fun learning with my family." This is truly a family goal. Parents are important motivators to children, and a child's first and most important teachers. Establishing a fun learning environment within your family is the key link between wanting to learn and needing to learn.

Step 4
Practice and play

This recipe will provide you with several fun family activities that make learning a family priority. Most importantly, your child will realize that you enjoy learning and so will ultimately enjoy learning himself. Keep in mind that play is a child's most natural form of learning. **Spicing up** the school curriculum and homework assignments so that they correspond with family learning adventures and family games will inevitably increase your child's motivation to learn.

The first thing you will need to do is thoroughly familiarize yourself with your child's study plan, specific learning themes, and school agendas for the year. Have regular discussions with his teacher about his progress and the specific learning needs required for each subject. Now you are ready to turn your home into a learning environment of fun and games.

The Family Wheel of Fortune. Create your own family game shows such as "Wheel of Fortune," "Jeopardy," or the PBS game show called "Where in the World Is Carmen San Diego?" Using your child's "academic" calendar and homework assignments, think up questions for the show that will reflect what he is currently studying. Take turns being the contestants. Make the prize something the family wins together, like a trip to the

Science Museum or ice cream shop. Use **humor, modeling, try, try again,** and lots of cheering and **encouragement** throughout the game. (See Special Resources, page 268, for a list of school-supply catalogs that sell games with an academic focus and playfully reinforce learning in the family.)

Family Learning Adventures. **Prepare, plan** and take your child on a family field trip that is related to the subject he is currently studying. Be creative and seek out activities that are not normally scheduled field trips during the school year. Books such as *Games for Learning, Games for Reading,* and *Games for Math,* by Peggy Kaye (Pantheon Books), contain excellent suggestions for turning learning into fun and games.

Family School Days. Make learning a family affair, literally, by taking a class together. This learning experience could become a part of your family's identity. Take a class together in American Sign Language (check state schools for the deaf for information) or a foreign language. Learn to play the same musical instrument, take a course in astronomy, or learn a craft skill like knitting, pottery, or painting. Most important, **model** for your child how to listen in class, ask questions, plan, study, and be enthusiastic about learning. This is a wonderful way to show your child first-hand how to learn and how to have fun learning. If possible, plan vacations or weekend activities that are related to your classes. For example, take a trip to a Spanish-speaking country if you are studying Spanish, or to Washington, D.C., if you are learning about our government. The possibilities are endless.

Accenting the *fun* in the *fun*damentals of learning in this recipe will bring out the best in your child's motivation to learn.

Step 5
Review and recognize efforts

☆ Kid-Teacher ☆

RECIPE #43

Serves: 6–12 years

This recipe gives learning-disabled children an opportunity (a) to demonstrate their knowledge and (b) to discover what it is like to teach.

Step 1 *State and define the problem*	This part of the recipe focuses on how your child's learning problem affects his feelings about himself rather than how his behavior causes a learning problem. Let him know by using **empathy** and **mutual respect** that he is not the cause of his learning problems. Encourage him to share his feelings about his difficulties in school. Use techniques such as **"I" messages** and **effective listening** to help him express himself about his sensitive point.
Step 2 *Identify skills and solutions*	This important step requires you to list your child's skills in learning—anything that shows her that she is a capable student. Focus on social skills, physical skills, efforts made, and perseverance. Show your child that every potential weakness can be a potential strength (**positive reframing**). **Model** for your child how everyone has some kind of learning difficulty, including yourself, and then show how you are nevertheless a skilled, capable person.
Step 3 *Mutually agree upon goals*	Goal: "I will use my special skills to feel good about my learning capabilities and my abilities to be a good teacher."
Step 4 *Practice and play*	Children who have learning problems, whether cognitive or emotionally based, have one thing in common: low self-esteem where learning is concerned. The following activity has been successfully utilized to help learning-disabled children feel proud of what they can do and to experience success in school. The recipe is not a cure for a learning disability, nor does it concentrate on diagnosis or treatment. But it will help improve your child's feelings toward himself and help him believe that he is a good student and an intelligent person.

In order to successfully use this recipe, you will need the trust and support of one of your child's teachers. It is essential that the teacher be committed to your child's succeeding as a "kid-teacher." Discuss a plan that consists of selecting either a learning ability or a learning disability that can be **positively reframed** as a teaching skill. Your son or daughter will then be given the opportunity to teach/tutor a younger child or a more learning-disabled schoolmate by using his or her chosen skills (see step 2). We suggest having your child become a kid-teacher to a student three or four classes below.

With the help of his teacher and the teacher of the student he will be tutoring, have your child set up a lesson plan. Buy a few inexpensive teaching tools such as a weekly planner, flash cards, and folders. **Encourage** your child to talk to either you or his teacher about strategies for helping others to learn (self-**modeling**). A kid-teacher experience might be to have a learning-disabled child who has problems with reading teach a much younger child the alphabet. Daily or weekly tutoring should be arranged. Reinforce the process by having your child share with the teacher his thoughts about his student's progress. If things work out, celebrate his success by asking teachers and students in his class or in his student's class to come to an end-of-the-year or end-of-the-semester party.

Even if the activity isn't totally successful, any gain achieved by your child in helping another child learn something new is a victory for both. **Try, try again** if the kid-teacher experience did not meet expectations—perhaps it was just a mismatch between student and teacher. By **encouraging** your child to **try, try again,** you are showing her that even though a student might not catch on right away, the "teacher" should not give up.

Step 5
Review and recognize efforts

151

☆ *Planful Playing in a Pinch* ☆

Hot tips and quick recipes for solving school problems.

44.1   *The School Picture Checklist.* On a large poster board draw pictures on the left-hand side of school-related situations that your child can't cope with or has difficulties with. If she has trouble behaving on the school bus, draw a picture of a school bus. If he can't get along with his teacher, draw a teacher. If she doesn't get her homework in on time, draw a picture of homework papers and a calendar or watch. For this activity it is best to think of the separate components of a problem such as remembering homework, doing it neatly, and turning it in on time. This way you will have more than one item to check off every day your child goes to school. Each time your child deals with the situation or acts responsibly he or she gets a check mark. Establish a number of check marks needed to receive a reward.

44.2   *The School Bus Blahs.* Help your child understand how he can organize his time and assume responsibility for being on time for the school bus. He can either write a story or make a video on the step-by-step daily procedure necessary in order to catch the bus on time. Encourage him to make it funny. Perhaps a comical story on what would happen if he didn't organize his time would be a great way to **spice up** the video.

44.3   *Ten Days to Go.* Post on a bulletin board how many days your child has before his homework is due. This is usually good for larger projects such as reports. Announce to your child every time you change the day on the bulletin board, indicating how many days are left. As the deadline nears, change the days into hours: "15 hours to go." This is a fun, anti-nag way to remind your child of when his homework is due.

44.4   *The Hurdles.* Explain to your child how in track and field events there is a special running activity called hurdles. Show how hurdles are set up so that the runner must clear each one before reaching the finish line. Use this as a theme and draw a hurdle event on a large poster board. You might draw a colorful track with hurdles, a starting gate, and a flag-studded finish. Now explain how jumping these hurdles is like getting a homework assignment done. The starting gate could represent the teacher assigning the report, and the flag-studded finish would be finishing it. Each hurdle is a step in the process of writing the report. The first hurdle could be deciding on the topic, the second could be researching it, etc. Attach a picture of your child to each hurdle as he or she jumps over it, and at the end of the race, celebrate!

44.5   *Happy Hobbies.* Teach your child good learning habits by investing time in a hobby. For example, if your daughter becomes interested in stamp collecting, don't only collect the stamps but research, investigate, go to collection shows, and read about stamp collections. Be sure to encourage your child to show his hobbies to relatives and friends. We suggest having your child take his hobby to senior citizens' homes and to hospitals for children so he can demonstrate his knowledge. A hobby can teach your child how to develop an interest in a subject, deepen her knowledge of it, and perhaps even cause her to become an expert.

The Study Break. Surprise your child with a snack and a glass of milk during his study hour. Announce it as the study-break time and let him know you are pleased with his efforts. Take this time to listen to your child. Ask questions about the school day and review homework with him.   *44.6*

Teacher Time. When a child and a teacher have a relationship problem, invite the teacher out for lunch or dinner. Have your child write the invitation and plan the event. Make it special. Play up the need for the two of them to get to know each other better. Persistent relationship problems should *not* be pushed aside until your son or daughter gets a new teacher next year. Speak with the teacher or with school administrators with the object of solving the problem during the present school year.   *44.7*

(See page 257 for a list of reading recipes for school problems. A list of educational-resource catalogs is on page 269.)

Recipe #45: Make Way for the King and Queen

CHAPTER 11

Self-Centered Behaviors

ALL RISE AS SEVEN-YEAR-OLD Prince Jeffrey enters the room and immediately begins bellowing orders at his servants. To his mother: "I want a peanut butter sandwich now!" To his sister: "You can't play that Nintendo game—it's mine!" His mother dares to interrupt Jeffrey's tirade: "Jeffrey, before you get any lunch or *share* the Nintendo with your sister, you still have to make your bed. It's the fifth time I've told you that." Jeffrey whines, "I can't make it good—anyway, it's not fair—it's *my* game and I don't want to share!" "Okay, okay," his exasperated mom answers. "I'll make you a peanut butter sandwich and then we'll make your bed together."

Poor sister. Poor Mother. Poor Jeffrey. Self-centered behaviors can be extremely trying. While no one else seems happy with the outcome, Jeffrey will get what he wants: get his sandwich and grab his mother's attention. Mother probably did not intend to give in, but she did, and in doing so has just reinforced her son's selfish and demanding behavior. On the positive side, however, she has exercised an important skill in helping children like Jeffrey improve their behavior: she compromised in order to prevent a painful and unnecessary power struggle.

Like most children with this problem, Jeffrey is primarily concerned with his own desires and perceived needs, and has no interest in how this affects those around him. While this is a normal developmental characteristic of toddlers and young children, Jeffrey seems either not to have grown out of it or else for some reason he has returned to an earlier phase. Self-centeredness and immaturity go hand in hand, for maturation should bring better social perceptions and consideration for others.

Teaching and **modeling** altruism, **mutual respect,** and **empathy** can help youngsters like Jeffrey move outside of themselves and become better-adjusted persons. Parents should be firm in setting limits, using **the Five C's** and **logical consequences** (say what you will do and do as you say), so that self-centered Jeffreys realize that their behavior is definitely not acceptable. You also need to be aware of the stressors in your child's life so you can better understand emerging behaviors such as this. A young child whose emotional needs are met with nurturance and limits will probably pass through this difficult stage.

Selfishness

Overly Demanding

Doesn't Share

For the young child, an egocentric view of the world is both normal and healthy. It is a fundamental developmental starting point, from which he or she begins to develop the concepts of self-worth and security.

A child who demands excessive attention or won't take no for an answer will surely push the unfortunate parent or parents to the brink and result in the onset of a negative cycle of parent/child relations.

While it is important to encourage and nurture your child's sense of self, if you are overprotective, too permissive, or all-giving, your child will not learn to deal with frustration or not getting her way. She could remain in an infantile, egocentric state of development and have serious difficulty (1) accepting that she is not the center of the universe, (2) sharing parental attention and time, (3) sharing possessions, and (4) recognizing that the needs of others can sometimes take priority.

Parents who measure social success by the number and brand name of their material possessions, income, and superiority over others may unwittingly be passing along an attitude to their children, which then promotes self-centered behavior and undervaluing the worth of relationships.

Children who feel that their needs are not being met by their parent or parents, perhaps due to a chronic or serious illness, prolonged or frequent absence of one or both parents, or divorce, may become more demanding, attention-seeking, or oppositional in an effort to meet those needs.

Children often become more self-focused during difficult periods of transition or separation (beginning kindergarten, when the primary caretaker returns to work, or when the family moves from one house to another).

Self-centered children tend to become more preoccupied with power-seeking behavior—they feel more significant and secure when they are in control or are trying to be boss.

When overt control-seeking behavior proves ineffective, some children resort to passive-aggressive or manipulative means to get what they want or to feel in control.

The odds are that your child won't be this way forever: it's a necessary developmental stage. If a child feels safe and valued, he can translate these positive feelings to how he feels about and treats others. (Recipes 45, 47, 48.1, 48.8, 48.9)

Try not to take his or her behavior personally. Be consistent. Self-centered behaviors are not a sign that you have failed or neglected your child's needs. Practice techniques such as **effective listening, mutual respect,** and **empathy.** Set firm limits and seek support for yourself from your spouse, partner, friend, or family. (Recipe 48.9)

Children should have an environment that has both structure and diversity. As important as it is to succeed, she should learn that she will not always get what she wants and will not always reach her goals. (Recipes 29.1, 45, 46, 47)

Give your child opportunities to contribute to the lives of others. Praise her efforts sincerely and enthusiastically. Give her special attention when she has asked for it (not necessarily at that moment but at some agreed-upon time) as proof that you have heard her request and respect her needs. (Recipes 16, 46, 48)

Help your child understand the difference between her needs and her wants. Be patient, this is a slow and gradual process. (Recipes 45, 46)

Help your child learn to value people over objects. Demonstrate through **modeling** your own commitment to this value. Establish a family atmosphere in which concern for others is more rewarding and important than are possessions. (Recipes 46, 47, 48, 50)

If your child's behavior is becoming noticeably more self-centered, oppositional, or demanding, review the last few months and note any major changes, any upheavals that have occurred in your lives. Explore these with your child. Solicit his feelings and thoughts and ask him for suggestions about how you can help.

Help your child feel empowered and important whether or not she is really in charge. Think up ways for her to experience control and independence without engaging in power struggles. Try to head off power struggles before they become serious. Whenever possible, rechannel her urge to be bossy into productive endeavors. (Recipes 26, 29.10)

Let your child know, in clear and simple terms, that she may not be aware of how she is behaving, but you are. **Encourage** her to find more appropriate ways to express her demands, frustrations, and dissatisfaction. (Recipes 18.2, 18.3, 30, 33, 34, 35)

☆ *Make Way for the King and Queen* ☆

RECIPE #45

Serves: 3–10 years

This recipe teaches younger children to be sensitive to others and refrain from being demanding.

Step 1
State and define the problem

This step gives you a perfect opportunity to **model** for your child the process of seeing things from another's perspective. You enable him to move from a solitary view of himself to a more sensitive, altruistic view of others. Help your child see that being demanding, selfish, and unwilling to cooperate makes friendships and relationships with family members difficult. Use communication skills such as **"I" messages, effective listening, empathy,** and **mutual respect** to model or show your child how to take part in a two-way conversation in which all family members are heard.

Step 2
Identify skills and solutions

Point out your child's skills and attributes that indicate his thoughtfulness, such as the ability to ask for things in a considerate way, sensitivity to others, and the ability to share things and to listen to friends and family. Take the time to **positively reframe** situations in which your child was selfish, trying to be sensitive or undemanding.

Step 3
Mutually agree upon goals

Goal: "I will use my special skills to be sensitive to and considerate of others and to learn to ask for things in the right way."

Step 4
Practice and play

Selfishness and demanding behavior is a normal developmental phase of early childhood. However, when older children continue to demand attention or objects without consideration of the circumstances, the problem requires a good recipe. The "gimme-gimme" and "do-it-my-way-or-else" blues can be cured by using this "royal" procedure.

Explain to your child that you will help him change his selfish behavior by making him a king (or a queen for a girl) of his palace. Tell him that there are nice kings and spoiled kings. Give examples of nice kingly behavior such as asking nicely for things, waiting a turn, saying thank you, not ordering people around, and accepting no for an answer. Spoiled-king behavior is just the opposite—selfish and demanding. Make a list of nice kingly behaviors and spoiled kingly behaviors.

Next, make a crown out of construction paper and rhinestones from a craft store. When your child engages in nice kingly behavior, glue a rhinestone to his crown. When he is demanding or selfish, **ignore** him, use **distraction, the Five C's,** or apply a **logical consequence.** Children quickly learn that by using negative behaviors such as tantruming, whining, and being excessively demanding, they can force parents into changing a no to a yes. When this happens, do not bow to the king. Walk away calmly, use **ignoring,** and then **T.A.P.** yourself to resist these attention-seeking ploys. Help your child to **try, try again** to win a rhinestone by supporting her efforts when she makes a mistake. Use **S.T.A.R./R.A.T.S.** to help him stop and think about his actions. **Spice up** your responses to your child's selfish demands by **playfully** reminding him when he is being a spoiled king. You could say, "Excuse me, your royal highness—but did you want something?"

When your child has collected a good number of rhinestones on his crown, reward him (see chapter 17, "Just Desserts"). If you feel he needs to continue working to reduce selfish behavior, use different-colored rhinestones for each new week. **Encourage** him to work toward a new reward for nice kingly behavior. **Prepare, plan, prevent** shopping or social disasters by reviewing with your child correct, nice kingly behavior before removing him from his palace and into the public eye. Lay out his **choices** of ways he should behave.

Share with your child your thoughts and good feelings concerning unselfish and less-demanding behavior. Learning to see things through the eyes of others is a very difficult developmental task, so be patient and recognize even small steps toward becoming more socially sensitive.

Step 5
Review and recognize efforts

159

☆ *Sharing and Caring Projects* ☆

RECIPE #46

Serves: All ages

This recipe teaches children the value of sharing with others and caring for them.

Step 1
State and define the problem

In this step you will be sharing your understanding and perceptions of the sharing and caring problems in your family. To help your child listen to your viewpoints about selfishness, use simple **role plays** that show one person being selfish and uncaring, while the other person is feeling hurt and unhappy. **Model** for your child how to be **empathic** when listening to others by using **"I" messages** and **effective listening.** By showing real interest in your child and valuing his or her opinions, you will enhance the caring environment in your family.

Step 2
Identify skills and solutions

Make a list with your child of all his caring and sharing skills. Include times when he shared an ice cream cone, gave a present to a friend, walked the dog, stuck up for a sibling, waited his turn, or simply said thank you.

Step 3
Mutually agree upon goals

Goal: "I will use my special skills to become a more giving and caring person and family."

Step 4
Practice and play

This is a family recipe that asks that everyone in your home become involved in choosing and participating in a family caring project. The activity requires that you give your time and energy to benefit others. We have successfully used this recipe in dozens of families (including our own) to cure selfish behaviors in children.

Research local charitable organizations such as churches, hospitals, centers for underprivileged children, animal shelters, and nursing homes and/or global problems such as homelessness, inadequate health care, third world poverty, and ecological issues. Discuss with your child what each organization does and then pick one or two that will become your family's yearly Sharing and Caring Project. Don't just send a check or give old clothes away as the only giving activity. Your family should learn about the organization and find out how you can be helpful to it in person. Just call them and ask—it's that simple. Consider participating in a fund-raising or time-giving event. For example, if your family chooses to make a Sharing and Caring Project for homeless children, first learn something about homelessness and then encourage your child to consider what it would be like to be in that situation. (This teaches **empathy** and **mutual respect**.)

Next, your family should outline a giving plan that would allow each member to contribute individually or in the company of others. Participating in a walk for the homeless or sponsoring a car wash to raise money for a local family shelter are two good ideas for giving. Have your child collect her old and forgotten toys and take them to a shelter. This is an excellent way for your child to feel that she is sharing her good fortune with others.

Create an atmosphere in your home in which the needs of others are discussed, appreciated, and cared about. **Model** caring behavior by sharing your thoughts and concerns for others on a daily basis. Let your child experience the results or **natural consequences** of giving. Below is a list of organizations that you can use in setting up a family giving project. Or see the book *Volunteer USA,* by Andrew Carroll (Fawcett).

United Way of America
701 N. Fairfax St.
Alexandria, VA 22314

National Coalition
for the Homeless
1621 Connecticut Ave, NW #400
Washington, DC 20009

UNICEF
3 United Nations Plaza
New York, NY 10017

Dream Factory
315 Guthrie Green
Louisville, KY 40202
(This organization brings
smiles to the faces
of chronically ill
children.)

Environmental Action Coalition
625 Broadway
2nd Floor
New York, NY 10012

American Society
for the Prevention
of Cruelty to Animals
441 E. 92 St.
New York, NY 10128

This is a lifelong recipe that should be a part of any family's traditions.

Step 5
Review and recognize efforts

161

☆ *I Am a Shining Star—* ☆
But Not the Center of the Universe

R E C I P E   # 4 7

Serves: 4–12 years

This recipe encourages children to think more about others and be less self-centered.

Step 1
State and define the problem

Discuss with your older child how selfish behaviors and insensitivity toward others are problems that need to be corrected. **Model** for her how to express an opinion by using **"I" messages.** Teach her how to listen to others by using **effective listening, empathy,** and **mutual respect. Encourage** her to share her perceptions regarding selfish behaviors and how these behaviors affect others.

Step 2
Identify skills and solutions

Identify skills and traits possessed by your child that demonstrate her ability to think about others. These might include sharing her toys, accepting that people are different, giving her opinions in an appropriate way, and respecting the feelings of her friends. Remind her of occasions on which she showed these positive qualities.

Step 3
Mutually agree upon goals

Goal: "I will use my special skills to think more about others and not just myself, and to feel good about me."

Step 4
Practice and play

Some children are selfish because they have not learned to see things through the eyes of others. Often they feel unworthy and are preoccupied with self-doubts. Since insecurity breeds excessive neediness, a child who does not feel secure will have trouble letting go of her possessions and thinking of others.

It is important to bolster the self-esteem of your child (see chapter 12 on Self-Concept) while increasing his ability to be concerned and aware of others around him. By doing this, you will be creating a universe that includes people in his world and specific skills that he has that enhance his relationships with others.

In this recipe you are required to use the parenting technique **S.T.A.R.** This self-taught method of stopping, thinking, and then acting right can help your child replace selfish and self-defeating thoughts with thoughtful regard for herself and others. Using the list of skills and special attributes discussed in step 2, make a list with your child of S.T.A.R. behaviors that shows her that she is capable of thinking and caring about others. Make a list of self-boosting behaviors such as "I am a nice person," or, "I can take good care of myself." Next design and cut out about two dozen stars from paper that has self-adhesive backing. Now you can make your child's "world" by cutting a circle out of a large piece of construction paper and pasting or drawing pictures of family and friends, teachers, and heroes, onto her world (the round paper). Finally, clear a wall in your child's bedroom and tape her world to the center of the wall. Every time your child stops and thinks about using S.T.A.R. behaviors (the list of skills from step 2), she gets to stick a star onto the "universe wall" so it can "shine" on her world. Thus, every time she behaves in a caring and giving way, the people in her life are affected positively. You may want to write the specific skill on the star to remind her of the S.T.A.R. behaviors she used that make her a caring and thoughtful person. Give her the **choice** between being a "star" and receiving positive attention, or acting selfishly and being **ignored. Positively reframe** any behavior that indicates your child is trying to act appropriately by placing the star on her universe wall. Then tell her why she received the star.

While doing this activity, **model** altruistic behaviors by sharing and caring about others in front of your child. Ask her if she thinks *you* are using S.T.A.R. behaviors and therefore deserve a star. If you want to use incentives to support your child's behavior improvements, decide on the number of stars needed to get a reward. Otherwise, simply look together at a star-studded universe and remark how beautiful it looks when she treats people in her world with **empathy,** respect, and kindness.

Take the time to recognize any improvements in her behavior, small as they may be. If she did not reach her goal, don't abandon the universe—**try, try again.**

Step 5
Review and recognize efforts

☆ *Planful Playing in a Pinch* ☆

Hot tips and quick recipes for decreasing self-centeredness.

48.1   *In Your Shoes.* Collect several pairs of shoes from all family members. Have everyone try on each other's shoes. Ask your child what it is like to be in that specific person's shoes. Take turns trying on everyone's shoes and telling what it must be like to be that person. **Role-play** different situations to show what it is like to be an adult when your child is acting selfishly or being demanding. Show that you understand what it is like to be in your child's shoes when he is asking for something from you. State how you think your child feels, and **encourage** your child to do the same when he is in someone else's shoes.

48.2   *What Others Need at Christmastime.* When your child is making her seemingly endless list of Christmas gifts, compile a list of what others, who do not have the means, need at this time. Choose a few items from the list and have your child purchase them, wrap them, and give them to a shelter or an organization for children. Discuss this giving behavior and show unadulterated pride in your child's altruistic behavior.

48.3   *Secret Buddy.* A few times a month have a secret buddy day on which your family can pick names out of a hat and then become that person's secret buddy. Secret buddies leave little gifts, fun notes, and special surprises for each other. At the end of the day, family members guess who their secret buddy is and thank him or her for the fun thoughts and kindness.

48.4   *Unconditional Giving.* Every week, come up with a Sharing and Caring Project your family or child can do for someone else. These weekly projects could be taking out the garbage for an elderly neighbor, helping a young sister or brother study for a test, making cookies for a sick relative, or just scratching a parent's back. Let your child know how unselfish he is for doing these nice things for someone else. Make sure there is no reward except good feeling.

48.5   *The Sharing Box.* On the front of a cardboard box, write the words "Sharing Box." Put into the box toys that your son can play with only if he shares them: items that are fun to use with a friend such as balls, board games, or jump ropes. Add toys like dolls or puzzles that do not require two people to enjoy. This way your child is challenged to share something that requires him to take turns and negotiate how to play with someone else.

48.6   *The Neighborhood Exchange.* With the help of neighbors who have children about the same age as yours, start a toy exchange. Have your child choose a few toys she would like to share with a neighbor in exchange for a toy of theirs. Older children can do this with books and clothing. Encourage your child to occasionally give up something to be exchanged that she currently enjoys and will miss. This way she will learn how to give up a little in order to get something of equal value from a neighborhood friend. All items should be returned and reexchanged unless arrangements are made to make the exchange permanent.

Thank-You Cards. Design your own family thank-you cards. Ask your child to come up with a simple design. Have it printed. (Many office-supply stores can do this professionally.) Encourage your child to think of what would be nice to say to someone when you want to thank them for doing something nice for you. Give these cards out when appropriate.

48.7

Empathy Antenna. Teach your child **empathy** by making a special antenna resembling insect antennae to be worn on his or her head. Explain that this device can pick up the "special feeling waves" of another person. It can help her tune into the feelings and thoughts of others and how her behavior affects them. For example, if your child hurts another child's feelings by refusing to share her toys, have her put on her feeling antenna to see if she can pick up the feeling waves of that individual. Have her tell you what feelings she thought her antenna was receiving. Put on the antenna yourself when you want to **model** showing empathy for another person.

48.8

The Sign. Have your family decide on a simple sign, such as a peace sign, that is done with your hands or your index finger up to indicate that a family member is being overly demanding or interrupting someone. Use this sign to help your child recognize when he is interrupting you and then give him a "time" (one minute, five minutes) in which he knows you will respond to him. Encourage your child to count the number of seconds he needs to wait (**distraction**) before you will respond to him.

48.9

Rainbow Box. One way to help your child become interested in others, appreciate others' differences, and respect diversity is to make your child a box filled with play items representing other cultures and ethnicities. Fill the box with dolls with different skin colors, board games from different cultures, books and magazines that recognize ethnic diversity, and dress-up clothes and items from different countries. Encourage your family to celebrate holidays from other ethnic and religious backgrounds. By introducing your child at an early age to the differences among people through play, you are inviting him to see things through another perspective and life-style.

48.10

(See page 257 for a list of reading recipes for solving self-centeredness.)

CHAPTER 12

Self-Concept Problems

ELEVEN-YEAR-OLD SUSAN HAS BEEN begging to take a gymnastics class for months. Her parents finally located one and readjusted their schedules. On the first day of class, she is terrified and refuses to go, saying that she's clumsy and uncoordinated and the other girls will make fun of her. Her parents feel defeated—they thought this time things would be different. They are privately wondering what they did wrong that makes her seem so unhappy. Should they force her to go or should they give in to her own arranged failure?

Seven-year-old Paul does not, I repeat does *not*, want to go to camp. He has complained of everything from a splinter in his finger to diarrhea as a reason not to go. Right now he is glued to the carpet on the floor of your car. He refused to get on the bus. His poor frustrated parents are about ready to offer him a new toy if only he'll go for one day.

Nine-year-old Jesse is a great kid. He gets fantastic grades, is quick to help out his mom, keeps his room neat and organized. He just can't seem to make friends. He seems so nervous around the other kids and is so afraid he'll do something wrong. He stays awake worrying about schoolwork. His parents wish he'd loosen up and be a kid—enjoy himself a little more.

Susan, Paul, and Jesse all suffer from low self-worth and associated problems of being overly critical, overly dependent, and perfectionism. Self-esteem is not something one can give or get in an afternoon. It is the result of growing and living in a nurturing and empowering environment. It is a lifelong task.

Positive self-worth is the foundation for the development of healthy reciprocal relationships, creativity, personality strengths, intellectual achievement, and responsibility. It is the glue that binds children's personalities into positive, integrated, and effective human beings.

The child with healthy self-esteem will enjoy her accomplishments, act independently, assume responsibility easily, feel capable of influencing by tapping into her "personal power," confront challenges without excessive anxiety, accept her mistakes, and avoid self-defeating or dangerous situations.

Low Self-Esteem

Perfectionism

Separation Problems

Overcompetitiveness

PROBLEMS

Low Self-Esteem

A child with low self-worth feels inadequate and believes that others don't value or like him. He demeans or minimizes his talents and avoids challenging situations.

He has a generally pessimistic outlook, feels powerless and at times hopeless about changing or improving the situation.

He is fragile and sensitive to criticism. He may become defensive or guarded even when being given positive feedback (compliments).

There are many factors that alone or in combination may cause low self-esteem: rejection by loved ones or peers, parental withholding of love, conditional love, lack of attention, negative comparisons to others, being frequently ignored or put down, overemphasis on appearance and performance, and ridicule or criticism.

Everyone experiences some or all of these negative influences at some point in his or her life. It is the child who by nature is particularly sensitive or who frequently or chronically experiences any one of the above that is likely to develop negative self-concept.

Perfectionism

The child tends to be extremely obedient and compliant, orderly, neat, and overly concerned with pleasing others.

He may become anxious and tense and concentrate so hard on achieving perfection that he becomes lost in detail and unproductive.

She is likely to set unrealistic standards that she can't reach. She will often feel frustrated and disappointed with even excellent performance.

A child whose world is unpredictable, chaotic, or dangerous may be trying to gain a sense of control and mastery of those circumstances by her perfectionistic behaviors.

A perfectionistic child frequently has perfectionistic parents.

Overcompetitiveness

The child may be so focused on being the best that he loses sight of the reason he is involved in the activity, class, or sport. He rigorously compares himself to others (many of whom are not his counterparts; they are older, stronger, or more experienced), and he feels satisfied only when he has gotten the highest batting average, test score, race time, etc.

He may have parents who themselves are extremely competitive and/or are living vicariously through the child (the overzealous Little League coach). This child's competitive nature may be an attempt to please his parent and receive acceptance or love.

The child may be so fearful or anxious of failing, of being second best, or of being criticized, that he will develop withdrawal symptoms (avoiding social situations, isolating himself in his room or home).

Separation and Dependency

Children who have grown accustomed to having all their needs met either with no effort on their part or by manipulating others may become overly dependent, making normal and necessary separations traumatic and difficult.

These children fail to develop confidence in themselves, their ideas, or their instincts. They feel unequipped to make decisions or solve problems.

A child who is constantly supervised and held to an excessively rule-oriented structure may be obedient but will become totally dependent on others and will not develop his own internal controls. Therefore he is not developing the skills he will need for increasing levels of independence.

SOLUTIONS

Low Self-Esteem

Help your child come to know and appreciate the skills, attributes, and positive traits that make him special and unique. "Personal power" builds self-esteem. Individuals who have the resources, capability, and opportunity to influence the circumstances of their lives experience this power or sense of control. (Recipes 49, 50, 55.1 through 55.14)

You can build your child's tolerance to criticism by gradually exposing her to sensitive and productive feed-back. This experience will enable her to learn to accept both positive and negative responses. (Recipes 53, 54, 55.15)

Children who are positively connected to friends and relatives will feel valued and validated in that they are needed, wanted, and when not present are missed. (Recipes 1, 2, 5, 67)

Children who are loved unconditionally will come to believe that it is they, not their performance, that is loved. (Recipes 49, 50, 55.1 through 55.14)

Perfectionism

Some children need permission and even **encouragement** to at times be independent, irresponsible, messy, and self-focused. (Recipes 53, 54)

Parents must help children find a healthy balance between striving for excellence or perfection and being unmotivated or uninterested in achievement. (Recipes 53, 54)

This child may feel she desperately needs these behaviors and can give them up only when her life stressors are alleviated. (Recipes 19, 64.8)

Take stock of your own tendency toward perfectionism—make this process one you can both benefit from.

Overcompetitiveness

Model good sportsmanship. Ask your child about more than winning or losing—ask about things such as social situations, friendships, and skills development. Talk about winning and losing; share your experiences and involve your child in discussion about hypothetical situations. (Recipes 53, 54, 55.15, 55.20)

Try to take an objective view of your own style of involvement in groups and sports. Be sure your own investment in your child's activities is not more than his.

Use **prepare, plan, prevent.** Help your child **prepare** equally for winning or losing. Emphasize progress, improvement, and advancement rather than best or worst (or winning and losing). (Recipes 53, 54, 55.15, 55.20)

Separation and Dependency

Children need to learn independence and the ability to separate through gradual steps beginning in early infancy. Show your children that they can depend on you and that you will be available to them when they need you. (Recipes 51, 52, 55.16, 55.17, 55.18, 55.19)

From an early age, encourage your child's independent thinking. Don't rush to his rescue if he has difficulty with the task, and be tolerant of imperfect results. Help him if he needs it, and emphasize your belief that he can do things on his own. Do not teach obedience at the expense of independent thinking. (Recipes 51, 52, 55.16, 55.17, 55.18, 55.19)

Practice age-appropriate problem solving with "what-if" games and discussions. Recognize and praise independent efforts and accomplishments; emphasize improvement and progress rather than results.

☆ *My Backpack of Skills* ☆

This recipe helps children recognize their positive skills, traits, and special attributes.

Step 1
State and define the problem

Approach this step of the recipe with caution. If you have turned to this chapter, you probably have a child who is very sensitive to criticism. Do not label low self-esteem as a problem. Let your child know that the real problem is that he doesn't realize how terrific he is. **Encourage** him to talk about his insecurities and self-doubts. Use **empathy** and **effective listening** throughout this recipe to get a clear understanding of what your child may be struggling with.

Step 2
Identify skills and solutions

In this recipe and the other recipes in this chapter, step 2 is very important. You are inviting your child and those who know him to focus on his abilities, skills, and positive traits. Your child's self-esteem will be greatly increased when he can acknowledge and respect the qualities and attributes that make him special and different. Refer to the Over 450 Skills, Talents, and Abilities list on page 265 in coming up with a list of fifty or more positive aspects regarding your child. Use **positive reframing** and **encouragement** to provide a safe and inviting environment for your child to explore her positive attributes and accomplishments. Write each and every positive statement on separate 3 × 5 cards. This is your child's deck of "positive cards." If she is unable to voice her strengths, **try, try again** and positively reframe any trait that proves she is special—like sparkly eyes, answers the phone nicely, says thank you.

Step 3
Mutually agree upon goals

Goal: "I will use my special skills to feel proud of myself, my accomplishments and my best qualities. To feel more confident in handling new challenges."

Step 4
Practice and play

Feeling special, confident, purposeful, and valued is essential to a child's well-being. This activity gives her the needed information about herself that will increase her insight into her positive and capable parts. You and your child will work together in making a skill pack (a backpack filled with positive statements).

First you will need a school backpack. Let your child pick out a backpack for this activity that appeals to her and makes her feel special. Next, collect all the 3 × 5 cards completed in step 2 and read through each "positive" one. Put the deck in the backpack and then have your child put on the pack. Explain that with this backpack she will feel more confident in dealing with her feelings about herself and in handling daily challenges. Also, she will remember all her terrific and special skills because the positive cards are "right behind her." Use **planful playing** and **role-play** common situations in which your child previously felt insecure. Have her reach into her backpack and pull out a few positive cards that will help her deal with insecurity.

For example, if your child has trouble meeting new people, role-play meeting a new person for the first time and **encourage** her to pick out socially related skills to help her feel more capable of handling the situation. These could be: smiles nicely, is a good listener, is fun to talk to. Add new cards to the deck daily to increase her awareness of her skills and abilities. Have your child put on her backpack whenever she is feeling bad about herself, needs a boost, or needs practice tackling a difficulty in her life. Let her know that even though she may not have the pack on, her positive skills are always with her.

Pour on praise whenever your child recognizes the positive in herself. Show your approval for her use of her positive skills. Point out times when she uses them without realizing it. Use this recipe with other recipes in this chapter to further improve his or her self-esteem.

Step 5
Review and recognize efforts

☆ *The Campaign Kid* ☆

RECIPE #50

Serves: 6–12 years

This recipe teaches children how to speak positively about themselves.

Step 1
State and define the problem

Talk with your child about his difficulties in speaking nicely about himself. Share with him your view of his perceived weaknesses and let him know that you would like to see him speak better about himself. Give him examples of when he is being overly critical and self-denigrating. Use **empathy** and **effective listening** to help him verbalize his self-doubts and insecurities.

Step 2
Identify skills and solutions

With your child, explore and make a list of all the special traits and skills he has that indicate he is a good and capable person. Stress occasions when he did a good job, succeeded in an activity, or preserved his self-esteem regardless of the results. **Model** for your child how to speak nicely about himself by sharing some of your own positive skills and special traits.

Step 3
Mutually agree upon goals

Goal: "I will use my special skills to improve my self-confidence and speak more positively about myself."

Step 4
Practice and play

Children with low self-esteem often have given up hope of succeeding and try to keep others from expecting anything from them. As a result, they always speak about themselves in a critical and demeaning fashion, see things from a pessimistic point of view, and often have a hard time accepting compliments or seeing the positive side of things. In this activity you will be playfully exposing your child to his capabilities and skills through a "campaign for kids." Start by explaining to your child what a campaign is. Explain how presidents have to campaign for the presidency so that they can share with people their skills and abilities to become a good president. Using **planful playing** and an abundance of creativity, have your child campaign for "Kid President," an imaginary president who makes important decisions regarding the welfare of children in the United States. You can become your child's campaign manager and help him or her to campaign for the Kid Presidency.

Using poster board, buttons, and banners, put together a campaign that highlights your child's capacities for being a good kid. Have members of your family chip in and think of nice things to say about your child. Write these comments on poster boards. Use the list made in step 2 to come up with as many skills and attributes as your child has. Stage a campaign rally. Put up the signs, stick on the buttons, and tape up the banners. Help him prepare his speech to deliver to his "supporters" (family members and friends), and make sure he knows all of his skills. In his speech have him highlight his skills and abilities for becoming a good Kid President. Take pictures of the event to remember the campaign day. Following his rally, vote your child into the Kid Presidency. Prepare an inauguration with a special dinner and a swearing-in. You may want to take this ego-boosting experience one step further and have your child write a letter to the real President of the United States expressing his desires and suggestions for helping children. You may even encourage him to sign his name and position: Local Kid President. (The address for the White House is: The President, The White House, Washington, D.C., 20500.) Remember, when a child is aware of his own actions and how they contribute to a positive outcome, he feels more powerful, self-assured, and able to make a difference.

Look through the pictures taken at the campaign and recall positive statements made about your child. Recognize and praise her ability to speak positively about herself and see herself as a good and capable kid.

Step 5
Review and recognize efforts

☆ *The Chain Gang* ☆

RECIPE #51

Serves: 3–8 years

This recipe helps young children separate from their parents.

Step 1
State and define the problem

Use **"I" messages** and **planful playing** (**role plays,** dolls, puppets) to explain and show your child how you feel about her inability to separate from you. Show that you **empathize** and respect her feelings, but her inability to separate from you is causing you a problem. **Effectively listen** to your child's point of view and encourage her to express her feelings and fears.

Step 2
Identify skills and solutions

Whether your child does not have the self-confidence to separate from you, or lacks the drive to be independent, **positively reframe** any behavior that shows she is capable of being away from you. Point out times when she plays by herself, goes to a grandparent's house, sleeps alone, or plays with a friend away from home. Have her think of any independent "by-herself" activities—brushing her teeth, eating, dressing, coloring, going to the bathroom—that would prove that she has the skills to do things on her own. Talk about decisions she made on her own and emphasize her ability to make positive choices. Make a list with your child of all these separation skills discussed.

Step 3
Mutually agree upon goals

Goal: "I will use my special skills to be able to separate from my parent or parents and become more independent."

Step 4
Practice and play

For a child to have a firm sense of independence, she needs to feel confident, capable, and connected to her family. Children who feel secure, loved, and cared for are less likely to be afraid when a parent leaves. Some children, however, do not want to be more independent, and would rather be treated like babies, constantly needing to be held, waited on, and demanding of adult attention. These children often learn to manipulate adults by being the "cutesy baby." This cuddly, clingy behavior is often unconsciously reinforced by parents who find it "adorable."

In this activity you will be sharing with your child that she is capable of separating from you. It also shows that even though you are apart, you are always connected. Remember those paper chains you made in grammar school out of different-colored construction paper? Get out your scissors, paste, and colored paper and put those dormant skills to use. Cut enough strips to make a six-to-ten-foot chain. Next, make a list (step 2) of all the independent, capable skills your child has for separating from you. Write or draw each of these "by-myself" skills on a strip of paper chain-link. Explain to your child that you are going to show her that she is capable of being away from you, but you will always think of her, love her, and be connected to her even though you may be apart.

Now stand next to your child, face to face, as close as possible. Take each strip of paper with the skills written or drawn on them and read them out loud one at a time. Paste the chain-link papers together to make your chain. Each time you make a few new links, have your child step back to make way for the growing chain of skills and independent abilities. Continue until the entire chain is finished. **Encourage** her to talk about the fact that she is very skilled ("Look at all these skills!") at being apart from you. Explain that just like the chain, when you are separated from each other, you are nevertheless very much connected.

Let your child take her chain with her when she goes to day care, school, or any place in which she must separate from you, as a firm reminder of how skillful she is at being independent. Add new links anytime either you or your child comes up with a new "by-myself" skill. Use an incentive program to reward your child (see chapter 17, "Just Desserts") for accumulating a specific number of links. In new, unknown situations, **plan** and **prevent** a dependency "attack" by providing your baby-sitter with a few distractions before you go out. These could be toys and games that your child especially enjoys. You can **prepare** your child for upcoming separations and new situations by visiting these places beforehand and discussing what's going to happen. **Spice up** goodbyes with family kisses-and-hugs rituals that playfully prepare your child for the separation. Before you leave her, always bring out the chain-link of skills to remind her of her ability to be separated from you.

Give her plenty of praise for her efforts to be more independent. Review the chain of independent skills regularly.

Step 5
Review and recognize efforts

☆ *Homesickness-Prevention Package* ☆

RECIPE #52
Serves: 3–10 years

This recipe will help children overcome their anxiety over separation from their parents.

Step 1
State and define the problem

Discuss with your child your perceptions of his insecurities about leaving you to spend the night at a friend's house or go to overnight camp. Using **"I" messages,** share your feelings about how you still love him and think about him when he is away from you, but that you believe that it is important he learn how to become more independent. **Empathy** and **effective listening** will help your child explore his feelings regarding separating. **Encourage** him to tell you what his fears are about leaving home.

Step 2
Identify skills and solutions

Highlight your child's skills and abilities to separate from you. Give examples of times when he or she successfully separated and had a good experience (**positive reframing**). Let your child know you believe he is capable of being more independent.

Step 3
Mutually agree upon goals

Goal: "I will use my special skills to feel brave and capable about leaving my parents, and to have a good time away from home."

Step 4
Practice and play

It is natural for a child to feel insecure away from home. However, when that insecurity becomes an "inability" to be away from parents, we prescribe the Homesickness-Prevention kit, which can help your child with the needed confidence to be apart from you.

Overnight Edition. To start, speak with a close relative or a good friend who will be willing to help you out with a few trial-run overnight adventures for your child. Next, you will need an old briefcase or knapsack to hold the items of his Homesickness-Prevention kit. With your child, pack the briefcase with items such as a wallet with pictures of his family, a familiar item from his bedroom (a stuffed animal, a toy, a pillowcase and pillow), a special surprise (a bedtime snack, a bedtime book), and an "I-can-do-it" list. This list is a combination of your child's skills for separating from you (see step 2) and activities (**distractions**) he can do to keep himself busy. Make this list with your child and help him think of a dozen or so fun activities (read a book, play a board game, have a pillow fight with a friend or relative). **Role-play** how he would take his I-can-do-it list out of his kit and choose an activity anytime he feels lonely for you.

Use **encouragement, positive reframing,** and **S.T.A.R.** to stop and think, "I'm safe, I'm okay," before giving up or crying for his parent or parents. Reassure your child before she sets out for her overnight adventure that you understand that she gets upset, but you know she can do it. You may want to build in added incentive by making plans to take her out for brunch the next morning after the sleepover.

176

The Camp Kit. Extended stays at overnight camp and week-long visits to Grandma's require a special Homesickness-Prevention kit. Along with the regular kit items mentioned in the overnight package, include these extra items:

1. A fun surprise that he can open each night that he is away. Kiss a piece of paper and leave your lip marks for him, give him a small toy or game that he can play with his friends at camp, or give him a joke book or a small box of snacks.

2. Include a small tape recorder so that he can record his daily happenings for you. Encourage him to make it funny and have his friends at camp join him in a few recordings. Before your child leaves, make a funny tape of all your family members saying their goodbyes and wishing him good luck at camp.

3. Make sure he has an extensive I-can-do-it list of activities that will last him for a week or two weeks during his extended separation. Be sure to mail him new items—pictures, cards, stickers, a new tape recording—to put in his kit. Prior to his camp vacation have a few practice "camp nights" over at a friend's or relative's house. Don't forget to give him his kit during his practice nights.

Praise and congratulate your child anytime he tries to separate from you. Even if he is not successful, let him know he can **try, try again** and that you know he can do it. Reassure him that you will always be there when he returns.

Step 5
Review and recognize efforts

177

☆ *The Thomas Edison Award* ☆

RECIPE # 5 3
Serves: 6–12 years

This recipe helps perfectionist children accept their mistakes and defeats.

Step 1
State and define the problem

Explain to your child that it seems she is always trying to be too perfect and has a hard time accepting errors and defeats. Share with her that you feel that while it is great that she tries so hard, being overly concerned with perfection will leave her little energy for being a kid. Use **modeling** and **role playing** to show that you make mistakes yourself— you are not perfect. **Empathy** and **effective listening** will come in handy when listening to your child's feelings about this problem.

Step 2
Identify skills and solutions

Begin this step by explaining to your child that she has many, many skills and abilities even if she doesn't do everything perfectly. Being able to accept oneself, regardless of weaknesses, is a skill. List your child's abilities to balance high expectations with tolerating mistakes. Whenever she makes a mistake, loses, or fails to be perfect, **positively reframe** these setbacks as skills. Focus on her **try, try again** attitude.

Step 3
Mutually agree upon goals

Goal: "I will use my special skills to accept my mistakes—because nobody is perfect."

Step 4
Practice and play

There is so little in life that is perfect, so a perfectionist child is frequently frustrated, disappointed, critical, and judgmental of herself. This creates stress and low self-worth. A child who is constantly looking for something wrong finds it of course and feels like a failure. If your child cannot deal with setbacks and throws in the towel, stating, "I'm a loser," it is time to activate the Thomas Edison Award activity.

Begin by telling your child that Thomas Edison made two thousand mistakes before he was successful in inventing the light bulb. Ask her what would have happened if Edison had viewed himself as a failure and given up. We would all be in the dark! Next, buy a trophy from a local engraving shop. It will need to be the type with a hollow gold cup. Explain to your child that every time she accepts her mistakes, **tries, tries again,** and does her best to accept herself, she gets a chip or a marble placed in the gold cup. When the chips or marbles reach the top of the cup she gets the trophy. Engrave the trophy with her name on it and also the Thomas Edison "I'm not perfect and that's okay award." Give her a chip or marble for doing any of the skills on the list created in step 2.

Positively reframe any action your child takes toward accepting herself, her mistakes, or her imperfections. **Model** and show your mistakes and point them out to her. Tell her she can still be a **S.T.A.R.** if she says to herself **"R.A.T.S.",** Reviews her Actions and Tries Some more.

These empowering and positive responses to your child will help her realize that she is valuable and wonderful no matter what she does.

Pour on the **spices, love, and affection** anytime she makes a mistake. If your child wins her trophy for making dozens of mistakes and for **trying again,** have a small celebration. If she has difficulty losing, give her marbles for good sportsmanship and handling the loss maturely. Encourage her to vent her frustrations about the defeat but to see that losing does not mean she is a loser. Give her extra chips for occasions on which she focuses on improving of a skill rather than on winning. Most important, communicate to your child that when people accept and learn from their mistakes, just like Thomas Edison, they gain competence and wisdom. This activity will inevitably end in success, so no matter how long it takes to fill the gold cup, your child will be a winner.

It is imperative that your child's expectations of herself be based on realistic standards. Concentrate not on success, but on perseverance, effort, and commitment as the real accomplishments. Show her she is perfect to you simply because she is a great kid.

Step 5
Review and recognize efforts

☆ Detective "R.A.T.S." ☆
(The Imperfection Detective)

RECIPE #54

Serves: 3–9 years

This recipe teaches children that nobody is perfect or wins all the time and that's okay.

Step 1
State and define the problem

There is no realistic way to shield your child from competition—the attitude that winning, being the best, is good, and losing and making mistakes is bad. However, if you think your child's self-esteem is being damaged because his perfectionism is pushing him toward unrealistic goals, it is time for a recipe. Use **"I" messages** to express your views on the problem, and stress your love and unconditional acceptance of him no matter if he loses or makes mistakes. **Empathize** and use **effective listening** to hear your child's concerns regarding this problem.

Step 2
Identify skills and solutions

If your child tends to view himself as not being good enough, he needs to be shown how to accept the gray areas in life into which all of us fall. Use **planful playing** to point out his skills; **role playing** when he has made a mistake and accepted his losses. Make a list of these "Oh, well, I'm not perfect" behaviors and be sure to point out a few of your own imperfections (**modeling**).

Step 3
Mutually agree upon goals

Goal: "I will use my special skills to learn that I'm not perfect and I don't always have to win and that's okay!"

Step 4
Practice and play

"Do your best!" is a famous and enduring statement that should be said to children at least a hundred times a year. But when that statement becomes "Be the best" or "You are nothing unless you are the best," you can be sure a child's self-esteem will suffer. This activity will help your child accept his humanness, laugh at his mistakes, learn lessons from them, and learn to lose with pride. Use planful playing to entice your child into participating in this recipe by making a fun detective outfit including hat, badge, pad or paper, magnifying glass, and London Raincoat. Explain that he is officially the Imperfection Detective, and his name is Detective **R.A.T.S.** He is officially in charge of investigating all the mistakes, games that are lost, and imperfections that exist in the family.

First teach him what **S.T.A.R.** and R.A.T.S. mean (see page 29). Next let him know that it is his job to write down the mistakes and imperfections that he notices in his family. Of course, your child can be a private detective and sneak around the home looking for everyone's mistakes. Encourage him to write down his own mistakes. It is very important that you **model** correct ways to handle mistakes and games that are lost. At the end of the day, ask the detective to report to the family all the mistakes people made and how they handled them.

Draw the conclusion that everyone makes mistakes and that no one wins every time; no one is perfect. Encourage your child to keep a daily record of his mistakes and to note whether or not he was able to say, "I guess I'm not perfect, and that's okay."

Acknowledge your child's ability to observe the flaws that exist in others and himself and to deal with the realization that he himself isn't perfect. Share with him your delight in his ability to always **try, try, again,** and comment on his efforts just to be happy and proud of himself.

Step 5
Review and recognize efforts

☆ *Planful Playing in a Pinch* ☆

RECIPE #55

Hot tips and quick recipes for increasing your child's self-esteem.

55.1   *T-Shirt Talents.* With your child draw and write on a T-shirt with fabric paints his special qualities and unique skills. Make one for your child and one for yourself.

55.2   *Little Memos.* Write on Post-It notes little messages that say what is terrific about your child. Leave them all over the house, preferably in funny places. Have your child collect them and stick them in new places for her parent or parents to find. See how many messages your child can remember by recalling the statements at the end of the day.

55.3   *Fortune Cookies.* Buy fortune cookies and with a tweezer take out the slips of paper inside. On new slips of paper, and with the help of your child, write down all the good fortune he has had, his skills and good qualities, and his potential talents. A fortune cookie message might say, "I am a great kid and I know how to make people laugh with my jokes." Review the cookie statements with your child on a daily basis and read out loud what the slips of paper say.

55.4   *Button Boasting.* Make a few buttons that contain your child's picture and a brief statement of what people like about him. Be sure that your child comes up with one or two himself. Wear the buttons and have your child wear one as well. Give them to relatives.

55.5   *King/Queen for the Day.* Make your child a crown and announce that he or she is king or queen for the day. Treat your child like royalty and cater to her needs. At the end of the day have the family gather around the throne and let the king or queen know why he or she is the best in the land. Have your child announce what makes her special, a good king or queen, or just a great person. Be silly—bow to them every time they grace you with their presence.

55.6   *Sweet and Neat.* Bake a cake with your child and let him know that it is as sweet as he is. With each ingredient name a skill, personality trait, or accomplishment. Have your child label a few ingredients with comments on what he thinks is special about himself. The more the ingredients the cake has, the more positive traits you can acknowledge. Let your child decorate the cake with something that is representative of his or her sweetness.

55.7   *Front Page Headlines.* Draw and illustrate or use a computer and design the front page of a newspaper. Make the headline an announcement of something terrific about your child, and have her help you write a story about what makes her so great. Project into the future and date the newspaper five, ten, or twenty years from now. Announce a great event in her life. If you like, write a short article to go with the headline.

Business Cards. With your child order business cards containing his name and six to eight terrific things he can do. Give the cards to friends and family as little reminders of what makes him special.

55.8

Valentines. Valentine's day does not have to fall only on February 14. A few days after, buy some cards at a discount. Save the cards for a once-monthly Valentine message of love to your child. You may want to include a little chocolate heart and a brief note expressing your feelings and your thoughts about why he or she is lovable.

55.9

My Long, Long List of Likables. Begin this activity immediately and continue it throughout your child's growing-up years. Using a roll of paper, start writing everything you like and love about your child. Have your child write as many things as she can come up with that she likes about herself. Number each one and keep this list growing through the years. One family we know has been doing this for seven years. They last reported that their child's list of likables is sixty-nine feet long and contains over 2,500 likables!

55.10

Mirror, Mirror on the Wall. . . . Locate a wall mirror with at least a one-to-two-inch frame. Have your child paint the frame of the mirror with symbols and words that state why she is "the fairest of them all." Help her to come up with as many possible reasons for being special.

55.11

The Great Kids Convention. This activity not only gives you the opportunity to build your child's self-concept, but spreads positive self-esteem throughout your child's social group. Invite friends and family to a special party called The Great Kids Convention. Decorate the party room with banners and balloons that use self-boosting statements like "We are GREAT"—"The Best!" Each of the kids who is invited should be asked to bring something he or she is good at to show off at the party. Plan activities at the party that include fun ideas in this chapter such as The Long, Long List of Likables, Fortune Cookies, and T-shirt Talents. Give awards at the end of the party to each child attending.

55.12

Big News. Insert a short notice—two to five lines will do—about your child's recent accomplishments in your local newspaper. Some newspapers let you include a snapshot of your child. Make it a surprise.

55.13

A Special Roast. Send out the invitations, call up the relatives—you're going to have a roast. No, not a meat dish, an honorary roast. Prepare and plan a special day or evening for your child in which he will be honored for his achievements, accomplishments, and overall wonderfulness. Ask special friends and family members to attend this festive event and ask each person to think of something special to say about your child. All negatives are left at the front door! Serve a meal. Invite your child to sit at the head of the table. Then, one by one, each guest and

55.14

183

family member makes a positive speech about her. Take pictures and give her a plaque (purchased or homemade) to recognize this day. Encourage your child to say a few words at the end of the event and to thank the guests. Using the photographs taken at the roast, make a scrapbook and write in the highlights of the evening. Be sure to mention the nice things that were said about him. Take out the scrapbook anytime your child needs a little "roast reminder" to improve his self-image.

PERFECTIONISTIC

55.15   *Yea, You Lost!* Losing a big game or competition can be celebrated with a full-blown party. Depending on your child's emotional investment in the defeat, make the party a simple family restaurant celebration or a large barbecue in his or her honor. Talk about your child's skills and how he played the game well. Avoid mentioning who won or lost. Celebrate sportsmanship and the ability to lose gracefully.

SEPARATION

55.16   *By-Myself Bag.* Fill a bag with games, books, and toys that your child enjoys on his own. Whenever he needs to separate from you, suggest he go get his By-Myself Bag and remind him of how great he is at doing things all by himself. The items in the bag will surely help distract him from the obvious separation that is taking place.

55.17   *The Home Alone Briefcase.* Older children sometimes have a hard time coming home to an empty house or being left for a few hours while a parent runs errands. This problem can be alleviated if you give your child a briefcase with items that will help him feel safe and a list of fun activities to do while waiting for a parent to return. The contents of the briefcase should include a list of important phone numbers, a first-aid kit (for older children), a book on safety and independence such as *Playing It Smart,* by Tova Navarra (Barron's, 1989), and special activity items like game books, a video your child can pop into the machine, and a list of other activities that your child can do during this time. You may want to put a snack in the briefcase, or a note letting your child know what goodies are available in the refrigerator.

55.18   *Homesickness-Prevention Postcards and Messages.* This quick tip will help your child deal successfully with an extended separation at camp or with relatives. Prior to your child leaving the home, write postcards to her with fun messages on them and mail to where she is going so that they are there when she arrives. Another idea is to pick a time during the day called "Time for Rhyme." Explain to your child that at a certain time each day you will say this little rhyme and so will she. For example, every day at eleven in the morning, you will say to yourself, "Even though Emily is away, she is having a great day." She will recite the same rhyme at the identical hour.

Love Pillows. For a very young child who needs to separate from parents every day to day care or for extended stays with relatives, make a special heart pillow that contains a picture of her and her family. Use red felt to make a small pillow (6 inches across). Cut two pieces of the material into the shape of a heart, sew it together, and stuff it. On the front of the heart sew on a pocket that could accommodate a photo of your entire family. Your child can then take his special Love Pillow with him to help ease the separation. You may want to make one for yourself that contains your child's picture to show him that you think of him during the day, too.

55.19

OVERLY COMPETITIVE

Noncompetitive Games and Books. The following books contain terrific ideas for encouraging cooperative game-playing between children while steering away from competition: *Everyone Wins! Cooperative Games and Activities,* by Sambhaua and Josette Luvmour (New Society Publishers, 1990); *The Cooperative Sports and Games Book,* by Terry Orlick (Pantheon Books, 1978); and *New Games for the Whole Family,* by Dale N. LeFevre (Perigee, 1988). These books highlight noncompetitive games and activities your child can play to have fun, without emphasizing winning.

55.20

The following games reinforce cooperation while avoiding competition: "Mountaineering," "Harvest Times," "The Secret Door," "Investigators," "Outburst, Jr." "Sleeping Grump," "Funny Face," and "Kids on Stage." (They can be ordered from a catalog called *Childswork, Childsplay;* for ordering instructions see page 268; see page 258 for a list of reading recipes for self-concept problems.)

Recipe #58: All Tied Up for the Moment

CHAPTER 13

Sibling Conflict

IN THIS CORNER IS Teddy, who is happily lost in play with his brother Charlie's favorite toy. In this corner is Charlie, who, like a lion protecting his young, is ready to pounce on his brother for playing with his toy. Seconds later a scuffle begins. Cries of agony and pain are heard by the ever-alert ears of Mom and Dad, who as usual must referee the fight and separate the tearful combatants.

Fighting

Sharing a Room

New Sibling

If you have chosen to read this section, this scene must be a familiar one. Despite what you may think, you are not alone. Parents have frequently reported to us that this is one of the worst ongoing problems in their family.

Sibling battles are a normal experience for every family, for fighting and arguing are the natural results of conflict, which itself is a normal component of social development. Conflict-resolution skills are not something that we are born with, nor are they taught in school. But this is not to say that fighting is desirable or that any sane parent should have to settle for living in a war zone.

This challenging problem can be a great opportunity for children to practice the social skills necessary for resolving conflict within relationships. The development of these social skills will not only make your home a more peaceful place to live, but will be useful to your child throughout his or her life. We believe that if parents can reteach their children to recognize the value of their sibling relationships and to develop better problem-solving and communication skills, their children will enjoy each other's company far more.

The recipe solutions are designed to help your family resolve sibling conflict by providing situations in which you and your children can work together toward common and rewarding goals. These activities will empower your children to respond in new ways to old and familiar situations.

The family constellation (first-born . . . second-born) and family role definition (the brains in the family . . . the athlete) establish relationship patterns that may lead to conflict. Each family member needs to validate his or her position. This is often done through dominance (first-born over second-born) and definition of self ("I'm smarter than you").

Fights are often over possessions and ownership of those possessions. Although this is normal, and a common way for children to gain approval or control, it creates an environment in which siblings compete for a position of power.

Undesirable and/or favorable comparisons are made between children, resulting in competition between brothers and sisters for the attention of the parents or parent and for the "Mommy (or Daddy) likes me better" position in the family.

When conflicts and fights between any two family members are not appropriately resolved, children copy similar behaviors and do not learn problem-solving skills. The lack of co-operation, compromise, democracy, and **mutual respect** within the family as a whole creates an environment in which siblings cannot cooperate, compromise, be democratic, or mutually respect each other.

A family style that takes sides or ignores each other's feelings and thoughts teaches siblings to encourage their parents or parent to choose a side in every quarrel. This reduces the opportunity for children to work out their own difficulties and practice their skills in conflict resolution.

Sibling conflict is usually caused by the basic need of children to get as much attention from a parent as possible. When that attention must be shared with brother or sister, you can assume that there will almost always be some conflict involved.

A new baby creates new family structures and alignments and diverts attention from existing children, thus adding causes of conflict.

Remember that sibling battles are a normal part of family life. However, you can reduce the amount of fighting and discord between your children and help them develop conflict-resolutions skills.

Actively support, **model,** and use the problem-solving skills contained in this book along with your children and with your mate. (Recipes 15, 58)

Create a home environment in which family members **empathize, encourage** and **mutually respect** each other. (Recipes 47, 48.1, 48.3, 48.4, 48.6, 48.8, 48.9)

If your children are in the midst of petty bickering or an argument, do your best to **ignore** it and walk away. Let them have as many opportunities as possible to work out conflicts on their own. It is good practice and experience in conflict resolution. (Recipes 18.1, 18.2, 18.3, 57, 58, 59)

If a fight persists and adult intervention is needed, **effectively listen** to each child's point of view by acknowledging his or her feelings and describing the problem as he or she sees it. Use **"I" messages** to share your feelings regarding the problem, then express your belief in your children's ability to come to a solution on their own. (Recipes 15, 18.2, 18.3, 58)

If the fighting becomes dangerous, use **think chairs** (one for each child) and immediately separate the combatants. Give them the time to cool down and think through their feelings before requiring them to find a compromise or solution to the problem.

Try to avoid *all* comparisons between your children, whether the comparisons are favorable or unfavorable ("Johnny did great in baseball, maybe you can do as well as he did!"). Instead, highlight each child's unique self ("You're a fast runner—I bet you'll do fine on the baseball team"). (Recipe 60.3)

Focus on giving equal amounts of love and time according to each child's individual needs and unique reasons for being lovable. (Recipes 1, 2, 5)

Help your children learn to work through this normal occurrence in family relationships by creating an environment in which communication, compromise, and cooperation prevail. (Recipe 56; see also Family Council, page 19)

Listen to all of your children's feelings, opinions, and thoughts without taking sides. (Recipes 18.2, 18.3; see also Effective Listening, page 17)

One of the main objectives is to decrease sibling fighting by lessening the need for children to compete for your attention or compete with each other. (Recipes 57, 60.2, 60.3)

Children often lose sight of their special place in your affections when a new baby joins the family. Take the time to pay extra attention to the "seasoned" family member(s). (Recipe 56)

Also always take the time to notice positive interactions between your kids and to highlight their abilities to do things nicely with each other. Reminisce over good times and point out fun times ahead. (Recipes 1, 2, 5, 56, 57, 58, 59, 60)

☆ *Big Brother College* ☆

This recipe helps prepare a child for the arrival of a new sibling.

Step 1
State and define the problem

Use this step to talk about the arrival of the new baby. Involve your child as much as possible in the discussion of this change in his or her life. Be **empathic** and respect your child's feelings about this new addition to his family.

Step 2
Identify skills and solutions

Identify skills that your child has that show he is capable of handling changes. Point out times when he tried something new and was successful. Impress him with all the times he played with a friend or sibling, or shared something even though it meant not always getting his way. Praise his ability to share, to give to others, to be nice, or to care for pets and younger friends. Tell him these are all terrific ways to be Big Brother.

Step 3
Mutually agree upon goals

Goal: "I will use my special skills to learn how to be a good Big Brother/ Sister."

Step 4
Practice and play

With the arrival of a new baby, your child's world will change. If he is the only child, he will no longer be the center of attention. If there is already more than one child in your family at the very least the attention will need to be spread thinner. We suggest The Big Brother College as a fun way to help prepare your child for the new baby and make the transition easier. Let your child know that he has the potential of being a terrific and needed Big Brother because he has so many Big Brother skills (step 2). Explain that you are going to help him become an extra-special Big Brother by sending him to Big Brother College. (Of course, tell him that this is just for fun, and that he will be learning how to use his skill to his fullest potential.) Classes begin with prenatal education, and, for "inquisitive children," explanations of how babies are made. Terrific books to consider for "college" readings are: *A Baby for Max,* by Kathryn Lasky (Macmillan, 1984), *Getting Ready for New Baby,* by Harriet Ziefert (HarperCollins, 1990), *Making Babies,* by Sarah Stein (Walker, 1974), and *A Child Is Born,* by Lennart Nilsson (Dell, 1977).

Taking your child on a trip to the doctor to listen to the baby's heartbeat and going to the hospital to see the newborn babies are all a part of her "education." Encourage your child to talk about her fears and feelings regarding the baby at any stage of the education process.

Have your child help you design the nursery, put the crib together, and buy baby toys. Talk about new names for the baby and encourage your child to come up with one or two. A month or two before the baby arrives, buy your child a newborn doll and have him learn how to hold, feed, change, and play with it. Pour on the praise and compliment his abilities. When he has completed his education at Big Brother College, have a graduation party. Invite relatives and friends and make or buy congratulation cards. Give him a small gift for successfully learning how to be a good Big Brother. We suggest giving the party after the birth of the baby. Although it is a busy time, having a party might give your child much-needed attention.

At the graduation party, recognize your child's accomplishments and skills. A certificate with his name on it and a statement saying that he is a terrific brother might remind him on a daily basis that he is still very special and valuable. Have him hang it on his door.

Step 5
Review and recognize efforts

191

☆ *The Red Tag/Green Tag Game* ☆

RECIPE #57
Serves: 3–10 years

This recipe teaches siblings to focus on getting along with each other and helps solve the problem of constant sibling bickering.

Step 1
State and define the problem

Discuss and describe what each family member thinks is the cause of battles between the children. **Encourage** your children to use their favorite mode of communication (talking, drawing, acting it out). Each individual should express his or her perceptions and listen carefully to others. Use **modeling** for your children to help them learn appropriate interactions with each other by **effective listening** and using **"I" messages.** Use **mutual respect** and **empathy** to help your children understand other points of view. Use **the Five C's** to establish clear rules about ways brothers and sisters should act in your family.

Step 2
Identify skills and solutions

In coping with sibling quarrels, identify your children's skills and special abilities. For this exercise it would be helpful to point out to your children the positive aspects of their relationship: times when they play well together, share toys, and participate in activities that they enjoy equally. Make a list of these "together" skills and show your pleasure in their ability to get along.

Step 3
Mutually agree upon goals

Goal: "I will use my special skills to have more fun and to get along better with my brother (or sister)."

Step 4
Practice and play

Sibling rivalry can be influenced by a number of factors, including personality differences, jealousy, and close quarters. However, that does not mean that the matter is so complicated that you can't help your children learn to get along with each other and form stronger, more positive bonds.

This activity will automatically engage you in several parenting ingredients: **ignoring, distraction, positive reframing, your choice,** and **natural** and **logical consequences.** By playing this game you will **ignore** petty squabbles and silly arguments, teaching and redirecting your children to focus on positive aspects of their relationship and leaving them the control to choose the outcome—all while having fun!

Your goal in planning this game is to "catch" your children being cooperative and good to each other. The game is played with all family members. You will need a small, empty box and red-and-green construction paper, cut into small tags or pieces. The game is played for one week. All family members need to decide on a reward or shared activity that they would like to have or do if they are successful at the game. The green tags indicate every time your children interact without fighting, or do something positive for or with each other. The red tags indicate every time they do fight. These tags are put into a box, and at the end of the week, if there are more green tags than red tags, your family can enjoy its special reward or activity. If there are more reds than greens, there is no activity or reward. Green tags can be given when your children play nicely together, follow through on their not-fighting goals, stop a fight in progress, do something special for each other, and/or simply sit next to each other nicely on the couch. Use humor and give green tags for times when the children just laugh together. See the list of positive skills in step 2 to reassure your kids that they have the ability to get along.

Tell your children that you don't need to witness behavior that deserves a green tag. They can tell you about the positive situation and still receive their green tag. **S.T.A.R.** helps children to stop and think before getting a red.

Summarize your family's progress and future needs. Be sure to recognize efforts and accomplishments your children have made in reaching their goals. Continue this game on a weekly basis as needed and always **try, try again** if they didn't reach their goal.

Step 5
Review and recognize efforts

☆ *All Tied Up for the Moment* ☆

RECIPE # 5 8
Serves: 5–12 years

This recipe teaches children how to negotiate and get along with their brothers and sisters.

Step 1
State and define the problem

Have a **family council** meeting. Be sure to reinforce all the rules so that fighting does not erupt in the course of discussing the fighting problem. Explain your perceptions of the problem of lack of cooperation and negotiation between siblings. This is your chance to explore your feelings with your children on how their constant squabbling affects you. Equally, your children have a chance to describe to you what their perceptions of the problem are.

Step 2
Identify skills and solutions

List positive traits and your children's strengths when it comes to compromising with others and postponing fights. Focus on each individual's ability to cooperate and negotiate fairly. You may want to use specific situations in which you observed your children using these skills. **Role-play** these situations and point out the skills used in compromising.

Step 3
Mutually agree upon goals

Goal: "I will use my special skills to be able to get along better with my brother or sister."

Step 4
Practice and play

Decisions like who sits in the front seat or which television show to watch can result in major family battles. Teaching children to settle their differences through compromise and negotiation is a very difficult task. However, it can be done.

The Friday Fights, or Nightlife Negotiations. Conflict within the family is healthy and normal, and the need to "fight" in families should be acknowledged. However, you must fight fairly. This solution activity will teach your children how to interrupt the fury of the moment and put conflict aside for future resolution. This reinforces the **S.T.A.R.** technique because it encourages your children to stop and think before acting. The skill of postponing conflict for future resolution is the first step in learning how to problem-solve. Kids need help in learning how to gather up their anger, frustrations, and disappointments and channel them appropriately into problem-solving discussions. With this in mind, designate Friday evenings as the time when family "fighting" (in reality family negotiation) is allowed. Pop some popcorn and make a family event out of going to see the "fight"—negotiations. Remind your children throughout the week about the Friday Family Fight rule every time they begin to go at each other. On Friday night, set aside the time to give your kids permission to talk about what upset them earlier in the week. **The Five C's** can be used to help them set up their own rules for settling disagreements. Being available at the Friday Night Fight gives you the opportunity to **encourage** appropriate problem-solving behaviors and begins the process of solving through negotiation.

All Tied Up for the Moment. This experience will help teach your children to negotiate through a task in the very close (literally) presence of a brother or sister.

Have your children stand side by side. With bandannas, gently tie together the ankles and knees of the inside legs and their touching elbows. Give each child separate chores such as watering the plants or collecting all the pillows in the house. However, emphasize the need to accomplish a chore before receiving a reward. Without any guidance, let your children try to perform these tasks and work out this humorous situation. There is "bound" to be some conflict as to who does what and how: the **logical consequence** of not negotiating with each other. The differences that arise will allow the children to practice using their "identified" skills in negotiation and compromise. We suggest videotaping this event for future viewing. Not only will your kids get a good laugh watching themselves stumbling around, but they will be able to evaluate their skills in compromise and negotiation. You may want to join the fun and tie yourself to either your child or your mate. This will let you **model** for your children how to get chores done through cooperation. This experience teaches **mutual respect** because it gives your children a vivid, hands-on sense of being in someone else's situation.

Evaluate your family's progress and encourage your children to examine the goals that they have reached. Let your children know what their accomplishments were and how they can apply those skills to everyday living. This activity is a springboard to more complicated problem-solving skills. If your child can negotiate, problem-solve, and compromise at home, she can probably do it anywhere.

Step 5
Review and recognize efforts

195

☆ *Designer Room Activity* ☆

RECIPE #59
Serves: 4–12 years

This recipe helps children learn the basic skills of getting along, sharing a room, and making a special place of their own.

Step 1
State and define the problem

Have your children describe for the family how sharing a room is a problem for them. **Model** for them through **role plays** how to use **"I" messages** and **effective listening** when a roommate problem is being discussed. In describing your children's difficulty in sharing a room, be sure to inquire into their understanding of the problem. Identify (**empathy**) with your children—show them that you realize that sharing a room is tough for anyone, so it's not unreasonable that sometimes they can't cope.

Step 2
Identify skills and solutions

Describe and identify your children's individual skills and strengths that could help in solving this problem. Sharing toys with friends and being sensitive to other's feelings are good examples of skills that help in room sharing. Clearly indicate to your children the skills they have in being able to recognize when others want to be left alone or have some privacy. Explain or give examples of privacy skills and how your children can use them. (See Planful Playing, Privacy Time, page 226.)

Step 3
Mutually agree upon goals

Goal: "I will use my special skills to share my room peacefully and respect my sister's (brother's) privacy."

Step 4
Practice and play

This activity can be applied to problems arising from children sharing a room. Bedrooms are a major battleground for children. Trying to share a restricted area is one of the most difficult tasks children are presented with. One way to relieve the tension is to give your children the opportunity to redecorate their room together. Let them move furniture around or even make major changes such as buying new furniture, wallpapering, or putting on a fresh coat of paint. These projects should be discussed beforehand. Floor plans, a choice of paint color, or new curtains need to be decided on together. A fun activity for younger children is to redecorate their room by covering the walls with their hand and foot prints, using *nontoxic* paint in the colors of their choice. Before they start work on this special room, remind them that everyone, including adults, needs a place of refuge and privacy. Your children need to understand that their privacy has to be respected and so does the privacy of others.

Have your children designate a private space in their designer room. They can do whatever they please to make this space theirs. It is important that it be off-limits to others. It should be the exclusive refuge of the child to whom it belongs. Encourage your children to go to their special place if they need some space. Do *not* use this space as a go-to-your-room punishment. Keep it positive.

It is important to formalize this activity with lots of negotiating and problem-solving instruction. This is a fun and helpful activity that will encourage your children to communicate and to work through their room-sharing problems by making a special room of their own.

Evaluate and determine your children's progress in reaching their goal of solving room-sharing problems and respecting the privacy of others. Your children's success will result not only in coming up with new ways of working out their problems, but a great deal of satisfaction in working together to redecorate their room. If your kids couldn't complete this activity, start from the beginning and make the task more simple—perhaps a new poster or two. Always remember to **try, try again** and show faith in their ability to use their skills and solve their problems.

Step 5
Review and recognize efforts

☆ *Planful Playing in a Pinch* ☆

Hot tips and quick recipes for solving sibling conflict.

60.1   *Famous Siblings.* This exciting and educating activity will encourage your children to develop respect for their sibling relationship. Have your children research famous siblings of our past—the Wright brothers, for example. Be creative when researching these famous successful siblings— you could take a family trip to a local airport, air show or aviation museum to elaborate on the Wright brothers' accomplishments. Talk about how they had to work together to be as successful as they were. Point out their skills and compare them to those of your children who might see many similarities. Next, have your children write a short article together. Date it twenty or more years into the future. It should list some things that your kids are going to be famous for. Include headlines: CHARLIE AND DONNA DISCOVER CURE FOR HANGNAILS: GET NOBEL PRIZE or JOE AND BILLY SAVE THE DAY AT SUPER BOWL CLIFFHANGER. Use **positive reframing** and **encouragement** after doing the activity when you see your children do something nice together. Say, "Wow, you guys did that just like the Wright brothers!"

60.2   *Cooperate Games and Books.* See page 268 for suggestions of activity books and/or the games which emphasize noncompetitive fun and reinforce cooperation skills. Urge your children to play these types of games rather than choosing more competitive ones. Parents may want to join their kids in their cooperative activities. You can then **model, encourage,** and promote the spirit of family cooperation.

60.3   *We're Crazy About You Because . . . T-Shirts.* This activity is based on the fact that children must understand that they are loved and seen as equal and special, regardless of the skills or good qualities of their brothers or sisters.

     For this activity you will need a plain T-shirt for each child and a fabric crayon. Have your children put on the T-shirts and stand next to each other. Explain that you are crazy about each one of them for separate and unique reasons. *Important:* Do not compare these qualities—just enumerate them. Write or draw pictures of these attributes directly on their T-shirts. Have your children join in and write on their sister's or brother's T-shirt the qualities they like best. When each shirt is covered with as many compliments as you and your kids can think of, have them model their Crazy About You T-shirts for the family and read off why their family loves them. Hang the shirts on the wall as reminders. Use this in future situations when one of your children demands to know whom you love more, him or Brother or Sis. You love each for who they are.

60.4   *Sibling Holiday.* Three to four times a year mark a day on the calendar that designates it as National Brother and Sister Day. Spend the day talking about special times together, instances of considerate, loving behavior toward each other, and why they appreciate each other. Come up with an activity or an outing that all your children will enjoy, and make this a sibling holiday event. Hang out your sibling flag (see below) in front of your home.

Sibling Flag. Make a brother-and-sister flag specially designed by your children. Let them know that this flag is in honor of their unique relationship. Have them work together on the flag, using a large piece of fabric, fabric paint, and a wooden pole. Hang your flag out proudly to let your neighborhood know how terrific the brothers and sisters are in your home. *60.5*

Sibling Secrets. Encourage your kids to plan surprises and secrets together. Surprise Dad with a "we-love-you breakfast." Give them a few dollars to buy a gift together for a mutual friend or relative. Have them make the gift card together. Show them how to make up secret words and handshakes that only they know. These activities will help your children learn to enjoy and have fun with each other. *60.6*

(See page 259 for a list of reading recipes for solving sibling conflict.)

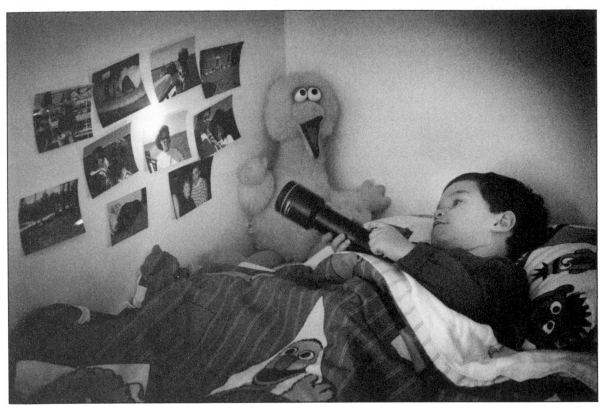

Recipe #61: Good Night Door, Good Night Ceiling

CHAPTER 14

Sleep Problems

IT'S THE MIDDLE OF the night, and for some reason you can't get comfortable in bed. You realize that you are balancing at the edge of your bed on one elbow. You open your eyes and sit up. Your arm tingles and your neck aches as you focus on your four-year-old, happily sprawled out in a blissful sleep in what was previously your space.

You consider your dilemma and weigh your options. Do you wake the little angel and chance no sleep or do you lie down on your precarious perch and settle for a neck ache? Just yesterday you told yourself, "No more. Next time he's going back to his bed." But oh, the trouble that causes, the tears and the tantrums. You know he can't help it, he really is so afraid. What's a parent to do?

Sleep-related problems are some of the most commonly reported by parents to us. Nearly one third of all children suffer from them at one time or another. Sleeping well does not necessarily come naturally or easily to everyone; for many it is a skill refined over years of practice. Worse, parents are often shocked to find out that their child's sleep problems don't necessarily end at infancy.

Children need regular, restful sleep not only for optimal physical functioning and growth, both also for their psychological well-being. Furthermore, they need to sleep well so their parents can.

A sleep problem can be defined as any difficulty that interferes with your sleep or your child's. The organizing themes to this chapter are all the *associations* that surround going to sleep, such as the setting, timing, sleep aids, routines, and persons involved. Your goal is threefold: to become acquainted with your child's sleep associations, (2) together with him to develop a plan tailored to his specific problems and needs, (3) to support his replacement of dysfunctional sleep habits and associations with new, mutually satisfying ones.

Going to Bed

Fact: One third of all children experience sleep-related problems. These difficulties are a normal reaction, the expression of a multitude of challenges children face. Many of these problems are caused by negative associations with bedtime and sleep.

Many children's sleep-related problems are caused by specific fears such as fear of the dark, fear of separation from parents, and fear of dying or not waking.

Fear of the dark may increase with age (through the elementary years) as your child develops greater imagination and awareness of the potential dangers in the world.

Some children are painfully lonely by themselves and crave the reassuring feeling they get from the company of a parent or parents.

Children who become excessively worried about life's problems and dangers find being alone in bed an uncomfortable and even frightening experience.

Very young children and those who tend to become easily overstimulated have difficulty making the transition from daytime and early-evening activities to bedtime because they don't have the internal mechanism that enables them to wind down, to relax physically and mentally.

Sleep patterns vary from child to child and from year to year. Just when you think your child has reached a peaceful and consistent pattern that you can identify, it may change.

Nightmares

Nightmares and restless sleep may be caused by unresolved internal conflicts pertaining to stressful life events, such as a test, a fight with a friend, divorce, or parental discord. Conflicts such as these are often repressed during the waking hours but emerge as frightening dreams when your child's defenses are lowered during sleep.

Early or Late Wakening

Children who wake too early cause problems for their siblings and parents. They tend to wake up others, get into mischief, and become tired and irritable early into the day.

Children who have difficulty awakening are often grouchy, combative, and late in morning routines. Their behavior throws off family schedules, causes stress for everyone, and in general is a bad way to begin a day.

202

Going to Bed

Become familiar with your child's sleep experiences; encourage her to share what she associates with sleep both negatively and positively. Share some of your own positive associations to help her develop and realize some of her own. (Recipe 64.7)

Help your child develop positive sleep associations. Use transitional objects—a special pillow, blanket, doll, or stuffed animal—to help her soothe herself when she's alone or apart from you. Take consistent and progressive steps toward self-sufficiency at sleep time. (Recipes 61, 62, 63, 64)

Help your child achieve a sense of mastery and control over her fears rather than letting them control her. Do not belittle her fears. Treat them with respect and encourage her to talk about them in detail. (Recipes 19, 20, 23.2, 23.3, 23.4, 23.5, 63, 64.6, 64.7)

Tell her that nothing bad will happen to her even though it is dark. Practice sitting in the dark together and playing games. (Recipes 19, 20, 23.4, 63)

Establish evening routines and rituals aimed at easing the transition from more to less activity. Give plenty of advance notice. Include activities aimed at developing the child's setting so that it feels secure and comfortable. (Recipes 61, 62, 64.1, 64.8)

Encourage your child to work through his concerns during waking hours. He should develop a plan to make peace with them before bedtime. (Recipes 63, 64.5, 64.6, 64.8)

Keep a mental or written chart if there seem to be erratic changes in sleep patterns. Look for a connection between life events, stressors, or developmental challenges. Remember: Patience is essential in dealing with your child's sleep problems.

Nightmares

Look for the causes or themes of recurrent nightmares and fears. Empower your child by involving her in a process of facing and reshaping bad dreams or her perceptions of feared objects or events. Help her to imagine better endings, ones that draw on her courage and resourcefulness. (Recipes 63, 64.6)

Early or Late Wakening

When your child wakes up too early, show her ways to occupy this time in a way that is respectful of others. Have her practice quiet, independent activities such as reading, writing, telling a make-believe story, or coloring, all in bed. (Recipes 55.16, 62, 64.9, 64.10)

If she wakes up late, work together to develop a plan (use an alarm clock) that helps her assume responsibility for this task. Remember, getting up on time should become her job, not yours. She needs to experience the **natural** and **logical consequences** for failing to do this. (Recipes 24, 26, 29.10, 62, 64.9, 64.10)

☆ *Good Night Door,* ☆
Good Night Ceiling

RECIPE # 61
Serves: 3–8 years

This recipe helps children feel safe and secure throughout the night.

Step 1
State and define the problem

Pull the family together for an "official" sleep talk. Share your thoughts and feelings regarding your child's inability to sleep in his own bed. (**"I" messages**) Use **humor** to **spice up** the conversation by doing a **role play** of what it is like to have a child in your bed, or joke that when he sleeps with you and your mate, you feel like the turkey in the middle of a turkey sandwich. Use **empathy** and **mutual respect** to show your child that you understand his need to sleep with you and that without the comfort of having you next to him he is scared and lonely. **Encourage** him to share his feelings about sleeping in his own bed.

Step 2
Identify skills and solutions

Ask your child to think of as many "independent" skills and abilities as he can. Review his past achievements and choose experiences in which he made efforts toward successfully accomplishing something on his own. Going to preschool, day care, or school; going to a relative's house alone, answering the telephone correctly, good hygiene habits, playing a sport on his own, and going to a friend's house are all good examples of independent skills. Make the list as long as possible.

Step 3
Mutually agree upon goals

Goal: "I will use my special skills to learn to sleep in my own bed and feel safe and secure."

Step 4
Practice and play

Attachments or associations to sleep begin in infancy. Rocking, singing, and holding your baby until he falls asleep provides a comforting and secure feeling. However, over time this wonderful and needed attention becomes *associated* with sleep. Without the rocking, body contact, and singing, your child will find it hard to fall asleep. You have become his connection with sleep; a security blanket. Understandably, to give you up without forming a new attachment is difficult.

This activity will help you and your child establish a safe sleep setting that is comforting and familiar: a new attachment for your child to associate with sleeping. Through repetition, mastery, and emotional support, she will become committed to this new sleep routine and able to establish the conditions and sense of security needed to fall and stay asleep on her own.

This recipe is based on principles found in *Goodnight Moon*, by Margaret W. Brown (HarperCollins, 1993), a must for parents of young children. In this story a rabbit is able to safely and comfortably to go sleep in his own bed after saying "Goodnight" to everything including the moon. This sleep routine is an important ritual (association) for the rabbit in order to go to sleep and stay asleep. Your child can establish the same routine and associations—with a special twist.

Begin by reading or rereading *Goodnight Moon* with your child. Explain that you are going to perform the same goodnight routine as the rabbit, but your child will be saying goodnight to real things in his life. Next, make a list of objects, people, and happy events in your child's life. Take photographs of these items. Using your list of independent skills discussed in step 2 of this recipe, take photographs of your child performing these special skills or have her reenact them for the purpose of taking the picture. Depending on your child's wishes and developmental ability, put the pictures on the inside of the door or on the wall or ceiling of her bedroom. Every night, right before she goes to bed, have her say goodnight to all the people, objects, and special things in her life represented in the pictures on her door, wall, or ceiling. Following her goodnights to all the important things in her life, support her efforts to sleep through the night by showing her the pictures of skills and reminding her to use them to safely and securely make it through the night on her own. Give her a flashlight. If she awakens in the middle of the night, she can shine it on the pictures on the wall or on the door or ceiling to remind her of all the people who are there to make her feel safe and happy.

Recognize her efforts to set up new sleep routines that do not include you as the sole source of comfort. Compliment and reinforce even her smallest attempts to make it through the night, even if she ends up in your bed.

Step 5
Review and recognize efforts

☆ *Good Morning/Good Night Club* ☆

Serves: 5–12 years

This recipe teaches children successful ways to go to bed, stay in their own beds, and get out of bed in the morning.

Step 1
State and define the problem

Gather your family for a meeting to discuss sleeping problems. Whether your child won't go to bed without a battle, sleep in his own bed, or wake up at an appropriate time, share your perceptions and feelings about it. Use **"I" messages** and **mutual respect. Effectively listen** to your child's perception of the problem. Be **empathic** and **encouraging** when your child expresses his feelings. Agree on a problem description that everyone feels accurately describes the situation.

Step 2
Identify skills and solutions

Identify your child's skills in following routines and acting independently. Focus on experiences and activities he participates in that show clearly the ability to follow through in meeting responsibilities and being able to do things by himself: washing up, practicing a sport, cleaning up his room, and listening and following directions in school.

Step 3
Mutually agree upon goals

Goal: "I will use my special skills for all of us to get a little more sleep by going to bed, staying in bed, and waking up right."

Step 4
Practice and play

Sleep time for parents is an unrecognized sport, a battle of the will, and a masterful game of winners and losers with ongoing competition between what you want and what your child wants.

The following activity offers your family a different game plan, one that promotes more peaceful nights and mornings. The Good Morning/Good Night Club will not only establish morning and evening rituals that are tailored to your family's sleep style, but will teach your child how to be responsible for her own sleep success by learning to cope with her evening or morning difficulties.

The Good Morning/Good Night Club is similar to recipe 26, I'm Responsible Association, in that your child needs to accumulate a given number of points on a chart to be in a club and receive club privileges. When he follows through on his evening responsibilities in return he gets club advantages (rewards and positive **logical consequences**). If he does not follow through, he fails to get into the club and has fewer privileges (earlier bedtime, no rewards, etc.).

In order to design a Good Morning or Good Night Club program that helps your child make the connection between successfully following a routine and increasing privileges, read the description of the Level Program on page 250. Use the chart examples in that section to make your own personalized Good Morning/Good Night chart.

Next, discuss the club idea with your child. Entice him into following the program by coming up with a list of club advantages that both you and he feel are worthy rewards for being responsible at bedtime or in the morning. Club advantages might include privileges such as a half-hour later bedtime, new bedtime apparel, special sleep-overs with friends and relatives, a new bed toy, or a new videotape to be watched in the morning. Next, make a bedtime or morning routine that is documented on a chart. To do this you will need to write down a routine in which your child must accomplish specific tasks, one by one, resulting in reaching his goal: going to bed, staying in bed, etc. Your child's routine could be something like, "Eat dinner, do homework, play with Dad/Mom, pajamas on, wash up, read book, in bed at 8:30, light off at 8:45." When your child follows through on each responsibility that appears on the chart, he receives a point. Decide on the desired number of points or checks needed to make it into the club. Remind your child to use his skills, discussed in step 2, for helping him to follow through on responsibilities and eventually make it into the club.

Design your child's chart to meet his needs, strengths, weaknesses, and developmental capabilities. Test it, and if it seems too difficult, revise it to suit his abilities.

Always be sure to award points and to count them daily. If your child begins to resort to old, unwanted evening and morning habits, remind him that it is his **choice** to win club privileges or not, and it is his personal victory if he does so.

Share and praise her smallest efforts toward reaching her goal. When your child makes it into the club, consider granting her a pajama party, complete with sleep-over, in which the family camps out on the floor in sleeping bags, and congratulatory speeches. Remember: Club membership can be revoked if she shows old and inappropriate behaviors. She can always **try, try again** to get her club membership back.

Step 5
Review and recognize efforts

☆ *No More Nightmares Book* ☆

This recipe helps children cope with nightmares.

Step 1
State and define the problem

Nightmares require enormous amounts of **empathy, respect,** and **effective listening.** Let your child know that she is not alone and that lots of kids have scary dreams. Try to pinpoint fears and worries that she has during the day. **Encourage** her to express her feelings about them and about the nightmares: you may be able to identify what is triggering them. Reassure her that her family will be there to help, and that together you will conquer the problem.

Step 2
Identify skills and solutions

Point out skills and personality traits that can be **positively reframed** as possible defenses against nightmares. Both physical and intellectual skills make good armor for nightmare combat. For example, the ability to make up a story or play make-believe is an effective strategy for coping with nightmares and for transforming bad dreams into good ones.

Step 3
Mutually agree upon goals

Goal: "I will use my special skills to make my bad dreams turn into good dreams."

Step 4
Practice and play

Childhood nightmares are usually the result of unresolved anxieties and concerns. It makes good sense that children who keep their worries uncommunicated and under wraps during the day, when they are busy and preoccupied, are more prone to have bad dreams at night, when their fears and their imaginations are set loose. The cause or causes of your child's nightmares may or may not be known to you or to your child. However, unbeknownst to him, he or she is the main source of the solution.

In this recipe you and your child will together write a children's book about her nightmares and how she can cope with them. The book will directly involve your child in the process of facing up to and then overcoming the terrifying object or experience in her dreams. This automatically reduces the fear by promoting her strength and sense of mastery. Once she feels in control of her fears, the nightmare-book activity will help her reshape the bad dreams into good ones.

For this recipe you will need paper, crayons, markers, and construction paper. First explain the book activity to your child and express your commitment to helping her solve the nightmare problems. Next, **encourage** her to describe a few nightmares (many kids can remember the content in vivid detail) and select a few to be described in the *No More Nightmares Book.* Begin the story by having your child draw pictures of herself during the day being exposed to anxiety-provoking or downright scary experiences. You may discover the cause of your child's nightmares in this initial "chapter." Now ask her to draw pictures of the nightmare. Get as much detail as possible in this part of the book. This repetitive, storytelling experience greatly reduces the impact of the nightmare and gives your child more control over her feelings and mastery over the bad dreams. End the book with a story showing your child overcoming this nightmare by using skills (step 2) and "whipped cream dreams," which are nice, comforting, safe dreams with happy endings. Come up with at least a dozen whipped cream dreams and/or happy endings. These specially designed dreams should be created by your child. Encourage her to use them in exchange for her nightmares. This way she uses her mind, creativity, and skills to "rewrite" her nightmares by positively changing the storyline. List and draw pictures of the whipped cream dreams in the book. It is essential that your child write her story so that she conquers her nightmare problem by the end of her book. **Positively reframe** efforts and encourage her to change the storyline if she focuses on a negative ending.

Now you have a terrific book to read with her at night, one that will help her vent her fears, face the nightmare, and solve the problem, all prior to falling asleep. You may want to leave her book at her bedside so that she can turn the light on and look up a few whipped cream dreams to replace her nightmare or end it in a more comforting way.

Even if your child's nightmares do not vanish, her efforts to write the book should not go unrecognized. You might discover that the book and its whipped cream endings are helping her work through the problems and anxieties that she experiences during the day.

Step 5
Review and recognize efforts

One parenting technique or ingredient that you should not use for this problem is **ignoring.** Nightmares are hard for a child to deal with alone, so you should **spice up** this activity with lots of loving, affection, and reassurance.

☆ *Planful Playing in a Pinch* ☆

Hot tips and quick recipes for solving sleeping problems.

64.1   *Goodnight Routines.* Have a set routine that you do with your child before going to bed. It can be simple or complex. Include something the child will look forward to each evening, such as a story, special time with a parent, or a bedtime snack. You may want to write down the routine for everyone to remember. We suggest including a special surprise your child will look forward to that comes at a certain time each evening.

64.2   *The Bed Bet.* Make a bed bet with your child. Bet him that he will go to bed at the right time every night. You win the bet if he doesn't. He wins if he does what he is told. Make the bet exciting, and remind your child way before bedtime what it is. Use **humor:** challenge your child by saying, "Mom's gonna win—"

64.3   *Bedtime Soap Opera.* Give a good reason to your child to get in his bed. Make up an ongoing saga in which each evening the story continues. Make the characters people in your home, but change the names slightly to make the story funny. Or make your child's name the same as the main character in a story. The story should be safe and silly. Always leave the end a mystery: your child will have to wait until the next evening to find out what is going to happen. You can make a sound effects box filled with noisy items so that your child can add appropriate sounds to the story. Better yet, tape the story every night so that it can be heard in its entirety on long car trips.

64.4   *Bed Haven.* To encourage your child to go to bed, create a fun environment for him to sleep in. Make his bed into a tent, using sheets. Fill shelves near the bed with books and quiet-time play items. Create a houseboat theme for younger children by sectioning off part of the bed for different areas of the boat. You may even want to put a box of quiet-time play items under the bed.

64.5   *The Goodnight/Good Day Recordings.* You need a recorder or notebook for this activity. Keep a journal with your child that records what was special about his day. Record it or write it in the special book. Spend some special time with your child and listen to the recordings and read through some of the book entries prior to going to sleep.

64.6   *Safe-and-Sound Book or Video.* Have your child write a brief story about people, things, or events in her world that are safe. The story should focus on how these safe things continue to be safe throughout the night. Encourage her to write down things like, "Parents are in the next room," "We have smoke detectors," "I know where to call the policemen," etc. Read the book together when your child needs assurance about going to sleep. Turn the book into a video your child can watch prior to going to sleep.

The Goodnight Pillow. Turn your child's pillowcase into a sleep security system. On a plain pillowcase, draw with fabric pens a few pictures, words, and phrases that will make your child feel safe and secure. This pillowcase and its pillow will become a permanent part of bed. Anytime he needs a reminder of how safe and secure he is, he can turn on the night-light and/or flashlight and look at his sleep-security-system pillow.

64.7

The "Give-It-a-Rest" Drawer. Explain to your child that he can put his worries and concerns aside for the evening so that he can get a good night's sleep. Write down or draw pictures of the worries and concerns he had all day and put them in a special drawer for safekeeping. Help him to understand that he deserves a good night's sleep, and you can both attend to his worries the next day.

64.8

Wake-Up Watchmen. Take turns being the family alarm clock. Give the wake-up person an alarm clock and the times everyone has to get up. Make a family game out of trying to wake people up creatively: tickling feet, playing soft music, etc. See who can come up with the most creative wake-up routine.

64.9

Wake-Up Map. If you need a little sleep in the morning and your child wakes up with the roosters, **prepare, plan, prevent** by mapping out a routine the night before. Put numbers or labels on activities you want her to accomplish in succession. Do this before she goes to sleep. For example, put the number 1 on her toothbrush, the number 2 on her clothes, the number 3 on a cereal box and milk carton, the number 4 on a morning video to watch, the number 5 on a coloring book, etc. Show her the routine before she goes to bed.

64.10

(See page 259 for a list of reading recipes for solving sleep problems.)

Recipe #67: How to Make a Very Best Friend Book

CHAPTER 15

Social Problems

YOU'VE WORRIED SINCE THE day you sent in the RSVP to your niece's wedding. Little Zachary never does well in these situations, but as usual you'll **try again.** You've done everything you can think of. You've pleaded with him and screamed at him. He looks cute as a button in that suit and tie, but somehow you can't get rid of the knots in your stomach. You think to yourself, "Maybe he'll play nicely with the other children instead of hiding behind me. Just maybe he won't pick a fight or act like a clown. Maybe the tablecloth and his new white shirt will stay white." Well, anyone can dream!

Children and adults alike accept or reject others based on personality traits and social skills. Friendly, respectful, sociable, and easygoing children are almost without exception valued by their peers, while immature, withdrawn, ill-mannered or hostile children are shunned. Social relatedness is essential for learning and growth. It also provides a sense of companionship and belonging.

This chapter and its recipes focus on enhancing social desirability and your child's motivation to be sociable in and outside your home. Social skills (everything from table manners to initiating friendships) are learned through parental **modeling** and by practice. You would no more want to send your child into social situations without adequate skills than you would drop him into a swimming pool without swimming lessons. We often take for granted the acquisition of these skills, when in actuality they are far more complex than learning how to operate a computer. Social competence is a lifelong process that has its roots in the formative experiences of childhood.

Your goal is to help your child develop the skills that will lend to his or her social success in early childhood. From small successes he will develop confidence in himself and motivation to continue trying. Your child's first social relationships are at home; use your family as a proving ground and a real-life **model** of group acceptance and group norms. Improving personal and social skills is a result of participation in social relationships with age-mates and adults alike. So get out there and **prepare, plan, prevent.**

In Public

With Peers

Making Friends

Social Skills in Public

You can dress them up, but you can bet that your can't-take-them-anywhere children have figured out that the **consequences** for misbehavior are different or nonexistent when away from home.

Some children become easily bored or overstimulated in public environments, especially supermarkets, toy stores, and restaurants, and in family gatherings. They lose control much more easily than when they are in less demanding places such as at home.

Social Skills with Peers

Children who have had little exposure or practice in social relationships with their peers may not have acquired the skills and knowledge to develop friendships.

Because of previous failures or inexperience, some children may withdraw socially and avoid interactions with other children, choosing to remain alone rather than risking further failure, rejection, or anxiety.

Your child's withdrawal may be correlated with, caused by, or related to other problems he is struggling with, such as school difficulties (academic or social), overactivity and at-

tentional problems, body-related issues (hygiene, overweight, underdevelopment), aggression, or low self-esteem.

Conversely, the shy child wishes for social contact and friendships but finds the process of socializing awkward, difficult, or painful.

Some children who feel left out and who are frustrated by unsuccessful efforts to join a group of other children may resort to extreme and undesirable behavior such as aggression, teasing, or very immature clowning.

Lack of Personal Boundaries

Children with limited social experience are often uneducated about and insensitive to others' boundaries and needs for personal space. As a result they may unknowingly make

others uncomfortable or angry (children and adults alike) by invading their personal space.

SOLUTIONS

Be sure your expectations are reasonable for your child, given his or her age, level of maturity, and disposition. Use advance **preparation—plan** for what could occur and discuss the scheduled activities with your child. Establish ground rules and agreed-upon expectations. Bring along things that will occupy him when he is bored or tired. In your own mind be prepared to leave; if need be, for an older child you can list **consequences** that will occur later. (Recipes 65, 69.1 through 69.10)

Social Skills with Peers

Social skills are behaviors best learned in small steps starting at an early age. Expose your children to a variety of social situations involving other children and adults. Developing social mastery and confidence at an early age is the key to avoiding future problems. (Recipes 66, 67, 68, 69.8, 69.9, 69.10)

Children learn by observing your relationships—how you get along with friends and relatives, even those you don't like. **Modeling** how to take the risks associated with initiating social relationships will help your fearful child put her fears in perspective. (Recipes 66, 67, 69.8)

After you have identified your child's withdrawal problem, consider other difficulties he has that could be related to or be complicating it—low self-esteem, aggression or body-related difficulties, for example. Seek help from chapters in this book that address those problems more specifically and involve him in the activities listed in those chapters.

Practice and gentle **encouragement** are the hallmarks of this solution. To begin, use **role playing** and behavioral rehearsal with coaching to practice basic communication skills such as listening, making introductions, showing interest in the ideas of others, and expressing her views. Provide support and feedback. Once you've practiced these, gradually introduce her to safe social situations with her age mates. Institute an open-door policy for visitors. It may mean a little more noise and commotion in your house, but the benefits clearly outweigh the bother. (Recipes 66, 67, 68, 69.8, 69.9, 69.10)

In addition to teaching social skills in preparation for social situations, practice at home. Reward appropriate social interaction and discourage or be unresponsive to undesirable behaviors. Teach nonviolent conflict resolution and give your child opportunities to practice play. (Recipes 18.1, 18.3, 57, 58, 68, 69.2, 69.8)

Personal Boundaries

Encourage and teach the concept of privacy as it relates to your body or the body of your child in areas such as bathing, toileting, and dressing. **Model** your own need for privacy and personal space. (Recipe 69.11)

☆ *The To-Go Bag* ☆

RECIPE #65

Serves: 3–12 years

This recipe helps children to behave socially by keeping them busy while they are in restaurants or supermarkets, attending family events, or simply in the car.

Step 1
State and define the problem

Talk with your child about your perceptions regarding his failure to behave in public places. Use **"I" messages** to clearly state how this rude, loud, or inappropriate behavior makes you feel. Show him that you are **empathic** to the demands placed on him to be well mannered and that you realize and respect that it is hard for him to follow these rules. Nonetheless, this problem needs to be taken care of. You may want to **spice up** this discussion with a few **humorous role plays** of what it looks like when he gets out of hand in public.

Step 2
Identify skills and solutions

List his skills and abilities to show good manners and to be socially acceptable. Recall times when he spoke in a soft voice, played quietly by himself, or was polite to someone. Talk about how nice it was to see him acting and behaving so well in public. Use **positive reframing** if you are having trouble finding skills in your child's social behaviors. Sitting still in a movie theater or watching a baseball game nicely are two good examples of behaviors you can positively reframe as skills.

Step 3
Mutually agree upon goals

Goal: "I will use my special skills to act more appropriately and have good manners in public places."

Step 4
Practice and play

Taking a child or two on an outing is often an unpredictable and socially trying event. It is safe to say that adult-focused activities such as eating out or going grocery shopping are not kid-friendly. Such excursions are truly a challenge for your child, for sitting still for an extended period of time, plus social demands, may be too much for his or her curious, energetic, and eager personality. However, you can help your child accommodate to socially demanding situations with the To-Go Bag.

This activity will help you promote your child's social skills and **distract** him from engaging in socially inappropriate behaviors. With your child, help design a To-Go Bag filled with games, crafts, and sit-still activities. You can use a backpack, a large purse, or a plastic shopping bag to keep the To-Go items in. The contents of the bag should be decided on by you and your child. Keep the bag in a convenient place so that it is handy when you are ready to go. Keep a special list of do's and don'ts and place it in the bag. The list outlines which behaviors are acceptable in public and which are not. For example: Don't scream, yell, or fight loudly. Do sit nicely. Do say thank you. Include your child's previously discussed skills (in step 2) and integrate them into the "do" side of the list. Explain what will happen if he chooses to use a behavior in the "don't" section. (Please see The 5 C's for Rule Making to establish your expectations for him in public.) Let him know that it's *his* **choice** to be a **S.T.A.R.** and to choose a game or activity from the bag rather than misbehave in public. Use **planful playing** to set up outings or demanding social events such as weddings by **modeling** and **role-playing** with your child how to use the To-Go Bag and follow the do-and-don't list. Initiate an incentive program that directs your child to work toward a reward for behaving correctly in public. (See chapter 17, "Just Desserts.") You may want to include a **think chair** sign in your To-Go Bag in case his behavior gets out of hand and he needs to collect himself and think through his actions. Keep adding new fun items to the bag. You may want to tell him there is a surprise in it that he may have if he shows you his skills for behaving the right way in a specific social situation. Never hesitate to **T.A.P.** yourself if you need to regain control when dealing with your child's negative behavior in public. Here are things you could put in your To-Go Bag: cards, bingo, travel-size board games, write-in activity books, coloring books, little dolls, beads for making necklaces, macramé bracelets, books, origami, needlepoint, talk activities. (See The Restaurant Game, in Planful Playing, page 224.)

Keep in mind that every kid has trouble adjusting to adult situations. Tantrums, rude behavior, and yelling come with the territory when you have a child. When your child acts well, comment on how good it made you feel. When she doesn't, let her know there will always be a time when she can **try, try again.** Most important, keep your list of do's and don'ts easily available to your child so she has a clear understanding of what you expect and what the ground rules are.

Step 5
Review and recognize efforts

☆ *Eyecatchers* ☆

RECIPE #66
Serves: 3–12 years

This recipe teaches children how to be sociable and interesting.

Step 1
State and define the problem

Call a **family council** meeting with the topic being "friendships." Use **"I" messages, effective listening,** and **mutual respect** when you discuss problems in getting children to come over and play or socialize. Express interest in making your home more exciting and interesting for them. Explain that you think if your home were more fun for children, perhaps inviting them over would be easier.

Step 2
Identify skills and solutions

List your child's fun skills. Think of the many nice, socially engaging, fun, and exciting skills your child possesses. Highlight skills that outline for her how interesting she can be to other children. Skills such as tells a good joke, shares games nicely, has a fun laugh, and knows how to have a good time are excellent examples.

Step 3
Mutually agree upon goals

Goal: "I will use my special skills to feel more comfortable inviting friends to come over and play."

Step 4
Practice and play

Social-skill problems are often rooted in the fear of taking chances. You as a parent can reduce this fear and put it into perspective. This recipe will help your child be more popular by making his home more attractive to his peers.

The recipe is called "Eyecatchers" because that is exactly what you and your child will be trying to accomplish. Making your home more inviting, more kid-friendly, will make it easier for your son or daughter to feel comfortable asking friends over to play.

Prior to setting up any Eyecatchers, go over with your child appropriate ways to invite friends over. Remind her of her special skills found in step 2. **Model** ways she can interact, be friendly, and share interests. Use **role plays** to show her how to resolve conflicts. Here are suggestions that have caught the eyes of children in many neighborhoods:

Tree House. Good old-fashioned tree houses are terrific ways to attract children to your home. Consider one that is designed and built by the children in your neighborhood.

Super Sandbox. Younger children might flock to your yard if it had an oversized sandbox with fun sand toys.

Big Games. Using a large outdoor space such as a driveway, design a big checkerboard with chalk. Use the lids from 6-inch-diameter plastic containers (such as for margarine containers) for the game pieces.

Carnival Times. Set up a carnival in your backyard complete with games and prizes. Plan activities such as tossing balls into buckets, hoop tosses, bean bag throws, and squirt gun shooting galleries. Make it a charity event. Encourage your child to advertise it at school, church, or camp: Come over and play at our carnival!

Sidewalk Art. Paint the sidewalk and driveway with chalk or *washable* paint. Have plenty of art supplies ready for neighborhood friends to come over and use.

The Friendly Project. Invite a few neighborhood families to work on a project together. Your family could sponsor a neighborhood garden. With their parents' permission, local kids could come over and help grow vegetables. Or, with help from other parents you could start a rabbit farm that required children to help take care of the farm.

Inside Fun. If your home is large enough, consider redesigning a room to be an attractive play area for numbers of children. Stock it with arts and crafts, games, toys, and snacks. Encourage your child to invite friends over to bake a cake or cookies or to make a big bowl of Jell-O or some other edible delight.

The most important step in this recipe is this: *Be sure to review with your child how the day went.* Discuss positive and negative interactions. Always suggest he or she can **try, try again** if the day did not go as planned. Combine this recipe with others to reinforce social skills.

Step 5
Review and recognize efforts

☆ *Adopt-a-Friend Club* ☆

RECIPE #67
Serves: 7–12 years

This recipe teaches children with poor social skills how to make and keep friends.

Step 1
State and define the problem

In this step you will need to **effectively listen** to your child's thoughts and feelings about making and keeping friends. Use **empathy** and share with your child times when you had difficulty making friends. Explore his fears and previously unsuccessful experiences in this area. Be sure to let him know he is not alone, for many children and adults find it hard to make friends.

Step 2
Identify skills and solutions

Whether your child is shy, feels uncomfortable seeking social contacts, or isolates himself from interacting with others, explain that making friends takes time and practice. **Encourage** him to see that he has special, unique personality traits that make him desirable to people. Make a list of those characteristics and show him that they can help him make friends and get along better with others.

Step 3
Mutually agree upon goals

Goal: "I will use my special skills to learn how to make and keep friends."

Step 4
Practice and play

Parents often feel helpless or even guilty when their child has friendship problems. It is disheartening and embarrassing to see your child withdraw from social gatherings, and even more upsetting to see him or her consciously excluded by a group of children. Don't undermine your role in helping your child form friendships. You have the unique position of being highly visible to your child, so you can **model** the steps for initiating and building friendships. You can provide your child with examples of countless ways to interact with others. However, it is your child who will eventually need to go out and make his or her own friends.

Explain to your child that you are going to start a special club for children his age whose purpose is to reach out to lonely people. Talk with him about children in long-term hospital care, adults in nursing homes, and mildly retarded adults who would welcome the friendship of children. **Positively reframe** his skills in friendship-making as discussed in step 2, skills that indicate how he would be a perfect club member. After getting his commitment to join, encourage him to help you name the club. Suggestions are The Reach-Out-to-Friends Club, The Adopt-a-Friend Club, or Friends, Incorporated.

Next make a list of children his age (classmates, neighborhood kids, cousins, Cub Scouts, etc.) who should be invited to be in the club. Work together in phoning these children and their parents and inviting them to become members. Remember: It doesn't matter how many members you sign up. The purpose is to give your child a socially engaging experience by meeting regularly with people his or her age. Since children can be taught and coached on how to make friends, it is important to help them learn appropriate social behaviors and give them plenty of practice. What better way than providing them with a children's club that works together to be friends with lonely people.

Prior to the first meeting, select a place such as a senior citizens' home or a home for mildly retarded adults where you feel comfortable taking this group of children. Call around to find the right environment, and do what you can to be a part of the matching of the children with a potential adoptee.

At the first meeting, either you (**modeling**) or your child should explain to the members the purpose of the club and who the adoptees will be. Show your child how to **encourage** discussions between members and assist the children in coming up with ways they can begin friendships with the adoptees. You can have the children do **role plays** in which they practice meeting new people, showing interest, giving attention, listening, and being supportive and helpful to the adoptees. Have the children decide on activities they can share with their adopted friends and the best way they can spend special time with them. Make a few suggestions such as having a talent show, singing songs, or making crafts. Help the club think up nice things to do for their adopted friends such as sending birthday cards or offering to shop for them. Caution: Some children may get carried away and will need help from you to define the limits of the relationship. Monitor the discussion to ensure realistic goals. Make sure that the club meets a few times prior to the first visit with its adopted friends. Gradually withdraw from the meetings so your child can socialize on his or her own.

Have the children set up weekly or monthly visits with their adopted friends. It should be a requirement that they go as a group. We suggest that you accompany them on their visits but let them do the friendship-making.

Every time your child meets with his club members, acknowledge his efforts and review the experience. Indicate ways he was a good friend. **Positively reframe** social blunders so he can **try, try again** next time. Take the time to reward all the children in the club for their generous gift of friendship to lonely people by going out for ice cream or pizza after meeting with their adoptees.

Step 5
Review and recognize efforts

☆ The Time Machine ☆

RECIPE #68

Serves: 3–10 years

This recipe teaches children how to prevent social problems and review their social skills.

Step 1
State and define the problem

Invite your child to discuss her feelings and perceptions regarding manners and/or the nature of friendship. Your responses must be **empathic** and sensitive; treat your child's feelings with **respect. Encourage** her to explore her knowledge of appropriate behavior in specific situations such as at dress-up events, in church, and at restaurants. If your child is struggling to make and keep friends, she is likely to be sensitive about this issue and will need you to **spice up** the conversation with affection, support, and understanding.

Step 2
Identify skills and solutions

Positively reframe behaviors in which your child demonstrated his strengths, skills, and positive attributes in social situations. Make a list of his abilities to successfully socialize such as saying hello, waiting his turn, saying thank you, playing nicely with a cousin, or smiling. **Role-play** (**planful playing**) a situation in which he can practice using his skills in a social situation with a peer. Point out times when he was able to look back at a situation and comment, positively or negatively, on his behavior.

Step 3
Mutually agree upon goals

Goal: "I will use my special skills to improve my social behavior."

Step 4
Practice and play

Children need guidance from their parents in how to review their social behaviors and then make positive adjustments. This fun activity will provide you with an excellent opportunity to **model** appropriate ways to socialize, while giving your child practice and experience testing and examining his or her social skills and behaviors.

With your child, make a time machine out of a refrigerator box or very large cardboard box. It must be big enough for your child to sit in. Add pushbuttons, gears, gadgets, levers, and a special window for your child to look out of. Make it look like a real time machine that will be used to go backward and forward in time to review a situation in which your child has misbehaved, recognize events in which he behaved appropriately, try out a new social skill for an upcoming or future event, and practice his friendship skills.

For children with poor manners, send your machine back in time, then **role-play** and show your child how he could have acted differently. Go ahead in time to have your child practice and show how he will handle the situation in the future. **Spice it up** with a little **humor** and have your child take you back to your own childhood to examine situations in which you weren't being an angel. End your time travels by showing him how you improved your behaviors.

Use the time machine to help your child develop his ability to make friends. Send the machine back in time to meet one or two of his favorite heroes such Babe Ruth or Columbus. Role-play: pretend that he gets out of his machine and introduces himself to these people. Encourage your child to use his best social skills when introducing himself. He should ask polite questions and start a friendly, appropriate conversation.

Fly into the future and have him meet a new friend. Give him plenty of **encouragement** to use his best skills in saying hello, being polite, and inviting his "new" friend back home with him.

Here are some places to which your child can travel:

- Back to a social conflict that he did not resolve.

- To another country, planet, or universe.

- To a place or situation in which she is apprehensive; in which she can practice mastering her fear.

- To an upcoming event where she must behave at her best (a wedding or party).

Since this activity is founded on a playful approach to reviewing behaviors, you have already performed the last step in the problem-solving process. Further explain how she can use her newly learned skills in any social situations she is placed in.

Step 5
Review and recognize efforts

☆ *Planful Playing in a Pinch* ☆

Hot tips and quick recipes for solving social-skill problems.

MANNERS

69.1   *The Restaurant Game.* The name of the game is to keep your family quiet, playing, and involved. Whatever you can come up with to amuse your children is the main ingredient behind good behavior in a restaurant.

Invent a story from words on the menu. Each family member takes turns choosing a word and making up a story that everyone can continue and add to. Bring a book or a magazine to continue this storytelling activity before the dinner arrives. Or try to guess who sat in the seat before you. Have everyone try to make up a story about who it was, what he or she does for a living, what they did during the day, etc. Parents can make this **humorous** and intriguing by dreaming up exotic tales about famous stars and mysterious people doing bizarre and funny things. Have your kids draw pictures of what these people look like.

69.2   *Let's Practice.* Practice with your child what will happen at the special occasion. Use dress-up clothes and other props. Playact what the event will be like. If you're going to a wedding, dress up like the bride and groom and take turns being the guests. Practice appropriate behaviors and point out the age-appropriate things your child could do to make the event fun.

To help your children behave appropriately when answering the phone, practice on play telephones. Show your child the right way to answer and ask questions on the phone by using plastic toy phones.

69.3   *The Vacation Creation.* Plan how you can organize the trip and help your children improve their behavior. Fill a large suitcase with toys and games for each child. It's worth taking up some space with this suitcase. Include items that are calming. (See The Cool, Calm, In-Control Clubhouse, recipe 37.) Have each of your children become a "boss" of a specific vacation responsibility. The camera boss would be in charge of taking pictures, carrying the camera, and getting the film developed. And of course she will be the first to see the pictures. Other bosses could be the video boss, the scrapbook boss, or the problem-solver boss. Your children can switch roles for each day or continue their roles throughout the trip. For vacations that require long drives, we recommend taking *Are We There Yet? Travel Games for Kids,* by Richard Salter (Crown Publishers, 1991).

69.4   *The "Carsette."* Have your entire family work together on a music, story, or joke-filled cassette to be played only when you are in the car together. Encourage your child to make up secret but appropriate tapes that he can surprise everyone with later when you get into the car for either a short ride to the supermarket or a cross-country trip.

The Video of Bad Manners and Rude Kids. Have your children work to- 69.5
gether to write and make a video on bad manners and social misbehavior. They could begin the video with about ten of the rudest things
kids can do in a restaurant, in the car, at someone's house, or on the
school bus. Have your kids act these out, then correct themselves in the
second segment of the video. At the end of the video, list about ten of
the most appropriate things kids can do in a restaurant, in the car, etc.

The Coupon Detective. Give your child a stack of coupons and discount ads 69.6
from the supermarket in which you will be shopping. His job will be
to locate the items found on them. If he is successful at finding them
and bringing them back to the cart, give him a coupon, at the very end of
the supermarket trip, which promises him a treat that is pictured on the
coupon.

The Plan, Prepare, Prevent Announcement. Each family member should 69.7
make a morning announcement of what he or she plans to do for the
day. Make them simple, clear, and specific. Include in your announcement the kinds of behavior you expect at each event. Your announce-
ments should be made **humorously** or at least in a humorous tone of
voice to help keep your children's attention. You may want to have them
think of rhymes for each activity: "First we go to the store, but not before
we shut the door. Then we go to the park, but definitely before it gets
real dark."

SOCIALIZING AND FRIENDSHIP

Let's Party. Parties are real-life, fun testing grounds for social skills. Ex- 69.8
plain to your child that you will help her learn how to introduce herself
to others and form friendships at a "friendship party." To make sure that
this experience does not result in another rejection (no one shows up),
make the party a combined social gathering: both your adult friends
and their children your child's age will attend. Have your child help in
the planning of the party, from invitations to activities. Also help her by
encouraging her to talk about what kids like to do and what children like
to talk about. **Role-play** how she could be the hostess and how to meet
people at the door, introduce herself, and show guests around the home.
Role-play social situations that might baffle her: how to share a toy, deal
with a bossy friend, or act when a friend refuses to cooperate. On the day
of the party, be near your child for support and guidance, but let her **try,
try again** for herself. After the party, talk with her about how well she
did and what were some of the outstanding social skills she demonstrated at the party. **Model** social skills whenever you need to show your
child how to invite friends over again or make future arrangements.

69.9   *The Aquarium of Friends.* Make an aquarium out of your child's room by pasting pictures of fish, seaweed, and coral around the walls. Have at least twelve removable, friendly fish "swimming" in the aquarium. Name them. Pretend that the fish are in a neighborhood aquarium. Move them around the aquarium and have them say hello to one another, invite one another to their homes, and resolve conflicts. Playfully examine your child's social difficulties, using the feelings of the fish.

69.10   *How-to-Make-and-Keep-Friends Video or Book.* Have your child write a brief book or produce a video on how to make and keep friends. Go through the steps of friendship-making with your child and encourage him to include this in his book or video. Begin the book or video with skills on how to introduce yourself. End them with your child's success in meeting and gaining a friend. Better yet, encourage him to write the book or produce the video with a friend or relative his age.

PRIVACY

69.11   *Private Time.* For children who have difficulty respecting the privacy of others, try the following activities, which reinforce the need for space and alone time.

- With your child, make doorknob signs, like the ones in hotels that say *Knock first—I want privacy* on one side and *Come on in—I want company* on the other.

- Set up a special time every day during which all members of the family have private time. Depending on your child's age, set aside fifteen minutes to an hour when everyone goes to his room, selects a private space to sit in, or takes a walk on his own.

- Teach your child the concept of boundaries by having her define the progressive degrees of privacy, beginning with the limits of your property (it is not respectful for people to step on your grass), the physical boundaries of your home (people who do not live there must ask permission to come inside), and your body (you must have permission to touch someone's body). Play a game and see if your child can think of ten or twenty ways a person can express his wish for privacy: closing a door, pulling the shades, wearing clothes, etc.

- Give a younger child a box. Let him know that he can put all his private items in it and you will never look inside. Give an older child a diary and promise (and follow through) never to read it.

- Teaching your child about privacy and boundaries through play will help her learn to protect herself against unwanted touching. It will build self-worth, social awareness, and assertiveness. A good book to read with your child regarding appropriate and inappropriate touching is *My Body Is Private,* by Linda Girard Walvoord (Albert Whitman & Company, 1984).

(See page 260 for a list of reading recipes for solving social problems.)

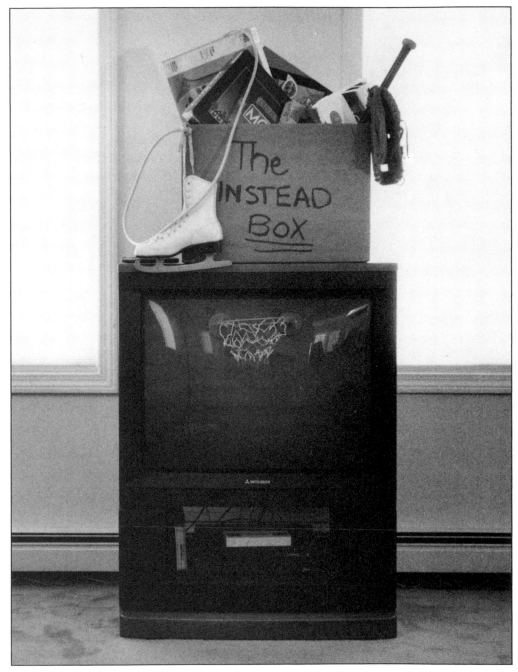

Recipe #70: The Instead Box

CHAPTER 16

Television and Video-Game Addiction

IT'S 7:15 SATURDAY MORNING, and you can answer the question, "Do you know where your children are?" Six hours later you can still safely answer that question because odds are they're solidifying in front of the boob tube, watching some commercially hyped cartoon dripping with mindless violence. Equally worrisome is the permanent indentation of your child's index finger from excessive use of the remote control and the video-game buttons. All this indoor activity is going on while the weather is beautiful and the new, expensive jungle gym you recently agonized to build and pay for looks like the spiders are getting more use out of it than your kids. Are you the proud parents of a sixty-three-pound couch potato? If so, join the ranks of parents across the country who are concerned about their children's TV and video-game addiction.

Television itself is neither good nor bad. It is the way you use it that determines its impact. It can be stimulating, educational, and positive. It can be numbing and unproductive. The power of television as a tool for learning about others and the world at large is as powerful as its role in teaching aggression and violence. We believe that TV can serve as an important ingredient in living and learning, like sugar in a cake recipe. However, too much sugar—and too much television—is a poor diet. You can shape your children's television experiences by **encouraging** them to be analytical about what they watch and by choosing programs that are rich, rewarding, and that reinforce your learning objectives for them.

We also feel that one of the main reasons children sit in front of the boob tube and fiddle with video games until their eyes cross is that they have "nothin' to do."

The recipes in this chapter will give you plenty of good ideas for limiting the amount of television your family watches, as well as dozens of terrific ideas of "somethin' to do."

PROBLEMS

Wasted Time

Television by its very nature is a passive and effortless activity. Its mesmerizing images glue children to the set for long periods of physically and intellectually inactive time.

Children are the unknowing and unresisting recipients of sophisticated marketing ploys by everyone from toy companies to the liquor industry. The latent message in these sales pitches is that buying these products will bring success and happiness.

Violence

The sheer abundance of interpersonal violence shown on TV in some ways normalizes and condones this behavior and desensitizes young viewers to its real impact, thereby diminishing your child's ability to empathize with victims of violence. The net effect is that TV minimizes the tragedy and pain associated with aggression and instead links this type of behavior with hero figures.

Intellectual Effects

Excessive TV watching can have adverse effects on your child's intellectual development, including but not limited to the development of language and reading skills, the growth of imagination and creativity, problem-solving skills, and attention span.

Television presents an essentially unreal image of the world, suggesting options for living and for dealing with problems that are neither socially acceptable nor within your child's reach.

SOLUTIONS

Wasted Time

Set limits on the amount and type of television your children watch. Offer alternative experiences, real and make-believe, that are exciting and rich. (Recipes 70, 71, 74)

Set an example by turning off the TV and reading a book or working on a hobby (**modeling**). The more active you are in limiting your own viewing habits, the easier it will be to ask your children to do the same. (Recipes 70, 74.3, 74.4)

Help your children choose programs carefully. Ask them to talk about what they like and dislike about a show or a character. In essence, teach them to be TV critics. (Recipes 71, 72, 73, 74.5)

Violence

Ask your children their thoughts and comment on aspects of TV that disturb you such as violence, sexism, racism, or promiscuity. (Recipes 71, 72, 73, 74.5)

Intellectual Effects

Ask questions and generate discussion that help your children distinguish between the fantasy world of TV and reality. Wonder out loud what would happen if someone started swinging his fists every time he was angry or didn't have magical powers to rescue him from harm. Ask questions and insist on replies. Ignore the moans and groans from your children—relate your skepticism to old age or senility and ask your kids to humor you by listening to you and challenging themselves to really "think" about what they are watching. (Recipes 71, 72, 73)

231

☆ *The Instead Box* ☆

RECIPE #70
Serves: All ages

This recipe gives children (and adults) something to do other than watching television or playing video games.

Step 1
State and define the problem

Share with your child your concerns regarding the amount of time he spends in front of the TV and playing video games. Show that you understand that it is difficult to avoid television because it is enjoyable to watch (**empathy**). **Effectively listen** to your child's point of view and try to determine what the TV problems are in your family.

Step 2
Identify skills and solutions

Emphasize skills in your child that show his ability to think through his actions and make responsible decisions: **S.T.A.R.** Next list both your child's and your own skills pertaining to leisure activities other than the TV or playing video games: sports, card games, board games, arts and crafts, reading, and cooking, for example.

Step 3
Mutually agree upon goals

Goal: "I will use my special talents to do something else instead of sitting in front of the television or playing video games."

Step 4
Practice and play

Glance over at your television set. Where is it? Probably it is perched in a place where all family members can see it from twenty-four different angles. It is hard to pass by the TV and do something else because your set puts out a signal just by being in a prominent place: *Turn me on!*

Try following this recipe: With your child, select a large box (at least 15″ × 15″) and decorate its outsides in bold, bright colors. Write INSTEAD BOX on the center of each side. Explain to your child that anytime she feels like turning on the television set or pulling out a video game, she can look in the Instead Box and entertain herself with a different activity. Fill the box with fun, engaging objects and activities you think your child would enjoy. Encourage her to come up with suggestions of her own: books, arts and crafts, music cassette tapes, board games, models to assemble, "write-in" activity books, puzzles, dress-up clothes, puppets, cards, dominoes, marbles and jacks, gross motor activities (jump ropes, skates, a ball), and the book called *365 TV-Free Outdoor Activities You Can Do With Your Children,* by Steven and Ruth Bennett (Bob Adams, Inc., 1992).

We suggest adding a few adult-oriented items such as whatever you happen to be reading, some knitting, or some golf balls so that your child can watch you do something else than look at the screen. The less parents watch TV, the more easily they can guide their children to limit their own viewing (**modeling**). Say out loud in front of your child, "I'm going to take something from the Instead Box and not turn on that TV." By your doing this, he can see how you stop and think instead of mindlessly flipping on the set (**S.T.A.R.** and **T.A.P.**). From time to time **spice up** the box with new items so you can say, "There's a surprise in the Instead Box—go check it out." You can use **distraction** and do this just when he is ready to grab his video game. Or try an incentive program that awards him points every time he reaches for the Instead Box rather than the remote-control box. The reward could be something added to the box. (See page 245 for "201 Rewards.")

Recognize and **praise** your child each time he goes to the Instead Box instead of the television. Share your concerns with him if he continues to spend too much time in front of the TV or playing video games. You can certainly **try, try again** with another recipe.

Step 5
Review and recognize efforts

☆ *"The Bradley Bunch"* ☆

RECIPE #71

Serves: 5–12 years

This recipe teaches children what makes a television show or video game healthy or not healthy to watch.

Step 1
State and define the problem

Turn off the TV and gather your family for a recipe that will help them take a closer look at the television and video-game industries. Share with your child your concerns about the amount of television watching and video-game playing in your home. Use **"I" messages** to indicate what you think about the content of today's television shows. **Empathize** and **effectively listen** to your child's views on the subject.

Step 2
Identify skills and solutions

Identify your child's skills in making good decisions regarding television watching. Point out her ability to choose a good show rather than one filled with violence and mindless plots.

Step 3
Mutually agree upon goals

Goal: "I will use my special skills to become more aware of the kinds of shows we watch and the video games we play. And to make good choices about them."

Step 4
Practice and play

Watch out, "Brady Bunch" and Cosby—here comes your competitor. In this activity you will be making your own television show or video game. As we have already emphasized, TV and video encourage us to be passive learners, observers, and thinkers—the information transmitted to us is via a one-way process. This recipe gets your family directly involved in the communication process by making *you* the originator of information. It also teaches children how to discriminate between positive and negative influences of television and video games.

The Family Television Show. With your family decide on a television show you will create and star in. Think of shows your family enjoys and re-write them to fit your own family. The show can be fictional or real, but make it fun. Keep in mind that just by participating in this activity your child is away from the television set, an accomplishment in itself! Using The TV Critic recipe and the "Yea-and-Nay Critique Sheet" on page 237 critique shows currently on the air and decide which positive parts you want in your show and which negative components you want to leave out. You can write a script or do an impromptu show in your living room. **Spice it up** with costumes, props, and scenery. If you have a video recorder, invite a relative or friend to tape your family show. Consider making weekly editions. Be sure to name your show and give credits to its stars. Review your tape and enjoy the show! You may even want to critique your own show to decide if it was educational and fun.

The Action Video Game. Review a few video games with your child. Then turn off the machine and explain that you are going to help him design his own game. Design it on paper and come up with a game strategy. Invent a character or two and name the video game. Talk with your child about what makes a good game and what makes a bad one. Too much violence and not enough adventure are good examples of the latter. You may want to get your child to physically test the game by setting up an obstacle course that resembles the game. Again, as in the television-show activity, your child will have to avoid playing video games while he is performing this activity.

Recognize your family's efforts toward communicating the ideas and insights of quality television. From time to time remark about your family's television show versus others you may be watching and comment on which one is better. (Yours of course!) Do the same for the video activity.

Step 5
Review and recognize efforts

☆ *The TV Critic* ☆

This recipe teaches children how to consciously make responsible decisions regarding their TV viewing.

Step 1
State and define the problem

Convene a **family council** meeting. The subject will be excessive TV watching. Use **effective listening** to hear your child's point of view and **"I" messages** to share yours.

Step 2
Identify skills and solutions

Highlight positive TV watching in which your child selected quality programs. Comment on her ability to use her thinking skills to analyze a show and decide if it is a good or bad one.

Step 3
Mutually agree upon goals

Goal: "I will use my special skills to learn to make responsible decisions about which shows are worthwhile and which should be avoided."

Step 4
Practice and play

Television itself is neither good nor evil and can be used foolishly or wisely. Television helps children put themselves in someone else's place and gives them a broader view of the world. There are programs that teach children about science, technology, history, literature, and art. TV's dynamic presentation and visual immediacy can make it a powerful learning tool in presenting options for living. On the other hand, this same powerful message-giver can turn a constructive learning experience into something negative, for television exposes children to extreme amounts of violence and desensitizes them to violence in real life. Emphasis on products in TV commercials gives children unrealistic understanding of success and happiness. Also, children are naive and literal-minded and tend to believe what they see and hear. They often do not distinguish fantasy from reality.

We whipped up this recipe to help parents work through this dilemma with their children. Using the following television Yea and Nay Critique Sheet, you will enhance the positive effects of television and reduce the negative ones by analyzing, interpreting, and coming to valid conclusions with your child on whether a show is a "Yea" (good) or a "Nay" (bad).

Sit down with your child and review the Yea and Nay Critique Sheet. Redesign it if you like, but be sure to make this critique exercise a "playful" rule for viewing any television show. Try to do it together with your child and **encourage** him to share as much as he can of his thoughts and feelings regarding the show he is watching. Elaborate on each question contained on the critique sheet. **Spice it up** with a little **humor.** Add up the "yeas" and "nays" and decide if the show was a winner or a dog by putting your thumbs up or down and cheering or booing. **Plan** and **prevent** watching "nay" shows in your home. Use an incentive program with your child in which she gets points every time she chooses a "yea" show and turns off a "nay." You can even make up a critique sheet for commercials and video games. This way you are encouraging your child to view commercials with a critical eye and consider if video games are worth his time and energy.

THE YEA AND NAY CRITIQUE SHEET		
Date: Time: Show:	Circle one	
Did this show make you smarter?	Yea	Nay
Did it treat people respectfully?	Yea	Nay
Was it realistic?	Yea	Nay
Did it solve a problem?	Yea	Nay
Did it make you laugh?	Yea	Nay
Did it make you feel good?	Yea	Nay
Was the show good for kids?	Yea	Nay

This recipe is all about reviewing and recognizing efforts made toward helping improve TV habits. Comment on your child's ability to critique when it comes to viewing. Point out her good choices whenever she selects a show that avoids violence, is educational, or has some other redeeming values.

Step 5
Review and recognize efforts

☆ *To Whom It May Concern . . .* ☆

RECIPE #73

Serves: 5–12 years

This recipe empowers children to take charge of what they watch on television.

Step 1
State and define the problem

To work this recipe you will first need to do recipe #72, The TV Critic. Share your feelings and concerns regarding the sort of television shows and commercials available today. **Encourage** your child to voice his opinions. Use **positive reframing** to persuade him to draw on his insights from doing the Yea and Nay Critique Sheet. Generalize the television problem as an American problem, something most families in the United States and even other countries should try to solve.

Step 2
Identify skills and solutions

Emphasize your child's skills in correctly and positively asserting his opinion. Point out occasions when he told someone, in an appropriate way, that he liked or didn't like something. List a few correct and suitable ways to tell someone that you are happy or unhappy with the way something was done.

Step 3
Mutually agree upon goals

Goal: "I will use my special skills to voice my opinions and try to make TV shows healthier for our family and for other families."

Step 4
Practice and play

It is easy for parents to complain about the amount of violence, unrealistic depictions of family life, and generally dubious material on TV. "Look at that junk!" you yell at the uncomprehending screen. Most people believe this is as far as you can go. There is nothing more to be done. Not true! Consider programming decisions. The higher the ratings, the greater the advertising revenues. So if you let a network know that you liked or disliked something, and if you encourage other families to do the same, it can affect programming. **Model** for your child that everyone has a voice about what goes on television. Sit down with your family and write a letter to the network that puts on a show you liked or did not like. Try to use your television critique form to help you justify your appreciation of or dissatisfaction with the show(s) you have watched. Encourage your child to express his thoughts about it. Draw on the skills listed in step 2 to appropriately and correctly voice his opinion in the letter. If he can't express himself in words, have your child draw pictures of what he is thinking. Send letters often, and send them to the top. The addresses listed on the following page are of several major networks.

238

For CBS:
President and CEO
CBS
51 W. 52nd Street
New York, NY 10019

For NBC:
President and CEO
National Broadcasting Co., Inc.
30 Rockefeller Plaza
New York, NY 10112

For ABC:
President and CEO
Capital Cities/ABC Inc.
77 W. 66th St.
New York, NY 10023

For PBS:
President and CEO
Public Broadcasting Service
1320 Braddock Place
Alexandria, VA 22314

For Fox:
Chairman and CEO
Fox Broadcasting Company
10201 W. Pico Blvd.
Los Angeles, CA 90035

Most important, try to demonstrate by your own viewing habits and critiques that television is a selective activity. Let those who can do something about programming know *what* you are choosing to watch or not watch and *why,* and let your kids feel a part of this process.

Recognize and praise your child's skills in explaining what she thinks about the show she is watching or has just watched. Compliment her ability to help make programming better for her family and for other families as well.

Step 5
Review and recognize efforts

☆ *Planful Playing in a Pinch* ☆

RECIPE #74

Hot tips and quick recipes for solving video and television addiction.

74.1 *The TV Diet.* Read through a *TV Guide* with your child and underline the shows he watches. Photocopy and enlarge the page of the *Guide* that lists these. Stick the enlargement on the refrigerator. Every time your child chooses not to watch a show that is underlined—a mutually agreed-on show that is not good to watch—he gets a point. Shows like "Sesame Street," educational programs, and previously decided-on shows that contain positive messages and values receive points for being watched. When he attains the desired number of points, by either limiting time in front of the TV or by choosing quality shows, he gets a reward. Try to make the reward something useful that your child can do instead of watching television.

You could also make a list of video games your child plays too long and too often and use the same system of rewards for cutting back.

74.2 *The Cartoon Club.* If your child needs help cutting down on cartoons, make her a member of a cartoon club. Loyal members are able to watch only the series to which they belong. Support her membership with a toy or perhaps a comic book that relates to the cartoon chosen. You could join the club and help her by watching the selected cartoon with her. Remember: other cartoon shows are taboo.

74.3 *TV Activities.* Use television shows to encourage children to actively experience what they are or have been passively watching. For example, if your child watches a show about dogs, go to a dog show. If the show took place in a park, a zoo, or a restaurant, plan an activity in which he or she gets to investigate the reality from which the show was taken.

74.4 *TV Turnoffs.* Designate one day per week in which you hang a sheet over the tube and shut it off for an extended period of time. Make a little ritual out of this. Say, "Good night, television, it's bedtime." Be sure however to plan activities to do with your child during the TV-turnoff period.

74.5 *TV Turnoff Poster Contest.* Encourage your child to head up a poster contest at your local library or school to help other kids think either about turning off their television or about what turns them off about it. Enlist the help of librarians and teachers for this contest and hang the posters throughout schools and libraries. Winners of the contest can send their posters to Children's Television Workshop, One Lincoln Plaza, New York, NY 10023 in support of this station's excellent programming ("Sesame Street," "Barney & Friends," "Lamb Chops," "Play Along"). Perhaps the workshop would be interested in supporting your contest.

Good Behavior Results in a Delicious Reward

CHAPTER 17

Just Desserts

CHOCOLATE CAKE OR ICE CREAM with hot fudge and extra whip cream, anyone? We called this chapter "Just Desserts" in honor of that age-old parenting tactic used to get reluctant kids to eat the remaining, and sometimes less tasty, portion of their meal. "If you finish your spinach, you'll get dessert." If you've turned to this chapter, you are seeking information on how to reward your child or yourself for the hard work your family puts forth in solving its various problems. The chapter was designed for easy access in turning any recipe or activity into a reward-based system.

Rewards are motivators. When you reward desirable behavior, you reinforce your child's feelings about the positive actions she made toward solving a problem, while simultaneously encouraging her to repeat those actions. Most children lack the maturity to enjoy the good feeling that comes from accomplishing a task or reaching a goal. They need something more tangible, an external motivator such as a desired object, an outing, or a special event. Your goal in using external motivators is of course to help your child move from feeling good about getting a reward for his hard work to feeling good about simply reaching his goal. Moving from an external motivator (reward) to an internal one (self-praise, enhanced feelings of self-worth, and self-confidence) in children is a maturational process which, combined with a supportive environment, nurtures self-esteem. We designed the following reward systems to help you reward your child for good behaviors while at the same time encouraging the development of his self-esteem and self-motivation. We've selected four different types of reward-based systems: tokens, charts, points and catalogs, and level programs. These can be used in progression to help move from external to internal motivations. For example, the Token Program is designed for young children who need constant reinforcement to change their behavior. The Level Program is for older, more mature children who have reached the point at which they get a feeling of satisfaction from receiving special privileges rather than desired objects.

To begin, you may need a little help discovering what would adequately motivate your child. We have devised a special test that will help you determine your child's wishes, desires, and motivators for changing negative behaviors into positive ones. The My Wishes and Wants Test on page 244 can be given verbally to a young child or photocopied for an older one to complete on his or her own. You can skip the test if you like

Motivation Programs

Rewards

Charts

and get some good ideas for rewards and motivators from the 201 Rewards Children Love to Work For.

In choosing a reward system that best suits your child and your family style, consider your child's age, developmental abilities, and maturity level. For each reward program, the following rules must be followed in order to ensure success:

1. Always deliver the reward or privilege promised—never make promises you can't keep.

2. Give your child plenty of time and always approach a reward program with a **try, try again** attitude.

3. Never give rewards prior to the desired behavior or they will become bribes.

4. Never withhold or revoke an earned reward: "If you don't do what I say, I won't give you the ———"

Enjoy your dessert.

MY WISHES AND WANTS TEST

If I had three wishes, what would I want?

1. _____

2. _____

3. _____

If I had one hundred dollars, what would I buy?

1. _____

2. _____

3. _____

If I could do anything I wanted with my family, what would it be?

1. _____

2. _____

3. _____

My favorite activity is _____

When I have special time with my parents, this is what I like to do _____
_____

When I play by myself, my favorite thing to do is _____
_____

If I could have special privileges, what would they be? _____
_____

201 REWARDS CHILDREN LOVE TO WORK FOR!

(To the child[ren]): Put a check in the square of each item or privilege you would like to have.

TOYS
- ☐ dolls
- ☐ doll clothing
- ☐ doll carriage
- ☐ doll toys
- ☐ stuffed animals
- ☐ dollhouse
- ☐ dollhouse furniture
- ☐ puppets
- ☐ play kitchen
- ☐ kitchen supplies
- ☐ play makeup
- ☐ dress-up clothes
- ☐ board games
- ☐ building blocks
- ☐ large play items
  - ☐ playhouse
  - ☐ outdoor toys
- ☐ play figures
- ☐ puzzles
- ☐ jump rope
- ☐ jacks
- ☐ marbles
- ☐ swimming pool toys
- ☐ sled
- ☐ spending money at a toy store
- ☐ bike
- ☐ motorbike

SPORTS EQUIPMENT
- ☐ balls
- ☐ basketball
- ☐ basket hoop
- ☐ soccer ball
- ☐ baseball
- ☐ baseball mitt
- ☐ hockey gear
- ☐ swimming goggles
- ☐ special sport shoes
- ☐ skis/poles/boots
- ☐ ice skates
- ☐ roller skates
- ☐ golf equipment

- ☐ skateboard
- ☐ surfboard
- ☐ ski equipment
- ☐ sports-related clothing
- ☐ gymnastic mat
- ☐ cheerleading (pompons, clothing)
- ☐ baton
- ☐ boating gear (clothing, equipment)
- ☐ volleyball
- ☐ badminton equipment
- ☐ horsehoes
- ☐ uniforms for sports
- ☐ sports bag
- ☐ exercise equipment
- ☐ fishing rod
- ☐ Windsurfing equipment

ART AND CRAFTS
- ☐ coloring book
- ☐ crayons
- ☐ markers
- ☐ paint
- ☐ easel
- ☐ clay
- ☐ ceramics
- ☐ origami
- ☐ fabric paint
- ☐ jewelry crafts
- ☐ yarn crafts (knitting, needlepoint)
- ☐ ribbon/hairpiece crafts
- ☐ sewing equipment
- ☐ macramé

SPECIAL CLASSES
- ☐ ceramics
- ☐ swimming
- ☐ dance
- ☐ gymnastics
- ☐ arts and crafts
- ☐ music

- ☐ sports (baseball, football, cheerleading camps)
- ☐ sailing/boating
- ☐ painting
- ☐ horseback riding
- ☐ drawing
- ☐ calligraphy
- ☐ cooking
- ☐ tennis
- ☐ martial arts
- ☐ music

FOODS
- ☐ sweet desserts
- ☐ special treats (candy, cookies)
- ☐ make favorite food
- ☐ eat with my hands
- ☐ cook with parent

FAMILY ACTIVITIES
- ☐ bowling
- ☐ ice skating
- ☐ ice cream outings
- ☐ pizza outings
- ☐ fast-food outings
- ☐ special restaurant
- ☐ movie
- ☐ picnic
- ☐ kite flying
- ☐ playground trip
- ☐ zoo
- ☐ camping trip
- ☐ play center outing
- ☐ beach
- ☐ museum
- ☐ aquarium
- ☐ roller-skating
- ☐ miniature golf
- ☐ water slides
- ☐ drive-in
- ☐ build a tree house
- ☐ sandbox
- ☐ playground equipment

- ☐ playhouse
- ☐ one-to-one parent time
- ☐ concert/go to Mom or Dad's work
- ☐ day at the mall
- ☐ living room camp-out
- ☐ read book at night
- ☐ go for a quiet parent-and-child walk
- ☐ play cards with parent
- ☐ play board game with parent
- ☐ go shopping with parent
- ☐ horseback riding
- ☐ play pretend with parent
- ☐ go out to lunch with parent
  - ☐ business lunch at parent's work
  - ☐ go out to lunch during school
- ☐ surprise day trip with parent
- ☐ breakfast in bed

BIG FAMILY REWARDS
- ☐ swimming pool
- ☐ vacation
- ☐ computer
- ☐ item for the home

BODY DELIGHTS
- ☐ new clothes
- ☐ perm

- ☐ nails done
- ☐ massage
- ☐ new nail kit
- ☐ makeup
- ☐ perfume
- ☐ lotions and powders
- ☐ blow dryer
- ☐ fancy brush
- ☐ hair ribbons

SOCIAL REWARDS
- ☐ hugs & kisses
- ☐ sleep-over
- ☐ party
- ☐ friend over for dinner
- ☐ join a club (Scouts, ski club)

SPECIAL ITEMS
- ☐ unknown surprise
- ☐ jewelry
- ☐ books
- ☐ backpack
- ☐ lunch box
- ☐ computer game
- ☐ telephone
- ☐ records
- ☐ tapes
- ☐ bedroom stuff
  - ☐ poster
  - ☐ new comforter
  - ☐ furniture
  - ☐ telephone
  - ☐ television
  - ☐ stereo

- ☐ camera
- ☐ gift certificate
- ☐ plaque
- ☐ ribbon
- ☐ trophy
- ☐ money
- ☐ television
- ☐ pet:
  - ☐ fish
  - ☐ bird
  - ☐ cat
  - ☐ dog
  - ☐ horse

PRIVILEGES
- ☐ later bedtime
- ☐ later curfew
- ☐ day off from chores
- ☐ get some space/privacy
- ☐ out with friend:
  - ☐ to the movies
  - ☐ to the mall
  - ☐ out to eat
- ☐ more telephone time
- ☐ sleep-in one morning
- ☐ own room
- ☐ choose:
  - ☐ wake-up time
  - ☐ sleep time
  - ☐ homework time
  - ☐ chores
  - ☐ meal
- ☐ cooking privileges

THE TOKEN PROGRAM

The Token Program is best used with preschool children and children who can't delay receiving a reward.

This program uses immediate rewards to reinforce desired behaviors. As soon as your child displays a positive behavior you are trying to reinforce, give him a small reward or token (snack, sticker, penny, etc.). For example, four-year-old Jimmy gets a penny from his mother to put in a jar every time he says "please," "thank you," or "excuse me."

To use this system, first select a target behavior (saying please, thank you, or excuse me), then select a reward for the positive behavior (stickers).

Every time your child displays the target behavior, immediately give him the selected reward.

As time passes, your child will understand which behaviors result in this special attention. He will probably need more incentives to reinforce other, more complicated behaviors. (See the Chart and Reward Program, which follows.)

THE CHART AND REWARD PROGRAM

Here you will be using a chart to record your child's progress by giving him a check or a point that eventually leads to a reward at the end of the day, week, or month. In other words, if he accumulates a desired number of points for positive behaviors listed on the chart, he receives his chosen reward. The charts can be custom made for each child's problem, developmental ability, and for the family life-style.

To set up an effective Chart and Reward Program for your child or family, follow these steps:

1. Select behaviors that you want to reinforce.

2. Make a chart with your child that is appealing and developmentally appropriate.

3. With your child, choose a reward that he is willing to work toward.

4. Determine the number of points needed to get the reward.

5. Follow through in giving the reward if your child accumulates the points needed.

6. Change the chart or the points needed if you think it is too simple or too demanding.

Charts 1, 2, and 3 are examples of how you might design a chart for rewarding good behavior. Examine them and choose a style that best suits your needs and those of your child.

CHART 1
ONE-MONTH CHART FOR ONE BEHAVIOR

Week	Mon	Tues	Wed	Thurs	Fri	Total Points
1						
2						
3						
4						

CHART 2
HOURLY AND WEEKLY CHART FOR ONE BEHAVIOR

Time	Sun	Mon	Tues	Wed	Thurs	Fri	Sat
8:00							
9:00							
10:00							
11:00							
12:00							
1:00							
2:00							
3:00							
4:00							
5:00							
6:00							
7:00							
Total							

CHART 3 ONE-WEEK CHART FOR SEVERAL BEHAVIORS							
List of Good Behaviors	S	M	T	W	T	F	S
Total Points Earned							

THE POINT AND CATALOG PROGRAM

The Point and Catalog Program uses charts to record points earned. With these points your child "buys" something he or she wants from a list of rewards. The rewards are displayed in a specially designed "catalog." The catalog is made by you and your child by drawing or cutting out pictures from magazines of these rewards, fun activities, or privileges and putting them in the reward catalog. Posted under each picture is the number of points needed to get that reward. Say your child's problem is keeping his room clean. Using chart 1, he would earn points throughout the week for cleaning up. Every day or week he adds up the number of points he earned, looks through the catalog, and chooses his reward. Once he spends his points, he has to earn more if he wants to continue "purchasing" items from the Reward Catalog.

HOW TO MAKE A REWARD CATALOG

First make a booklet containing several pieces of blank paper and a cover designed by your child. Next either draw pictures on the blank pages of things your child wants and/or cut out illustrations from magazines (children-oriented ones are best) and catalogs such as J. C. Penney's or toy store flyers. Negotiate how many points each catalog item would "cost" and write the "price" in points under the picture. Include rewards that would be fairly easy for your child to buy (ice cream cone = 10 points) as well as more expensive items that demand more commitment and time (soccer shoes = 200 points). In the back of the catalog keep a "bank statement" so that you and your child can keep track of points earned daily or weekly and points spent.

VARIATIONS

THE FAMILY-REWARD CATALOG

Make a catalog that your entire family can use to reward yourselves for reaching goals. Choose reward items that all members would enjoy.

THE PARENT-REWARD CATALOG

Desserts aren't just for kids. Child-rearing is hard work and you deserve a few rewards yourself. Make a parent catalog filled with things you long for, like a quiet morning to yourself or a night on the town with your spouse. Give yourself points for reaching goals, patiently supporting your child's efforts, or simply putting him in the **think chair** for the umpteenth time. Let your son or daughter see you pick out a reward from your catalog and give it to yourself.

THE LEVEL PROGRAM

This program is based on the concept that your child's behavior can be organized into a hierarchy of privileged levels that are attained by accumulating points through responsible behavior. What makes this program different from the others is that the focus is not on earning *rewards* but on earning *privileges*. Glance at chart 4 and you will notice that it is set up so that your child must collect a specific number of points to "graduate" from one level and move up to the next. Each level should follow a separate chart, like chart 5, which focuses on the behaviors and responsibilities expected. He must maintain a certain number of points weekly to stay at that level or he moves down.

The program begins at level 1, which includes basic responsibilities and related privileges, and continues through level 4: the highest level of responsibilities and the most desirable privileges. Use chart 4 to make your own program. In the same way that you would seek your child's input in deciding on rewards for positive behavior, involve him in developing the responsibilities and privileges associated with each level. Similarly, come up with a developmentally appropriate number of points he must get to move up to the next level or maintain each week to stay where he is. Once he reaches a new and higher level, he should start with 0 points, then collect more points to reach the next level.

Remember: Your child's success should be based on her reaching a level that matches her developmental capabilities rather than simply climbing to the highest level. Focus on her achievements within each level and on the positive behavioral changes she makes.

CHART 4

LEVEL PROGRAM

Name:

	Responsibility	Privilege	
Level 4 need ____ pts	Help Mom cook Wash Dad's car Walk dog Do chores In bed on time	Time w/Mom Time w/Dad 1 dollar You decide time You decide time	Must have ____ pts a week to stay in level 4 Total Pts ____
Level 3 need ____ pts	Wash Dad's car Walk dog Do chores In bed on time	Special time w/Dad Earn 75 cents By bedtime 9:30 bedtime	Week(s) Total Pts ____
Level 2 need ____ pts	Walk dog Do chores In bed on time	Earn 50 cents Done by 6:00 8:45 bedtime	Week(s) Total pts ____
Level 1	Do chores In bed on time	Done by 4:00 8:30 bedtime	Week(s) Total Pts ____

CHART 5

LEVEL PROGRAM CHART
Points Earned for One Week on Level Program

Good Behavior (and possible points):	S	M	T	W	T	F	S
Do chores							
In bed on time							
Walk dog							

READING RECIPES

HOW TO USE CHILDREN'S LITERATURE TO SOLVE PROBLEMS
Choose a book from the recommended list that relates to the problem you and your child are trying to work out. Follow steps 1 through 5 while reading it with him or her. Important: the books were selected because they are especially suited to be read together with your child, not alone.

HOW TO DO STEPS 1–5 WHILE READING BOOKS WITH YOUR CHILD

1. Discuss the dilemma faced by the character or characters. How do they view the problem? From what perspective? If the book doesn't seem to be shedding any light on your child's problem, go to step 2 and highlight the positive behaviors of the characters.

2. Encourage your child to point out the special skills and unique traits of the characters that enable them to solve the problem posed in the story.

3. Decide together what the characters should be trying to do—what is their aim? What is their goal?

4. Throughout the book help your child to see how the characters use different skills to solve the problem at hand.

5. Review the book with your child. Decide together whether or not the characters did in fact solve the problem or reach their goal by using appropriate skills. Ask your child how he might have coped better with the situation. Would he have made the story end differently?

READING RECIPES FOR FAMILY UNITY

FAMILIES

All Kind of Families. Norma Simon (Albert Whitman & Company, 1991) (All ages)

Family Dinner. Jane Cutler (Sunburst/Farrar, Straus & Giroux, 1991) (All ages)

A Family Is a Circle of People Who Love You. Doris Bell and Pamela Ryan (Compcare, 1988) (Younger)

It Could Always Be Worse. Margot Zemach (Farrar, Straus, Giroux, 1976) (All ages)

Lemonade Parade. Ben Brooks (Albert Whitman & Company, 1992) (Younger)

My First Family Tree Book. Cathrine Brussone (Ideals Children's Books, 1991) (All ages)

The Patchwork Quilt. Valerie Flournoy (Dial Press, 1985) (Older)

What Is a Family? Gretchen Super (Childrens Press, 1991) (Younger)

What Kind of Family Do You Have? Gretchen Super (Childrens Press, 1991) (Younger)

ADOPTION

Adoption Is for Always. Linda Walvoord Girard (Albert Whitman & Company, 1991) (Younger)

A Family for Jamie: An Adoption Story. Suzanne Bloom (Crown, 1992) (All Ages)

DUAL-CAREER FAMILIES

My Mom Travels a Lot. Caroline Feller Baurer (Puffin, 1981) (Younger)

DIVORCE

AJ's Mom Gets a New Job. Lawrence Balter (Barron's, 1992) (Younger)

At Daddy's on Saturday. Linda Walvoord Girard (Albert Whitman & Company, 1991) (All ages)

Dinosaurs Divorce. Laurene K. Brown and Marc Brown (Little, Brown & Company, 1988) (All ages)

How It Feels When Parents Divorce. Jill Krementz (Knopf, 1988) (Older)

READING RECIPES FOR BODY-RELATED PROBLEMS

EATING PROBLEMS

About Weight Problems and Eating Disorders. Good Answers to Tough Questions. Joy Berry (Childrens Press, 1990) (Older)

Belinda's Bouquet. Leslea Newman (Alyson Publications, 1991) (All ages)

The Berenstain Bears and Too Much Junk Food. Stan and Jan Berenstain (Random House, 1987) (All ages)

Blubber. Judy Blume (Yearling Books, 1974) (Older)

Bread and Jam for Frances. Russel Hoban (HarperCollins, 1986) (Younger)

Dinah and the Green Fat Kingdom. Isabelle Holland (HarperCollins, 1988) (All ages)

How My Parents Learned to Eat. Ina R. Friedman (Houghton Mifflin, 1987) (Younger)

Good for Me! All About Food in 32 Bites. Marilyn Burns (Little, Brown & Company, 1978) (All ages)

Jelly Belly. Robert Kimmel Smith (Delacorte/Dell, 1981) (Older)

No Carrots for Harry! Jean Langerman (Grosset & Dunlap, 1992) (Younger)

What Happens to a Hamburger. Paul Showers (HarperCollins, 1985) (Younger)

HYGIENE

Angelo, The Naughty One. Helen Garret (Viking Press, 1970) (Younger)

The Kids' Bathtub Songbook. Kerry Tucker and Hal Morgan (Steam Press, 1985) (Younger)

Teach Me About Bath Time. Joy Berry (Childrens Press, 1987) (Younger)

What to Do When Your Mom or Dad Says, "Clean Yourself Up." Joy Berry (Childrens Press, 1982) (Younger)

WETTING/SOILING

Clouds and Clocks: A Story for Children Who Soil. Matthew Galvin, M.D. (Magination Press, 1989) (All ages)

Emily Wet the Bed. Domitille De Pressense (Checkerboard Press, 1990) (Younger)

Sammy the Elephant and Mr. Camel: A Story to Help Children Overcome Bedwetting While Discovering Self-Appreciation. Joyce C. Mills and Richard Crowley (Magination Press, 1988) (All ages)

READING RECIPES FOR DESTRUCTIVE AND ANTISOCIAL BEHAVIORS

AGGRESSION

The Battle of Sir Cob and Sir Filbert. Angela McAllister (Crown, 1992) (All ages)

The Cat Ate My Gymsuit. Paula Danziger (Dell, 1974) (All ages)

The Knight and the Dragon. Tomie dePaola (G. P. Putnam's Sons, 1980) (All ages)

Let's Talk About Being Destructive. Joy Berry (Childrens Press, 1984) (Younger)

Let's Talk About Fighting. Joy Berry (Childrens Press, 1984) (Younger)

Let's Talk About Teasing. Joy Berry (Childrens Press, 1965) (Younger)

The Proud and Fearless Lion. Anne and Reg Cartwright (Barron's 1992) (Yanger)

LYING

A Big Fat Enormous Lie. Marjorie Sharmat (Dutton, 1986) (Younger)

The Boy Who Cried Wolf. Retold by Freya Littledale (Scholastic, 1975) (All ages)

Let's Talk About Lying. Joy Berry (Childrens Press, 1986) (Younger)

STEALING

Let's Talk About Stealing. Joy Berry (Childrens Press, 1985) (Younger)

READING RECIPES FOR ANXIETIES, FEARS, NERVOUS HABITS

ANXIETIES

Coping. Corinne Sanders and Cynthia Turner (Good Apple, 1983) (Older)

Not a Worry in the World. Marcia Williams (Crown, 1992) (All ages)

One Day, Two Dragons. Lynne Bertrand (Crown, 1992) (Younger)

Sometimes I'm Afraid. Jane Werner Watson (Crown, 1986) (Younger)

Sometimes I Worry. Alan Gross (Childrens Press, 1978) (Younger)

FEARS

The Boy and the Dog. Siv Widerberg (Sunburst Books, 1991) (Younger)

Dragons Go to the Doctor's. Lynne Bertrand (Crown, 1992) (Younger)

D. W. All Wet. Marc Brown, (Little, Brown & Company, 1988) (Younger)

Harry and the Terrible Whatzit. Dick Gackenbach (Clarion, 1978) (All ages)

I'd Rather Get a Spanking Than Go to the Doctor. Karen G. Frandsen (Childrens Press, 1987) (All ages)

I'm Lost. Elizabeth Crary (Parenting Press, 1985) (Younger)

Laney's Lost Momma. Diane Johnston Hamm (Albert Whitman & Company, 1991) (All ages)

Let's Go Swimming with Mr. Sillypants. M. K. Brown (Crown, 1986) (Younger)

The Moose in the Dress. Bruce Balan (Crown, 1992) (All ages)

My Mama Says There Aren't Any Zombies, Ghosts, Vampires, Creatures, Demons, Monsters, Fiends, Goblins, or Things. Judith Viorst (Atheneum, 1973) (Younger)

Night Light: A Story for Children Afraid of the Dark. Jack Dutro (Magination Press, 1991) (All ages)

Shadows. John Canty (HarperCollins, 1987) (All ages)

The Something. Natalie Babbitt (Farrar, Straus & Giroux, 1970) (All ages)

A Trip to the Doctor. Margot Linn (HarperCollins, 1988) (Younger)

What's Under My Bed? James Stevenson (Mulberry Books, 1983) (All ages)

Where the Wild Things Are. Maurice Sendak (HarperCollins, 1962) (All ages)

Your Turn, Doctor. Carla Perez and Deborah Robison (Dial Press, 1982) (All ages)

Nervous Habits

David Decides About Thumbsucking. Susan Heitler (Reading Matters, 1985) (Younger)

Don't Do That! Tony Ross (Crown, 1992) (All ages)

Geraldine's Blanket. Holly Keller (Greenwillow, 1984) (Younger)

Take a Deep Breath: The Kid's Play-Away Stress Book. Lawrence Shapiro (Order from Childswork, Childsplay—see Special Resources, page 268).

Teach Me About Security Objects. Joy Berry (Childrens Press, 1987) (Younger)

READING RECIPES FOR SOLVING IRRESPONSIBILITY

Irresponsibility

Christina Katerina and the Time She Quit the Family. Patricia Lee Gauch (G. P. Putnam's Sons, 1987) (All ages)

Don't Forget the Bacon! Pat Hutchins (Puffin Books, 1978) (All ages)

Ella. Bill Peet (Houghton Mifflin, 1964) (Younger)

The Gorilla Did It. Barbara Shook Hazen (Atheneum, 1974) (Younger)

Helping Out. George Ancona (Clarion Books, 1985) (All ages)

If I Ran the Family. Lee and Sue Kaiser Johnson (All ages)

Kid Power. Susan Beth Pfeffer (Scholastic, 1982) (A series of books on responsibilities of older children) (Older)

A Kid's Book of Smarts: How to Think, Make Decisions, Figure Things Out, Budget Your Time, Money, Plan Your Day, Week, Life & Other Things Adults Wish They'd Learned When They Were Kids! Carole Marsh (Gallopade Publishing Group, 1983) (Older)

Let's Talk About Being Lazy. Joy Berry (Childrens Press, 1985) (Younger)

Someone New. Charlotte Zolotow (HarperCollins, 1978) (Older)

Strega Nona. Retold by Tomie dePaola. (Prentice Hall, 1975) (All ages)

What If Everybody Did That? Ellen Javernick (Childrens Press, 1990) (All ages)

Wild Robin, retold by Susan Jeffers (Dutton, 1976) (All ages)

MESSINESS

The Berenstain Bears and the Messy Room. Stan and Jan Berenstain (Random House, 1985) (All ages)

Let's Talk About Being Messy. Joy Berry (Childrens Press, 1986) (Younger)

What to Do When Your Mom or Dad Says, "Clean Your Room." Joy Berry (Childrens Press, 1982) (Younger)

READING RECIPES FOR SOLVING MOODINESS

Alexander and the Terrible, Horrible, No Good, Very Bad Day. Judith Viorst (Atheneum, 1992) (All ages)

Anastasia, Ask Your Analyst. Lois Lowry (Dell, 1985) (Older)

Dealing with Feelings . . . I'm Frustrated, I'm Proud, I'm Mad. (A series.) Elizabeth Crary (Parenting Press, 1992) (Younger)

Don't Pop Your Cork on Mondays! The Children's Anti-stress Book. Adolph Moser (Landmark Editions, 1988) (older)

Double-Dip Feelings: A Book to Help Children Understand Emotions. Barbra S. Cain (Magination Press, 1990) (All ages)

Feelings. Aliki (Greenwillow, 1984) (All ages)

How Do I Feel? Norma Simon (Albert Whitman & Company, 1991) (Younger)

I Am Not a Crybaby! Norma Simon (Albert Whitman & Company, 1990) (Younger)

I Was So Mad! Norma Simon (Albert Whitman & Company, 1991) (Younger)

Let's Talk About Feelings: Ellie's Day and Nathan's Day. (A series.) Susan Conlin (Parenting Press, 1989) (Younger)

Let's Talk About Throwing Tantrums. Joy Berry (Childrens Press, 1985) (Younger)

Let's Talk About Whining. Joy Berry (Childrens Press, 1984) (Younger)

Sometimes I Get Angry. Jane W. Watson (Crown, 1988) (Younger)

Teach Me About Crying. Joy Berry (Childrens Press, 1986) (Younger)

The Temper Tantrum Book. Edna Preston and Rainey Bennett (Puffin Books, 1976) (Younger)

READING RECIPES FOR OVERACTIVITY

Eagle Eyes: A Child's View of Attention Deficit Disorder. Jeanne Gehret (Verbal Images Press, 1991) (All ages)

Mortimer. Robert Munsch (Firefly, 1985) (Younger)

Oops. Mercer Mayer (Dial Press, 1975) (Younger)

Putting on the Brakes: Young People's Guide to Understanding A.D.H.D. (All ages) (Order from Childswork, Childsplay—see Special Resources, page 268).

Shelley, The Hyperactive Turtle. Deborah Moss (Woodbine House, 1989) (All ages)

READING RECIPES FOR SCHOOL PROBLEMS

School Problems

Arthur's Teacher Trouble. Marc Brown (Little, Brown), 1989, (Younger)

The Berenstain Bears Go to School. Stan and Jan Berenstain (Random House, 1990) (All ages)

The Brown Paper School Series (Books relating to children taking on daily school challenges) (Little, Brown & Company) (Older)

Class Clown. Johanna Hurwitz (Morrow Jr. Books, 1987) (Older)

First Grade Jitters. Robert Quackenbush (HarperCollins, 1982) (Younger)

The Flunking of Joshua T. Bates. Susan Shreve (Scholastic, 1985) (Older)

Making the Grade. Carl W. Bosch (Parenting Press, 1991) (Older)

Monster Goes to School. Virginia Mueller (Albert Whitman & Company, 1991) (Younger)

My First Day at Preschool. Edwina Riddell (Barron's, 1992) (Younger)

School. John Burningham (Thomas Y. Crowell, 1974) (Younger)

Sixth Grade Can Really Kill You. Barthe DeClements (Scholastic, 1986) (Older)

The I Don't Want to Go to School Book. Alan Gross (Childrens Press, 1982) (Younger)

Today Was a Terrible Day. Patricia Reilly Giff (Penguin, 1984) (Older)

What to Do When Your Mom or Dad Says, "Get Good Grades." Joy Berry (Childrens Press, 1982) (Younger)

Learning Disabilities

Don't Look at Me: A Child's Book About Feeling Different. Doris Sanford (Multnomah, 1986) (All ages)

My Name Is Not Dummy. Elizabeth Crary (Parenting Press, 1983) (All ages)

The Don't-Give-Up Kid. Jeanne Gehret (Order from Childswork, Childsplay—see Special Resources, page 268.) (All ages)

READING RECIPES FOR SELF-CENTERED BEHAVIOR

Amy's Goose. Efner Tudor Holmes (HarperCollins, 1977) (All ages)

The Berenstain Bears Get the Gimmies. Stan and Jan Berenstain (Random House, 1983) (All ages)

A Cow in the House. Mabel Watts (Follett Publishing Company, 1956) (Older)

I Want It! Elizabeth Crary (Parenting Press, 1982) (Younger)

Let's Talk About Being Selfish. Joy Berry (Childrens Press, 1984) (Younger)

Me First and the Gimme Gimmes. Gerald G. Jampolsky (All ages)

Mine! A Sesame Street Book About Sharing. Linda Hayward (Random House, 1988) (Younger)

Mine, Yours, Ours. Burton Albert (Albert Whitman & Company, 1977) (Younger)

Oscar, the Selfish Octopus. John M. Barrett (Human Science Press, 1978) (Younger)

Renfroe's Christmas. Robert Burch (Viking, 1968) (Older)

The Selfish Giant. Oscar Wilde (Scholastic, 1991) (All ages)

READING RECIPES FOR SELF-CONCEPT PROBLEMS

Self-esteem

Arthur, for the Very First Time. Patricia MacLachlan (HarperCollins, 1980) (Older)

Don't Feed the Monster On Tuesdays! The Children's Self-Esteem Book. Adolph Moser (Landmark Editions, 1991) (All ages)

Hidden Talents. (Sport Mites Series) (Barron's 1989–90) (Older)

I Am Special, Marvelous Me, Be a Winner—Self-Esteem Coloring Books (Order from Childswork, Childsplay—see Special Resources, page 268.)

I Can! Can You? Carol Adorjan (Albert Whitman & Company, 1990) (Younger)

I Know What I Like. Norma Simon (Albert Whitman & Company, 1985) (Younger)

I Like Me! Nancy Carlson (Puffin, 1988) (Younger)

Jake Oshawnasey. Stephen Cosgrove (Serendipity Communication, Ltd, 1978) (Older)

Mary Marony and the Snake. Suzy Kline (G. P. Putnam's Sons, 1992) (Older)

Speak Up, Chelsea Martin! Becky Lindberg (Albert Whitman & Company, 1991) (Older)

Reckless Ruby. Hiawyn Oram (Crown, 1992) (Older)

Tough Eddie. Elizabeth Winthrop (Dutton, 1985) (Older)

Separation

All Alone After School. Muriel Stanek (Albert Whitman & Company, 1985) (All ages)

Alone at Home: A Kid's Guide to Being in Charge. Ann Banks (Puffin, 1989) (Older)

Arnie Goes to Camp. Nancy Carlson (Puffin, 1990) (Younger)

Freddie's First Night Away. Danielle Steel (Dell, 1992) (Younger)

Good Answers to Tough Questions About Dependency and Separation. Joy Berry (Childrens Press, 1991) (Older)

Ira Sleeps Over. Bernard Waber (Houghton Mifflin, 1972) (Younger)

Mommy Don't Go. Elizabeth Crary (Parenting Press, 1986) (Younger)

Will You Come Back for Me? Ann Tompert (Albert Whitman & Company, 1992) (Younger)

PERFECTIONISM

Nobody's Perfect, Not Even My Mother. Norma Simon (Albert Whitman & Company, 1981) (All ages)

Ooops! Suzy Kline (Albert Whitman & Company, 1988) (Younger)

The Sultan's Perfect Tree. Jane Yolen (Parents Magazine Press, 1977) (Older)

READING RECIPES FOR SIBLING CONFLICT

Confessions of an Only Child. Norma Klein (Knopf, 1988) (All ages)

The Day I Had to Play with My Sister. Crosby Bonsall (HarperCollins, 1973) (Younger)

For Sale: One Sister—Cheap! Katie Adler and Rachael McBride (Childrens Press, 1986) (All ages)

Growing-Up Feet. Beverly Cleary (Dell, 1988) (Older)

How to Be an Older Brother or Sister. Mike Venezia (Childrens Press, 1986) (Younger)

If I Had . . . Mercer Mayer (Dial Press, 1968) (Older)

Nobody Asked Me If I Wanted a Baby Sister. Martha Alexander (Dial Press, 1971) (Younger)

I Love My Baby Sister (Most of the Time). Elaine Edelman (Penguin, 1984) (Younger)

Oh Brother! Giggles, Gasps and Groans Growing Up Together. Debra Solomon (Warner Juvenile, 1990) (All ages)

101 Things to Do with a Baby. Jan Ormerod (Puffin, 1984) (All ages)

The Pain and the Great One. Judy Blume (Dell, 1985) (Older)

Sometimes I'm Jealous. Jane Werner Watson (Crown, 1986) (Younger)

Sara Loves Her Big Brother. Ruth Hooker (Albert Whitman & Company, 1987) (All ages)

Sunday Morning. Judith Viorst (Atheneum, 1968) (All ages)

We're Very Good Friends, My Brother and I. P. K. Hallinan (Childrens Press, 1989) (Younger)

We're Very Good Friends, My Sister and I. P. K. Hallinan (Childrens Press, 1973) (Younger)

Worse Than Willy. James Stevenson (Greenwillow, 1984) (Older)

READING RECIPES FOR SLEEP PROBLEMS

Can't You Sleep, Little Bear? Martin Waddell and Barbra Firth (Candlewick Press, 1992) (Younger)

Goodnight Moon. Margaret Wise Brown (HarperCollins, 1947) (Younger)

Monster Can't Sleep. Virgina Mueller (Albert Whitman & Company, 1991) (Younger)

Moon Tiger. Phyllis Root (Holt, 1985) (All ages)

Sleepy People. M. B. Goffstein (Farrar, Straus & Giroux, 1979) (All ages)

What to Do When Your Mom or Dad Says, "Go to Bed." Joy Berry (Childrens Press, 1983) (All ages)

NIGHTMARES

The Bad Dream. Jim Aylesworth (Albert Whitman & Company, 1985) (All ages)

"Bear E. Sleepy Growing-Up Bedtime Kit" (Order from Childswork, Childsplay—see Special Resources, page 268.) (Younger)

Scary Night Visitors. A Story for Children of Bedtime Fears. Irene Wineman Marcus and Paul Marcus (Magination Press, 1990) (All ages)

There's a Nightmare in My Closet. Mercer Mayer (Dial, 1990) (Younger)

READING RECIPES FOR SOCIAL PROBLEMS

RELATIONSHIPS WITH PEERS

Amos and Boris. William Steig (Farrar, Straus & Giroux, 1971) (Younger)

Bully on the Bus. Carl W. Bosch (Parenting Press, 1988) (All ages)

Franklin Stein. Ellen Raskin (Atheneum, 1972) (Older)

The Friend. John Burningham (Thomas Y. Crowell, 1975) (Younger)

Getting Along: Songs and Activities to Help Children Work and Play Together. (Children's TV Resource, 1989)

Frog and Toad Together. Arnold Lobel (HarperCollins, 1972) (Younger)

I Want to Play. Elizabeth Crary (Parenting Press, 1982) (Younger)

Kid Next Door and Other Headaches: Stories About Adam Joshua. Janice L. Smith (HarperCollins, 1984) (Older)

Playground Series, Being Bullied, Feeling Left Out, Making Friends, Playing the Game. (Barron's) (All ages)

Stick Up for Yourself. Gershen Kaufman and Lev Raphael (Free Spirit, 1990) (Older)

They Call Me Jack. Sandra Weiner (Pantheon Books, 1973) (All ages)

Why Is Everybody Always Picking On Me? A Guide to Handling Bullies. Terrence Webster-Doyle (Atrium Publishers, 1991) (Older)

Will I Have A Friend? Miriam Cohen (Macmillan, 1967) (Younger)

Young Andy. Tomie dePaola (Prentice Hall Press, 1973) (All ages)

SOCIAL MANNERS

Chucky Bellman Was So Bad. Phyllis Green (Albert Whitman & Company, 1991) (All ages)

Do I Have to Say Hello? Delia Ephron (Viking Press, 1989) (Older)

Freddie's Trip. Danielle Steel (Dell, 1992) (Younger)

Manners. Aliki (Greenwillow, 1990) (All ages)

Manners Can Be Fun. Monro Leaf (HarperCollins, 1985) (Younger)

Richard Scarry's Please and Thank You Book. Richard Scarry (Random House, 1973) (All ages)

Telephone Time: A First Book of Telephone Do's and Don'ts. Ellen Weiss (Random House, 1986) (All ages)

What to Do When Your Mom or Dad Says, "Be Kind to Your Guests." Joy Berry (Childrens Press, 1982) (Younger)

What to Do When Your Mom or Dad Says, "Behave in Public." Joy Berry (Childrens Press, 1987) (Younger)

READING RECIPES FOR TELEVISION AND VIDEO ADDICTION

The Berenstain Bears and Too Much T.V. Stan and Jan Berenstain (Random House) (All ages)

The Day the T.V. Blew Up. Dan West (Albert Whitman & Company, 1988) (All ages)

Fix-It. David McPhail (Dutton, 1984) (All ages)

What You Should Do When Your Mom or Dad Says, "Do Something Besides Watching T.V." Joy Berry (Childrens Press, 1984) (Younger)

Appendix

HOW TO FIND PROFESSIONAL HELP

We would like to congratulate you for deciding to consider getting professional help for your child's or family's problem. Seeking therapy does not suggest you have failed—quite to the contrary! It is a very caring decision, one that shows you believe there is something that still can be done to solve your difficulties even after you have given it your best shot. The best chefs need a good consultant once in a while.

WHO DOES THERAPY WITH CHILDREN AND FAMILIES?

- Psychiatrists (medical doctors)

- Psychologists (Ph.D's)

- Mental-health counselors (masters in counseling or education)

- Clinical social workers (masters in clinical social work)

- Marriage and family therapists (qualified specialists in family and marriage counseling—most have masters or doctorate degrees)

- Child or play therapists

HOW TO FIND A THERAPIST

1. Talk to friends with similar parenting styles—they may know a good therapist or two.

2. Ask your pediatrician for suggestions.

3. Ask your child's teacher, principal, or school counselor.

4. Call a nearby university or college that has educational programs for therapists.

5. Contact local mother/parent groups—they often have listings of good therapists in your area.

6. Phone or write the following recognized state and national associations for a referral. Most have lists of members who are qualified, some of whom specialize in specific problem areas.

American Association
for Marriage and Family Therapy
1717 K Street, NW, Suite 407
Washington, D.C. 20026

American Family Therapy
Association
2550 M Street, NW, Suite 275
Washington, D.C. 20037

American Psychiatric Association
1700 18th Street, NW
Washington, D.C. 20009

American Psychological Association
1200 17th Street, NW
Washington, D.C. 20036

National Association
of Social Workers
7981 Eastern Ave.
Silver Spring, MD 20910

National Register of Health Service
Providers in Psychology
1200 17th Street, NW
Washington, D.C. 20036

RECIPE WORKSHEET

Step 1 to 5 problem-solving worksheet to be used in conjunction with a "recipe."

STEP 1: DEFINE THE PROBLEM

The adult(s) in this family see the problem as: _____

_____

_____

_____

The child(ren) in this family see the problem as: _____

_____

_____

_____

We all agree that the problem we want to solve is: _____

_____

_____

_____

STEP 2: IDENTIFY SKILLS—WHAT ARE THE "SKILLUTIONS"?

Make a list of all the skills, talents, personality traits, capabilities, and abilities of the child(ren) in the family in solving the problem.

1. _____
2. _____
3. _____
4. _____
5. _____
6. _____
7. _____
8. _____
9. _____
10. _____
11. _____
12. _____

STEP 3: WRITE YOUR GOAL

"We can solve our _____
                              (problem discussed in step 1)

_____

_____ by using our skills _____
                                           (skills discussed in step 2)

_____

_____

_____ to become a happier family!"

Signed,

_____   _____

_____   _____

STEP 4: PRACTICE AND PLAY

Put your skillutions into play to reach your goal. Follow the directions in each step of the recipe you have chosen. You can also select a **planful playing** exercise or reading recipe. Check off the "ingredients" (parenting techniques needed to support your family's efforts to solve the difficulty).

- [ ] **Effective Listening**
- [ ] **Encouragement** and **Positive Reframing**
- [ ] **Family Council**
- [ ] **The Five C's for Rule Making**
- [ ] **"I" Messages**
- [ ] **Ignoring** and **Distraction**
- [ ] **Modeling**
- [ ] **Mutual Respect** and **Empathy**
- [ ] **Natural** and **Logical Consequences**
- [ ] **Planful Playing (Role Play,** etc.)
- [ ] **Prepare, Plan, Prevent**
- [ ] **Spices of Life (Humor, Affection)**
- [ ] **S.T.A.R.**
- [ ] **T.A.P.**
- [ ] **The Think Chair**
- [ ] **Try, Try Again**
- [ ] **Your Choice**

STEP 5: REVIEW AND RECOGNIZE EFFORTS

Yea! Hooray! Whoopeee! If you made it this far, it is an accomplishment. Take the time to recognize efforts and accomplishments both big and small:

1. _____
2. _____
3. _____
4. _____

Ask yourselves:

A. Did you reach your goal?   Yes _____   No _____
B. Do you need more practice?   Yes _____   No _____
   Do you need to try another recipe to
   solve the problem?   Yes _____   No _____
C. What did each of you learn from the recipe?

_____

_____

OVER 450 SKILLS, TALENTS, AND ABILITIES IN CHILDREN

BODY RELATED
body care:
  washes self
  brushes teeth well
  combs hair nicely
  nail cleaning
takes care of clothing
nice dresser
eats healthy foods
finishes a meal
knows when is full
uses bathroom right
nice hair
nice nails
muscular
nice eyes
cute dimples
friendly face
great freckles
strong arms
  legs
  stomach
  hands

great smile
smells nice
petite
tall
tans nicely

PHYSICAL ABILITIES
(Gross motor)
jumps high
runs fast
walks quickly
moves nice and slow
holds breath long
spins around
can balance
graceful
good arm
catches well
flexible
leaps high
good tree climber
good rope climber
swings high
can hop well

can skip well
can gallop well

PHYSICAL ABILITIES
(Fine motor)
nice handwriting
puzzles
drawing
carpentry
model building

ARTISTIC ABILITY
Good at:
painting
coloring
cutting
pasting
doodling
drawing lines, circles,
  squares
clay molding
ceramics
cake decorating
candlemaking
cartoon drawing

doll making
knitting
macramé
fabric art
calligraphy
weaving
woodcraft
sewing
quilting
photography
origami
needlepoint
pottery
print making
tie-dying
embroidery
crocheting
sculpting
movie making

PERSONALITY TRAITS
creative
friendly
careful

brave
curious
alert
active
happy
humorous
funny
silly
smart
giving
fearless
powerful
imaginative
charming
sweet
caring
athletic
artistic
happy-go-lucky
free spirited
tries hard
patient
learns quickly
applies self
takes his time
follows directions
watches carefully
does things safely
kind
appreciative
doesn't give up
mature
responsible
peacemaker
cooperative
quick thinker
assertive
gifted
agile
noncompetitive
good mood
respectful
accepting
excitable
independent
forgiving
generous
gift of gab

intriguing
joyful
good memory
determined
negotiator
trustworthy
self-confident
sure of self
organizer
flexible
handles emergencies well
accepts criticism
   praise
calm
gentle
private
thoughtful
physical
insightful
understanding
tells the truth
good storyteller
speaks nicely
well-mannered
proud
empathic
easy going
great joker
terrific laugh
good problem solver
motivated

SOCIAL SKILLS
leader
follower
plays nicely
good loser
good winner
introduces self nicely
says thank you
says you're welcome
shares
listens to others
sits nicely
nice manners
polite
apologizes
waits turn
good pen pal

participates in clubs (Girl
or Boy Scouts)
   good member
   joins activities
   earns badges
   follows rules of club
helps others
supports others
plays quietly
remembers names
says hello
says goodbye
gives good hugs, kisses
talks nicely about others
nice party guest
good host
nice phone skills
good sister/brother/cousin
plays fair

PERFORMANCE ABILITY
Good at:
dramatics
mime
chorus
improvisation
puppetry
role playing
ventriloquism
playwriting
costuming
face painting
magic tricks, card tricks
set constructions
play production and
   direction
dancing
   ballet
   jazz
   modern
   tap

**NATURE AND OUTDOOR
ABILITIES**
Good at:
caring for animals
astronomy
bird watching
backpacking
camping

hiking
rock climbing
studying butterflies
collecting rocks
mountain climbing
gardening
playground playing
shell collecting
whale watching
traveling
environmentalist
recycling
wildlife protector
explorer
farming

SPORT ABILITY
Good at:
aerobics
archery
badminton
baseball
baton twirling
basketball
bicycling
boating
canoeing
sailing
skiing
dart throwing
fencing
field hockey
ice hockey
skating
football
golf
horseback riding
jogging
tennis
soccer
surfing
Windsurfing
swimming
skateboarding
rollerskating
kite flying
karate
judo
jump roping

self-defense
softball
cheerleading
wrestling
yoga
water-skiing
track and field
racket ball

MUSICAL ABILITIES
can play an instrument
good ear
good songwriter
good band player
good in marching band
singing
chorus/choir
reading music

SCHOOL ABILITIES
math
science
history
spelling
reading
writing

concentrating
staying in seat
handwriting
foreign language
home economics
computers
geography
religious studies
researching
taking tests
neatly done papers
good reports
good speaker
raises hand
answers questions
joins class discussion
remembers to bring home
  books
good on bus
respects teacher
loves learning
studies hard
does homework
turns in papers on time
good library skills

on time
good grades
hardly absent

SPECIAL ABILITIES
board games
crosswords
cooking
video games
collecting things like:
  baseball cards
  stamps
  railroad cars
  dollhouse furniture
learning about:
  cars
  dinosaurs
  electricity
  music groups
saving money
gift giving
dog walking
map reading
pet care
fixing things

putting things together
taking things apart
reading directions

HOME ABILITIES
Good at:
cleaning up
cleaning dishes
  room
  bathroom
  outside
  windows
  closets
polishing
vacuuming
wiping
spraying
dusting
remembering chores
taking out garbage
folding clothes
hanging clothes
making things shiny
putting things away
turning off lights

Note: With a little creative adjustment, each of these skills can become a heading for a group of related skills. For example, "brushes teeth well" can be extended to gargles well, flosses well, puts cap on toothpaste, listens to dentist, nice breath, etc.

SPECIAL RESOURCES

Catalogs of quality toys, play supplies, videos, books, and special music that playfully enhance your child's problem-solving skills.

Childswork, Childsplay
Center for Applied Psychology, Inc.
PO Box 1586
King of Prussia, PA 19406
(1-800-962-1141)

The catalog's logo says, "a catalog addressing the mental health needs of children and their families through play," and that's exactly what it does. This catalog includes everything from a specially designed time-out timer and goodie jars filled with grab-size rewards to board games such as "The Anger Control Game," "Stress Strategies Game," "The Divorce Game," "The Junk Food Game," "The Talking, Feeling and Doing Game," "Mad, Sad, Glad Game," "Stop, Relax & Think-a Game" for impulsive children, "The Dinosaur's Journey to High Self-Esteem Game," "Mind Your Manners Game," and hundreds of problem-solving books for children and parents as well as toys and puppets. All of the books and games were invented and are used by play therapists, which testifies to their quality.

Constructive Playthings
1227 East 119th Street
Grandview, MO 64030
(1-800-255-6124)

Childcraft
P.O. Box 29149
Mission, KS 66201-9149
(1-800-367-3255)

Discovery Toys, Inc.
Martinez, CA 94553
(1-800-426-4777)

The Great Kids Company
P.O. Box 609
Lewisville, NC 27023-0609
(1-800-533-2166)

Troll Learn & Play
100 Corporate Drive
Mahwah, NJ 07430
(1-800-247-6106)

Sensational Beginnings
300 Detroit Ave. #E
PO Box 2009
Monroe, MI 48161
(1-800-444-2147)

Hearth Song
6519 N. Galena Road
Peoria, IL 61614-3125
(1-800-325-2502)

Hand-in-Hand
Route 26
RR1, Box 1425
Oxford, ME 04270
(1-800-872-9745)

PlayFair Inc.
1690 28th St.
Boulder, CA 80302
(1-800-824-7255)
This catalog of toys and games focuses on nonviolent, non-competitive educational toys.

Positive Promotions
222 Ashland Place
Brooklyn, NY 11217
(1-800-635-2666)

Uniquity
P.O. Box 6
Galt, CA 95632
(1-800-521-7771)
The items in this catalog focus on
personal growth and are widely
used by play therapists.

SCHOOL CATALOGS

The following are school-supply catalogs that have wonderful play items
and educational material such as board games for teaching academics
and poster kits that reinforce body care.

Lakeshore Learning Material
2695 E. Dominguez
PO Box 6261
Carson, CA 90749
(1-800-421-5354)

Up with Learning
Catalog Division
19 Ridge Street
Pawtucket, RI 02860

Chasell, Inc.
9645 Gerwig Lane
Columbia, MD 21046
(1-800-242-7355)

Educational Insights
19560 S. Rancho Way
Dominguez Hills, CA 90220
(1-800-933-3277)

About the Authors

DENISE CHAPMAN WESTON

Denise developed an interest in play over the course of eight years as a camp director, day-care provider, and teacher. She obtained an MSW from Simmons College and is now in private practice as a psychotherapist in Massachusetts. Her extensive background in the expressive arts combined with her training in play theory provide her with a unique approach to working with children, families, schools, and play centers. Denise is fluent in American Sign Language, and does consulting to schools and programs with special-needs children.

MARK S. WESTON

Mark is a licensed psychotherapist in private practice with over ten years of experience working with children and families. He has worked in a variety of professional settings from day-care centers to schools and currently consults to several colleges and residential schools. Mark trained with several of the foremost experts in the fields of family therapy, play, and abuse prevention. He holds his MSW from Simmons College.

The Westons have developed a reputation as engaging lecturers whose down-to-earth style has won praise and appreciation from parents and teachers alike. In addition, they have developed and conducted workshops for management groups and executives in businesses catering to children. Denise and Mark make frequent appearances on television and news shows including "FX Breakfast Time." They have written several children's books and regularly write articles for magazines on parenting, play, quality toys, family entertainment and travel. The Westons are members of the Playskool/Hasbro Advisory board.

Through their company, Play Works!, the Westons consult and create programs and products for family entertainment centers, museums, day-care centers, and catalog and toy companies. Play Works!, also develops its own line of play products that focus on interactive play, quality parenting, and joyful children. For more information about the Westons' lectures, workshops, or consulting services, please contact: Play Works!, P.O. Box 342, North Attleboro, MA 02761.